everywhere

everywhere

Comprehensive
Digital Business Strategy
for the **Social Media** Era

everywhere

Larry Weber

WILEY

John Wiley & Sons, Inc.

Published by John Wiley & Sons, Inc., Hoboken, New Jersey.
Published simultaneously in Canada.

For general information on our other products and services or for technical support, please
contact our Customer Care Department within the United States at (800) 762-2974, outside the
United States at (317) 572-3993 or fax (317) 572-4002.

Wiley also publishes its books in a variety of electronic formats. Some content that appears in
print may not be available in electronic books. For more information about Wiley products,
visit our web site at www.wiley.com.

Library of Congress Cataloging-in-Publication Data:
Weber, Larry.
  Everywhere: comprehensive digital business strategy for the social media era/Larry Weber.
    p. cm.
  Includes index.
    ISBN 978-0-470-65170-4 (cloth)
    ISBN 978-1-118-01627-5 (ebk)
    ISBN 978-1-118-01628-2 (ebk)
    ISBN 978-1-118-01629-9 (ebk)
  1.   Management—Social aspects. 2.   Social media. 3.   Internet marketing.
  4.   Information technology—Management. 5.   Strategic planning. I. Title.
  HD31.W37 2011
  658.8'72—dc22

                                                              2010043308

Printed in the United States of America

10 9 8 7 6 5 4 3 2 1

To my family

CONTENTS

ACKNOWLEDGMENTS

I am indebted to many for making *Everywhere* possible. To Lisa Leslie Henderson, my cowriter, for helping capture my thoughts into words on paper and for unearthing the vision of the social enterprise along with me: thank you. Heartfelt thanks and appreciation to Marijean Lauzier, Jackie Lustig, Jan Baxter, Ginger Lennon, and Brian Babineau at W2 Group for their keen insight and ability to see broad connections alongside important details and for their extraordinary dedication to this endeavor despite their already overbooked schedules. I am, as always, grateful to my terrific agent, Jill Kneerim, for her vision and confidence that we, in fact, had a book here.

This is the third book that I have published with John Wiley & Sons, Inc. My editor, Richard Narramore, has once again proved his polished skills in refining ideas and shaping a compelling story. Thank you to him and everyone else at Wiley, including Lydia Dimitriadis and Lauren Freestone for their always helpful and cheerful assistance in making the production process run smoothly.

Without the contributions of multiple business leaders, academics, and specialists, *Everywhere* would not be filled with as much proven-in-the-trenches and actionable experience and expertise as it is. Mark Fuller (Monitor), Jake Nickell (Threadless), Scott Griffith (Zipcar), David Holveck and Kevin Wiggins (Endo Pharmaceuticals), Dwayne Spradlin (InnoCentive), Jeremy Liew (Lightspeed Venture Partners), Dan Neeley (Network Analytics), Greg Matthews (WCG), Adam Weber (The Art of Shaving), Valertie Motis (Sony), Rick Wion (McDonald's), Ian Drew (ARM), Clay Shirky (NYU),

Brian Gaspar (Researcher), Scott Monty (Ford), David Weinberger (Berkman Center at Harvard), Steve Goldbach, (Monitor), Robbie Vitrano (Naked Pizza), Anne Berkowitch (SelectMinds), David Hayes (HireMinds), Pauline Ores (Consultant), Andrew McAfee (MIT), Doc Searls (Berkman Center at Harvard), Reid Hoffman (LinkedIn and Greylock), and Beth Comstock, Anubhav Ranjan, and Victor Welch (GE) have all quite generously taken the time to share their vision and experience with all of us here.

Finally, and as always, I want to thank my family. My wife, Dawn, and each of my three children inspire me, provide me with immeasurable joy, and constantly teach me about this highly connected world in which we live. Their enduring support and enthusiasm is the best gift that a man could hope to receive in his lifetime.

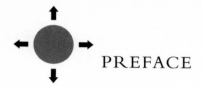

PREFACE

Every year that goes by, I am more amazed at the inventiveness and creativity of the Internet entrepreneur. In a world that seems steeped in shallowness, negativity, and spectacle, they are a shining light of innovation to help remind us we are all in this world together, to make a better place governed by self-respect, transparency, and moral purpose!

Making sense of all the new tools, platforms, trends, and technologies can be daunting. I believe, however, that if we all take a collective breath, step back, observe keenly, and share our thoughts with one another, a greater world will evolve.

This is especially true in business. We are at the very beginning of a renaissance for enterprises based on an overwhelming opportunity to share best practices, knowledge, and data for the betterment of our companies, large or small.

I wrote *Everywhere* to explore this very exciting time in an era in which our digital "lives" have completely integrated with our real ones.

If enterprises listen, create, and share, our economic force will continually replenish. Please view *Everywhere* as a starting point, a foundation, toward comprehensive digital strategy in a world ready for explosive innovation.

—Larry Weber
Boston, Massachusetts

INTRODUCTION

Every so often, an unavoidable and pervasive shift takes place that affects every sector, every industry, every company, and every corporate function. Think automobiles, railroads, and information technology. And, now, think social media.

As social media use spreads beyond corporate marketing departments into sales, customer service, product innovation, human resources, finance, planning, operations, and the C-suite, it is transforming corporations and industries, creating a new source of competitive advantage or disadvantage for organizations depending on whether their leadership recognizes and embraces the change—or not.

This new source of competitive advantage is the social enterprise. Social enterprises are organizations characterized by their extensive use of social media tools, both internally and externally, and, more important, by the effect this über connectedness is having on them.

The dialog made possible by social tools is prompting companies to ask themselves: what would our business look like if we had a more collaborative relationship with our customers, employees, and other stakeholders? As companies put social tools to work seemingly everywhere throughout their organizations, they are beginning to answer that question, function by function. As they interact with a broader base of stakeholders, in unprecedented ways and with a frequency that has never before been possible, they are building communities, not just companies. These communities are allowing companies to do what they have been talking about for decades: place their customers at the center of their businesses.

Threadless.com: Born on the Web

Threadless.com, the Internet-based T-shirt company, puts its customers directly in the bull's eye of its operations. In 2000, after meeting through an online T-shirt design competition, its founders, Jake Nickell and Jacob DeHart, came up with a simple business model: invite customers to submit designs for T-shirts, let them vote on which ones to make, ask them what they will buy, and rely on them to spread the word about their company and its products. That's idea generation and vetting, sales forecasting, and marketing all rolled into one—and carried out by customers no less. Sound idealistic? It's not.

Today, Threadless nurtures a vibrant member community of more than 1.2 million members. (Another 3 million people have purchased Threadless's products but are not registered members.) Designers within the community submit, on average, 2,000 designs a week to the company and spend about 6 hours on each design—that's dedication. The company has expanded its product line to include kids' hoodies and T-shirts and is partnering with other companies to community-source designs for iPhone covers, computers, Havaianas flip-flops, and a whole host of other products. The design community embraces this expansion. As Nickell said, "The artists are all about it—they love seeing their work everywhere."

The community continues to vote on the designs, indicate their purchase intent, and spread the word to their friends via Facebook, Twitter, and their own blogs. They are rewarded for customer referrals with Street Team points that can be applied to future purchases. The company itself has more than 1.5 million followers on Twitter and 100,000 fans on Facebook with which it enjoys ongoing dialog. Management is more involved in production decisions today than it was initially; it has standard batch sizes now, which it can tweak if social chatter indicates a potential spike in demand. Here's an astonishing fact: The company is so in sync with its market that it has never created a design failure.

"It's all about building community," Nickell explains. While Threadless' communities have a life of their own, Nickell and his staff continue to stir the engagement pot with themed design competitions and a conscious linking of their digital and physical presences.

Its retail store incorporates many of the features of its digital environments: designs change weekly and each T-shirt is displayed with a monitor that captures comments about that particular design, which are piped in directly from the social web. Providing in-store shoppers with the opportunity to be photographed in Threadless T-shirts promotes interactivity; these images are projected onto mannequins that are stationed in the front windows. "Spotting a Threadless tee in the wild" and submitting a photograph of the sighting earns additional Street Points, pulling the buzz of the online community into the streets and funneling it back again. The company's Threadless Everywhere Tour, which generates meet-ups at art parties and craft fairs across the country, further integrates the company's digital and physical presences while moving the fun around geographically and transforming digital connections into physical friendships. Little did Nickell and DeHart know that their off-the-cuff idea that was never designed to make a lot of money, would gross more than $30 million a year a decade later and serve as a model for would-be social enterprises.

Dell: A Presocial Company Retools

Older, "presocial media age" companies are also learning how to put their customers at the center of their businesses—function by function. "Customer connectivity and the ability to have conversations that drive our brand are the most important things," says Erin Nelson, chief marketing officer (CMO) of Dell. "Digital and social are tools that are allowing that to happen."[1]

Suggestions gathered and voted on through its branded customer community, IdeaStorm.com, have led to more than 300 new product ideas and improvements—and in record time. The ideation process is now spreading beyond Dell's own digital domains. Through Facebook Connect, Dell's customers can choose to share Dell happenings with friends via their Walls; they can also invite friends to vote on ideas and suggestions. Dell is even gathering the input of the Threadless design community for its products.

In order to better understand consumers' sources of satisfaction and frustration and to uncover sales and innovation opportunities,

Dell continually mines the social web. The company has a centralized listening function that monitors more than 4,000 brand mentions daily, determines what are anomalies and what are trends, and distributes summary information to the relevant business units. David Gardner, *Fast Company's* expert blogger understands firsthand how skilled Dell is at this, "They seem to know within minutes of anything that I write and post on the Internet. I jokingly say it feels like I'm being stalked but the reality is they are using the Internet powerfully to help drive customers and process corrective action."[2] To further engage customers in dialog, the company is establishing an internal social media university and is currently training more than a thousand employees to be the face and voice of Dell in social environments.

Like Threadless, the company augments its digital dialog with physical experiences. Thirty of its most passionate customers were recently invited to Dell's headquarters to participate in a newly formed Customer Advisory Panel. The idea was to get inside the minds of these customers in a deeper way to better understand their thoughts, feelings, and experiences with Dell products and service. Although it sounds like a variation on the age-old focus-group theme, consider this: Many of the participants were bloggers. What's more, half of the group consisted of ardent supporters of Dell and the other half was composed of people who have had serious issues with the company, primarily because of poor post-sale technical support. Clearly, Dell knew that the conversation would be colorful and that it would not be contained behind closed doors; nevertheless, it welcomed the dialog. Its leadership understood that focusing on quantitative measures of success were not enough; to be successful in a highly competitive marketplace, they needed to truly and transparently understand the full range of customers' experiences—as expressed in their own words.

Please Try This at Home

Threadless and Dell provide a glimpse of the rewards that are awaiting companies that embark upon the social enterprise path. When social media tools are used internally to foster conversation among employees, additional gains can be had. Here's an early peak at what companies are discovering.

The award-winning internal portal, Hello.bah.com, created for the consulting firm Booz Allen Hamilton (BAH), enables the firm's staff to blog, create wikis, and communicate with others who have similar interests or assignments. BAH claims that these tools help its employees find information faster, locate mentors, collaborate with subject experts, and network with colleagues—all the while having fun. To maximize the portal's value, the company's new-hire training process includes in-depth training on the platform's features and how to use it to connect with more seasoned employees. Senior Associate Walton Smith says, "Hello.bah.com provides users with a way to contribute their ideas and thoughts to issues shaping the firm. An individual who joined Booz Allen two weeks ago now has the ability to make the same connections as someone who has been here for 25 years."[3]

Further capitalizing on the potential of social media applied internally, General Electric Company (GE) recently created MarkNet, an internal social network and collaborative platform designed specifically to connect and engage the company's 5,000 marketing professionals worldwide. A part of GE's Gold Standard marketing program, which is designed to help GE employees become the best marketers around, MarkNet helps GE's marketing professionals collaborate and learn together. Through MarkNet, they are able to share best practices, brainstorm ideas, and learn new marketing skills. One GE division, for example, recently saved itself a lot of time and money in consulting fees by working with another division to solve its marketing segmentation challenge. Although they operate in completely different industries, the marketing segmentation challenges that these different divisions face are quite similar. Use of MarkNet kept them from having to reinvent that marketing wheel.

MarkNet is organized into online communities, or hubs, which are segmented according to the eight skill sets championed by the Gold Standard program. GE marketers create personal profiles on MarkNet in which they indicate their preferred hubs of marketing interest and expertise. These areas of interest and expertise cut across business units and industries so that marketers of aircraft engines can readily approach and learn from marketers of health care devices and vice versa. This exchange "smartens" GE's entire marketing function, providing each and every marketer in the company with a sense of what knowledge is contained within the company and how they can best connect with and make use of the company's global expertise. "Any marketer, in any division, at any level, and in any geography can find someone who's got the expertise to solve a problem," explains Anubhav Ranjan, Director, Strategic Marketing, at GE.

A senior marketing executive from one of GE's varied business units sponsors each of MarkNet's discussion hubs, facilitating direct engagement with senior leadership for marketers disbursed across the globe. Beth Comstock, GE's CMO, shares her ideas and observations with GE's entire marketing staff regularly through the social platform. "These ongoing updates keep the organization growing by continually refreshing its thinking," explains Ranjan. "The ensuing dialog further develops these ideas and often translates into action." MarkNet has been so well received that human resources and other functions across GE's businesses are exploring instituting their own. That's what can happen when organizations use social media to tap the wisdom and expertise of their internal communities.

It Doesn't Have to Be Made Here

Increasingly, in addition to looking to their customers and employees for insight and innovation, social enterprises are partnering with external organizations to better achieve goals, such as expanding the scope of their product offerings, monetizing underutilized intellectual property, accelerating research and discovery, developing formidable barriers to entry, and creating more agile and profitable overall business models. To do this most effectively, social enterprises are shifting work, skills, and operations around the globe, optimizing their expertise and capabilities with that of their partners.

Of course, partnering is nothing new, but because globally networked infrastructure has expanded connectivity and brought down the cost of communication, it has become much easier to integrate the knowledge and resources of people and companies disbursed across enterprises and oceans. As a result, more companies are now able to participate in a broader partnership model. Instead of having a handful of tight and exclusive relationships with business partners that are nurtured over telephone calls, dinners, and time-consuming business trips, firms today are employing social networks, video conferencing, podcasts and vcasts, blogs and other communication tools to help them build and leverage their relationships. In so doing, companies are forming broader and more fluid ecosystems that include customers, governments, research firms, universities, and even their competitors. The stand-alone company that carries on its business in isolation is being replaced with these porous ecosystems in which companies cocreate and engage regularly with a fluid set of partners.

ARM, the world's leading supplier of semiconductor intellectual property (IP), operates under a broad partnership model. Hundreds of companies, including Apple, Samsung, Qualcomm, Sony, and Microsoft, use ARM's designs to create and manufacture smart, low-energy chips that are then incorporated into digital electronic products. ARM's chips power more than 95 percent of mobile phones and a wide range of other products, including Apple's iPad, Amazon's Kindle, and Sony's TVs. The company's energy-efficient technology combined with its extensive network of partners, position ARM well for a future that will see countless new smart products in the marketplace.

Companies partner with ARM because it allows them to forgo the time and expense associated with the development of semiconductor IP, which ARM estimates would cost every semiconductor company between \$50 and \$150 million annually.[4] Its low-energy chips, which provide ample power for consumer products offer a substantial cost savings over Intel's more powerful version. ARM's partners also benefit from the flexibility of being able to design and build chips that meet their individual needs rather than using completed products created under Intel's closed proprietary system.

What's in it for ARM? Instead of incurring the costs of manufacturing chips, ARM licenses its technology to companies in exchange for an upfront fee. Over time this fee recovers ARM's research and development costs. In addition, ARM receives a royalty, typically based on a percentage of the chip price, for every chip sold by its partners that contains ARM's technology.

Both ARM and its partners benefit from ARM's Connected Community, an online and offline community of more than 700 third-party technology providers and designers. This community provides networking opportunities for member companies, which helps ARM create better designs and shortens the time-to-market for ARM-powered products. The community also serves as a barrier to entry for ARM competitors.

ARM and its partners will be the first to tell you: don't get caught in thinking that it all has to be made in your own shop. As chief executive officer (CEO) Warren East said, "The unique thing about ARM is the combination of business model and technology. We have the lowest-power microprocessors there are, and, rather than trying to be Intel and rule the world, we share our revenue. We believe it is better to have a small slice of a big pie."[5]

Mapping for Partnering Success

Recognizing the power of leveraging diverse external networks, GE has developed a formal mapping process to ensure that it is partnering with the most relevant players for its businesses. Here's a snapshot of how it works. To identify the key players around a business opportunity, project teams brainstorm about the relevant customers and channel members, competitors and complementers, influencers and changers, emerging technology players, suppliers, and other communities of interest that may potentially be involved. From there the company begins to further investigate the potential role of each player and create an action plan for leveraging the emerging network.

This process helps the company to discover blind spots and opportunities. A recent network mapping exercise surrounding GE's coal gasification business revealed that although the company was deeply engaged with partners on the electricity side of the business, they were not involved with several key coal producers. As a result of this mapping process, GE has developed collaborative relationships with several major coal producers, which is enhancing both GE's and the coal companies' business opportunities.

"The learning and skills that come out of these discussions prove to be very valuable," explains Victor Welch, Marketing and Customer Insight Manager, GE Research. "It's very clear that we often do not all have a common understanding of what the world looks like. By thrashing it out together, we come close to articulating a common perspective that allows us to move forward."

Although this process is powerful on the level of the individual initiative, consider the effect of this process and the resulting networks it builds when they are aggregated enterprise-wide.

From Twitter to Competitive Advantage

The real-time insights, networks, and market influence being harnessed from the far-reaching ecosystems surrounding social enterprises are setting these highly networked companies apart from their less-connected peers. Indeed, research conducted by marketing author David Meerman Scott, in which he examined the financial performance of the top 100 companies on the Fortune 500 list, found that the stock price of companies that engaged in real-time communications with their customers was up 67 percent during the period from December 31, 2009, through September 3, 2010, while the stock price of companies that were not engaged was up only 42 percent.[6]

The Wetpaint/Altimer Group's Engagement db study of the leading 100 global brands confirms this finding and documents a significant correlation between those companies that are deeply engaged in social media and those that outperform their peers on financial metrics.[7] Similarly, 69 percent of executives from around the world in a recent McKinsey & Company Global Survey report that their companies have already reaped measurable business benefits from social web involvement.[8] In fact, the greater the use of social technologies, the greater the benefits that have been realized.

What is it that the market recognizes in these companies? It is recognizing and affirming social enterprises' ability to develop competitive advantage. The foundation of this competitive advantage includes being more in sync with the marketplace; developing new sources of market influence; improving organizational efficiencies and cost structures; and being able to effectively recruit and retain employees—especially younger employees or digital natives—in an extremely competitive operating environment.

In Sync with the Marketplace

One of the most profound sources of competitive advantage for social enterprises is the ability to develop real-time, customer-infused strat‡egy. Active cultivation of multiple networks allows companies like Threadless, Dell, Booz Allen, and GE to regularly tap into the insights and experience of people who are actively engaged with their companies, their products and services, their industries, and the forces that are shaping them. The collective intelligence contained within these social communities reduces the risk of uncertainty for companies by providing them with early indications of trends and issues and with new product and service ideas and improvements. Furthermore, the immediacy of feedback afforded by the social web facilitates socially enabled organizations' quick readjustment of their strategy, tactics, and practices, allowing them to take advantage of emerging windows of opportunity as well as to reduce the costs of mistakes made. Companies that dedicate themselves to monitoring and engaging with the communities in which these conversations are taking place are garnering a wealth of knowledge that is helping them to constantly improve themselves, their strategies, and their value propositions to their customers.

The clothing company, Marc Jacobs, for example, is embarking upon a new business line as a result of conversations with customers on Twitter. After listening to feedback about its fashion line from customers, Robert Duffy, the company's chief executive officer (CEO), recently decided that the company needed to begin offering plus sizes. "We gotta do larger sizes," Duffy tweeted to the company's Twitter followers. "I'm with you. As soon as I get back to New York I am on it."[9] While building an expanded product line will surely take Marc Jacobs time and effort, this real-time feedback is allowing the company to get on with it, right away.

In another instance, in response to a "passionate outpouring from customers" across various online channels, within four days of rolling out an updated version of their corporate logo, the Gap decided to return to its traditional logo. As Marka Hansen, president of Gap Brand North America, explained in a blog post that she wrote for the *Huffington Post*:

> We chose this design as it's more contemporary and current. It honors our heritage through the blue box while still taking it forward.
>
> Now, given the passionate outpouring from customers that followed, we've decided to engage in the dialogue, take their feedback on board and work together as we move ahead and evolve to the next phase of Gap.[10]

Of course, companies still have to be able to separate the wheat from the chaff. Not all ideas that are derived from customers should be acted upon immediately—if ever. Companies still have to rigorously examine ideas with strategy implications, making sure that they are, indeed, up to par and on target. "Because our customers asked for it" is not enough of an endorsement, even in a customer-centric organization. For example, social enterprises still have responsibilities to their shareholders for profitability; they can't give everything away for free, even if their customers think it is a wonderful idea. An exaggerated example, I know, but hopefully it makes the point.

But when insights have been weighed and deemed to be on target, that's where competitive advantage is born. Rita Heise, chief information officer (CIO) of Cargill, which produces and markets food, agricultural, financial and industrial products and services, observed:

> When it comes to redefining your product to suit your customers, the biggest gain often comes from discovering your company's own distinct capabilities. Often a company possesses special value-creating capabilities that it is not fully utilizing. . . . Frequently, it is when a company looks more closely at its customer's needs, that it will discover what it can do that its competitors cannot.[11]

Focus on the Future

In addition to informing companies' short-term strategy, these on-going conversations with stakeholder communities are also helping companies to better integrate their strategies over time. Fueled by immediate feedback that has been tested and validated, companies can rebalance their strategy efforts to focus on what will fuel their growth over the longer term. It's not that they can forget about the short term, but information that used to take companies a year to gather can now be sourced via social media and fed into strategy almost instantaneously.

As a result, organizations are able to rebalance their efforts from spending, say, 90 percent of their time focusing on short-term, 9 percent on medium-term, and less than 1 percent of their time on the long-term strategy, to 60 percent, 30 percent, and 10 percent, respectively. That is 10 times as much effort going into considering the long-term future of companies than has been previously committed. That can be the difference between getting strategy right and missing the boat completely.

Improving Strategy Execution

In addition to formulating better strategy, and more quickly, social media is helping companies more effectively execute strategy. Mark Fuller, chairman of the strategy-consulting firm Monitor, tells me that, in his experience, 80 percent of the failures in strategy execution are a result of the friction along the boundaries among individuals, functions, business units, and even the C-suite and the rest of the company. Broad participation in social tools internally goes a long way toward reducing this friction by helping create environments in which silo thinkers can be transformed into bridge thinkers. That's a tall order, but here's a glimpse as to how social media is making it possible.

Aggregated conversational data derived from customer communities provides identical information sets to multiple organizational functions, reducing distortion, and helping to better align their often competing agendas. What's more, these ongoing customer conversations provide companies with the opportunity to answer any outstanding questions in real-time, so that they can move forward quickly. This upfront concurrence can help make comprehensive strategy design and execution that much easier.

But that's not all. As we saw in the case of Booz Allen and GE, when applied internally, social media can "smarten" companies by providing employees at all levels with access to knowledge already contained within the company. They do so by expanding employees' networks of contacts, helping them determine where expertise is located, and facilitating timely access to these resources. This makes it easier than it ever has been for colleagues to work collaboratively and in real time. By providing a broader range of employees with the information they need to make more effective decisions, social tools can flatten organizations, helping to thaw the "frozen middle" of companies, and more effectively harness their collective intelligence. It's hard to argue with that proposition.

Staying Ahead of the Commoditization Cycle

If companies are not changing and innovating, then they are becoming irrelevant. If businesses are going to stay ahead of the commoditization cycle, then they have to be relentless about innovating. The social web makes it possible for organizations to expand their innovation capability, tapping the most knowledgeable sources available.

We have seen how Threadless, Dell, and Marc Jacobs connect directly with their customer communities to keep their innovation pipelines robust and how GE and Booz Allen keep their thinking fresh via internal cross-fertilization. In addition, several new open innovation models are emerging that make it possible for companies to readily tap into the insight of outside experts such as business partners, universities, and average citizens who have insight to share. This access furthers companies' ability to roll out relevant and meaningful products and services faster and more consistently.

In an article for *Wired* magazine, contributing editor Jeff Howe, described how Colgate-Palmolive used the social web to solve a technical challenge that had stumped its in-house researchers. The consumer products company was looking for a way to "inject fluoride powder into a toothpaste tube without disbursing it into the sur-rounding air."[12] The company posted its challenge on InnoCentive's web site, an innovation broker that links organizations' research and development (R&D) issues with a network of scientists from a variety of specialties via the social web. The solution came from Ed Melcarek of Barre, Ontario, who tackles InnoCentive's issues on weekends from his "weekend crash pad," which Howe described as "a one-bedroom apartment littered with amplifiers, a guitar, electrical trans-ducers, two desktop computers, a trumpet, half of a pontoon boat, and enough electric gizmos to stock a Radio Shack."

"It was really a very simple solution," says Melcarek who had hap-pened upon the solution by the time he finished reading the chal-lenge, earning himself a quick $25,000. If it was so simple, why had it stumped Colgate-Palmolive's R&D staff? "They're probably test tube guys without any training in physics," offered Melcarek.

"It's all about diversity," explains Dwayne Spradlin, president and chief executive officer (CEO) of InnoCentive.[13] "It's about getting to everybody who might be able to bring an innovative idea to the table." Spradlin notes that academics who have polled InnoCentive's problem solvers have found that typically their back-ground is no less than six disciplines away from the subject area in which the problem emerged. "What that means is, if all the Stanford PhDs in your chemistry lab could have solved the prob-lem, they would have solved it already." Tapping the knowledge of the crowds may be just what your company needs.

Developing New Sources of Market Influence

Social enterprises are tapping into powerful new market influences. In addition to building resourceful partnership networks, the social web helps companies to engage and influence the all-important consumer peer network. Not long ago, customers looked to professional reviewers to rate restaurants, movies, books, and more. They looked to corporations to tell them about products. The read books by experts to assist them in reducing sibling rivalry, investing in the stock market, and reducing the risk of cardiovascular disease.

Today we live in a recommendation-based economy, where consumers can bypass these traditional resources, looking to their peers to assist them in making decisions about everything under the sun. While friends and family have the most influence—90 percent of consumers surveyed in a recent study by Nielsen noted that they trust recommendations from people they know—70 percent of consumers say that they have some degree of trust in consumer opinions posted online, even when they don't actually know the people that posted them.[14]

In a recommendation-based economy, consumers help to define brands. As consumers blog, write product reviews, and discuss products and experiences in social environments, consumers' voice and volume are becoming the primary means of influence for large and small purchases, investments, employment decisions, and policy recommendations. In many cases, consumers are becoming companies' primary customer acquisition tool. *Internet Retailer* reports that 67 percent of shoppers spend more online after receiving recommendations from their online community of friends.[15] Similarly, Rubbermaid has found that when they added customer reviews to the freestanding inserts that they distribute via newspapers, conversion for their coupons increased by 10 percent.[16] This represents an amazing marketing opportunity for companies that are able to harness the influence and advocacy of their customer communities.

People Really Do Care

Are people really discussing company's products and services in social environments? You bet. Here's a statistic to remember: consumers in the United States have created more than 500 billion online impressions about products and services.[17] What's more, a recent study conducted by the market research firm Chadwick Martin Bailey found that 79 percent of people who follow brands on Twitter are more likely to recommend those brands, and 60 percent of Facebook fans follow the same behavior.[18] Everyday people going about their daily lives really do want to talk about their product experiences with each other.

Just how widespread is the influence of social environments? Is it just a niche phenomenon? Social enterprises are engaging in social environments, not because it is the latest craze among techies and teenagers, but because it is essential to being able to connect with today's consumer. Social web use has gone mainstream—more than 80 percent of adults in the United States who use the Internet also use social media.[19] The social web is becoming the primary vehicle for disseminating news, entertainment, and information about companies and their products and services. Circulation and use statistics confirm this observation. In March 2010, for example, the *Huffington Post* recorded 13 million unique visitors to their news blog. Compare this with the *Wall Street Journal's* reported circulation of 2.1 million for April of the same year. To put this in perspective, consider that in 1950, on average, every household in America bought 1.23 newspapers per day. By 2000, only 53 percent of households bought even one newspaper. Television viewership is waning as well. In contrast, YouTube averages 2 billion page views per day—nearly double the number of people who tune into the three prime time TV stations combined in the United States.[20] I predict that this trend will continue and that by 2015, you'll be hard pressed to find any newspapers or nightly news on TV.

This is not just a phenomenon in the United States. Nielsen recently published statistics that show that the world now spends more than one minute out of every four and half on social networks and blog sites.[21] (The average user spends 66 percent more time on these sites than they did even a year ago.) Australian Internet users average the most time on social networking sites, followed by users in the United States and Italy. Social media usage is widespread; three quarters of global consumers who go online visit social networks. Brazil heads the pack with the highest percentage of Internet users visiting a social network site (86 percent). As global connectivity expands to previously underserved areas, primarily in the form of mobile devices, these numbers will skyrocket.

As a result, the traditional way of reaching consumers—mass-marketed advertising—is becoming increasingly ineffective and an incomplete marketing strategy. Furthermore, the widespread use of TiVo and DVR technology, spam filters, and iPods are making it possible for consumers to fast-forward right through corporations' advertising or to avoid it all together. What's more, whether they be involved in business-to-business or business-to-customer sales, companies must understand how social media has changed the customer purchase journey, so that they can effectively align their marketing, sales, and customer service efforts with this new behavior.

It's Not Just Your Customers

Remember, social media doesn't just reach companies' traditionally defined customers or potential customers. It reaches their other stakeholder communities as well. Institutional investors, for example, are gathering information through social media that is impacting their investment decisions. A 2010 study conducted at the University of Michigan Ross School of Business found that smaller companies that use Twitter to distribute financial information to investors experienced a lower bid-ask spread ("the difference between the highest price a buyer is willing to pay for shares of stock and the lowest price a seller is willing to sell them").[22] It also increased the number of shares available at each price. The impact was greater for smaller companies that traditionally have lower analyst coverage. Social media is critical for investor relations of larger companies as well. The most avid readers of GE's GEReports.com, which is a cross between a blog and a news site, are investors, who comb the site for financial news.

Human resources is using social media to connect with companies' employees. Utilizing Hello.bah.com, Booz Allen hosted an iSpeak Discussion Fest to solicit staff input about how the firm can improve its employees' career experiences.[23] Twenty-two pages of responses provided a road map for the firm's People Strategy, which is the foundation for its efforts to recruit and retain employees.

Through its social media site "CloroxConnects," Clorox, the consumer products company, reaches out to its consumers, employees, and suppliers. Utilizing gaming features, the company rewards suppliers that have gained enough points from solving problems and submitting ideas and comments on their site with 30-minute conference calls with relevant Clorox insiders.[24]

This is only the beginning. Here's the bottom line: If organizations want to connect with their stakeholders, they have to be active in social destinations.

It Takes Two to Tango

There is a price to be paid for consumer loyalty and advocacy. Today consumers expect more from the companies with which they interact. Diane Hessan, chief executive officer (CEO) of Communispace, which builds and runs private online customer communities, observed, "Customers are screaming to be more engaged with the companies that affect their lives. . . . They want to be asked and they want to be involved." Organizations are expected to listen, consider, and respond to their stakeholders' input in a way that wasn't even imagined 20 years ago.

Social media offers numerous venues and a communication style that allow organizations to interact with their customers and other stakeholders in this personalized way. Rather than talking *at* people as they have in the past, companies are learning to speak with them. Everything is fair game in these conversations: the good, the bad, and the ugly. Furthermore, rather than expecting stakeholders to come to them, organizations are learning to be where their constituencies are. As a result of this new mode of engaging, organizations are beginning to address consumers' increased expectations for responsiveness.

This is good news. When customers feel listened to and when they know that they are critical to an organization's success, it becomes almost like fashion: people wear their organizations like a favorite sweater—or T-shirt in the case of Threadless—becoming a fan of them in social destinations and advocating for them among their peers. They act as consultants about companies' products, services, and operations and help them discover unmet needs that can fuel organizations' innovation funnel for years to come.

Woe to the company that doesn't grasp this shift and tries to alter brand promises, features, or logos without the consent of their customers. Indeed, as the GAP found out with its recent logo redesign, companies today must keep their stakeholders in the loop and solicit their feedback constantly, not just after the fact. Had the GAP brought their customers into the design process, a new logo may have been developed and ultimately greeted with positive fanfare; the whole experience would have enhanced customer engagement and brand loyalty. In the absence of such collaboration, the new logo release did the opposite: it essentially said, "We are out of touch with our customers."

Rebuilding Trust in Business

Ongoing collaboration and engagement can also build stakeholder trust in business. That's significant in what has become a widespread climate of distrust of corporations. In 2009, the annual Trust Barometer survey conducted by the public relations firm, Edelman, found that only 44 percent of consumers trust business.[25] Although there is still much progress to be made on this front, the 2010 Edelman study found that the number of consumers who trust business jumped to 54 percent. This is more than a coincidence. Edelman attributes the growth to a rise in the stock market; companies communicating more honestly, openly, and regularly with their employees and other stakeholders; and businesses' involvement in addressing important societal challenges.[26]

Social enterprises get this. While there is not much they can do about the stock market's overall performance, they can—and are—communicating transparently and regularly with their stakeholder communities. Many are pursuing multiple bottom lines—social, environmental, and financial—recognizing that being a responsible corporate citizen and having a motivating moral purpose in addition to profitability are vital in today's business environment.

How much is stakeholder trust and loyalty worth to your business?

Improving Corporate Cost Structures

With the ability to almost instantaneously test ideas, tactics, and strategy, social enterprises are putting significant pressure on their less socially engaged competitors. The social gaming industry, which has seen enormous growth over the past two years, illustrates how companies that are developing, marketing, and/or distributing their products on the social web are able to alter their cost structures and that of their industries. Jeremy Liew, Managing Director at Lightspeed Venture Partners, shared the following analysis on paidContent.org.[27]

Video games take a lot of time and money to develop. In fact, the best games can take between 3 to 5 years to create and can cost between $30 million and $50 million to bring to market. Big hits make the process and expense worthwhile and keep developers and venture capitalists busy. Modern Warfare 2, for example, grossed $550 million in its first five days—that's a pretty nice return. Not every game is a hit, however, and success is not readily apparent from the get-go.

Social web-based games like *FarmVille* and *Friends for Sale* have a very different development profile. They can be launched in three to six months with development costs running in the neighborhood of hundreds of thousands of dollars. Furthermore, social games are often launched in beta. If they catch on, they receive further investment; if they don't, they are scrapped. "Because social games reduce development time by an order of magnitude and development costs by two orders of magnitude, they offer a very different risk-return profile," Liew explained.

Distribution costs differ significantly as well. More than 75 percent of console and videogame sales are made through retail stores and the average new release costs consumers around $40 to $60 per game. Social games, on the other hand, can be played by anyone who has access to the Internet—many through Facebook— without delay and without having to part with a dime. (Companies make their money through upselling digital goods.) "That dynamic helps drive much more trial," Liew observed, "and explains how Zynga now has more than 100 million unique visitors per month, which compares to the 8 million units sold of Modern Warfare 2, the best game launch of all time."

Finally, the differential in the cost of marketing the two types of games is sizeable. Modern Warfare 2 had a launch budget of $200 million versus many social games whose marketing budget is close to zero—they are discovered by invitation and word of mouth. Zynga is an exception; it supports its social games with some traditional advertising. "But once again, the amount that Zynga spends to launch a social game is one to two orders of magnitude less than what Activision spent to launch Modern Warfare 2," Liew said.

Who is using social media to transform the economics of your industry?

Winning the Talent Challenge

The Bureau of Labor Statistics recently published its *Occupational Outlook for 2018*, in which it describes long-term structural changes in the economy. Over the course of the next decade, the Bureau forecasts that the US workforce will age substantially—the percent of workers over 55 will grow by 30 percent.[28] As these baby boomers retire, however, companies will find themselves in intense competition for younger workers whose numbers are forecasted to decrease during the same time period. In order to win this talent challenge, successful companies will have to be able to take advantage of new recruiting channels and strategies that are proving to be effective in reaching this younger and digitally-savvy population, both domestically and globally.

We are already seeing these new practices taking root. The U.S. Army, for example, uses social media to connect with prospective recruits. Interested individuals can watch videos that capture on-the-ground stories created by various members of the National Guard; post questions—and receive answers—on an online bulletin board; participate in chat rooms; and even talk with soldiers directly.[29]

It isn't enough to be able to recruit young employees, however. Companies have to be able to retain them and harness their passion and abilities. Companies that are in sync with the way their employees communicate, work, and learn, and with what motivates them, will be able to retain and inspire them to great things.

Lockheed Martin, for example, anticipates that it will need to hire 250,000 technical professionals over the next decade. One of the primary reasons that Lockheed developed its internal social-networking platform, Unity, was to be able to offer a cutting-edge environment to recent college grads, digital natives who have grown up connected to the Internet and to each other—constantly. In an interview with *IT News*, Shawn Dahlen, program manager for Lockheed's Unity platform, explained the impetus for Unity's deployment at this particular time, "Fifty percent of our workforce will be retiring in the next ten years. We have a lot of folks we need to hire in. They grew up using these tools."[30]

For this group, traditional business communication tools are slow, cumbersome, and impediments to collaboration. They're looking for social networks, wikis, teleconferencing, microblogging, and tools that have not even hit the market yet. Furthermore, there is no distinction between communication tools for work and those for play for this population; it's just how things get done.

Unity combines blogging, wiki functions, personal pages, group forums, a social bookmarking tool, and weekly activity reporting to capture usage patterns. The social network is also part of the company's foundation for project interaction and document sharing. Before Unity was implemented, cross-enterprise collaboration took the form of e-mails, meetings, and PowerPoint presentations—none of which recent college grads are particularly attracted to, Dahlen added.

Not only is this coming-of-age generation digitally savvy in a way that digital immigrants—those of us who had to "learn" technology later in life—can only hope to be, but they also have very different ideas about life and work. As Don Tapscott, author of *Grown Up Digital* and *Wikinomics*, wrote:

> Typical Net Geners are, indeed, quite different from their baby boomer parents. They prize freedom and freedom of choice. They want to customize, make things their own. They're natural collaborators who enjoy a conversation, not a lecture. They'll scrutinize you and your organization. They insist on integrity—being open, honest, considerate, and living up to commitments. They want to have fun, even at work and at school. Speed is normal. Innovation is part of life."[31]

By 2020 digital natives will comprise more than 50 percent of the workforce—they will bring these skills, orientation, expectations, and a unique management style with them. Will your organization be ready?

It's Not Just the Tools; It's the Behavior

How can something as ubiquitous and inexpensive as social web tools create competitive advantage? Although the cost of digital technology is low, there is a steep learning curve associated with being able to successfully tap into the knowledge and resources of multiple partners and customer communities on an ongoing basis and translating the insights gained into actionable strategy. Becoming a social enterprise takes work.

Mark Addicks, CMO of packaged goods giant General Mills, explained the radical shift in orientation that social engagement demands from organizations: "This is about committing to a different kind of future—a really different way of doing business. . . . This is not a department or function thing, it's a new point of view . . . [the question is] how do you get your company to embrace social as a way of living?"[32] That is indeed the question.

Welcome to *Everywhere*

Social enterprises are organizations that are embracing social media as a way of living. They are accomplishing their goals by cultivating participatory networks in and among multiple functions. To do this effectively, social enterprises are learning new ways of communicating, integrating, organizing, and developing and implementing strategy. As they do, social enterprises are creating value and competitive advantage.

My purpose in writing *Everywhere* is to show you some of the possibilities that are emerging as social media begins to transform large and small, new and firmly established companies into social enterprises. This book is not the final word by any means but rather a wake-up call. By sharing stories of organizations' early efforts and outlining some essential steps to building a comprehensive digital business strategy, I hope to help leaders like you begin to realize this new source of competitive advantage. This customer connectedness and centrality will keep you ahead of your present and potential competition in the short and long term.

Quite assuredly, it's not easy. But in my opinion, there is no other viable option. Why are the stakes so high? The social forces effecting organizations today are far too strong and their roots too firmly planted in consumer preference to ignore. The horse is, as they say, already out of the barn.

Let me be clear: the gap is widening between those who are forging the way and building this capacity within their organizations and those who are observing, merely dipping their toes in, or calling it quits. It's not a race, but it does take time and effort to socially enable organizations. And it is a case of get connected or be left behind.

Unlearning and Reinventing

Building a successful social enterprise takes constant experimentation, evaluation, and readjustment. How do companies get up the social media learning curve? What does it take to create a comprehensive digital strategy that can bring your organization into closer collaboration with its stakeholders? In Chapter 1, we'll paint a more complete picture of the social enterprise. Examining where companies are on the social enterprise learning curve and how they can progress to reap the benefits of being more highly connected will be our focus.

In Chapters 2 and 3, we'll concentrate on how companies are developing social engagement skills—their enterprise-wide eyes, ears, and voice. We'll explore who comprises companies' most important communities of interest, how to find them on the Internet, and how to monitor them without invading their sense of privacy. What have we learned about best practices for enterprise engagement? Who should represent companies in social environments and what type of internal infrastructure is necessary to maximize the value of these external communities? You will find some answers to these questions on the pages that follow.

Once a company has acquired these skills, the largest impediment to becoming a social enterprise is usually culture. Old ways of doing things are enduring, and most organizations can't turn on a dime, even when it is clear that the environment has changed. In Chapter 4, we'll consider the inherent tension that many organizations feel between top-down control and grassroots collaboration. We'll explore aspects of corporate culture that leaders are reexamining and refreshing. We'll also share examples of companies that are taking a closer look at reporting structures, organizational policies, and procedures to determine what facilitates or impedes collaboration internally and externally and how leadership styles can morph to be in sync with the new Web 2.0 operating system.

The next section takes us on a journey through the functional areas of organizations to examine how Web 2.0 tools are being applied and are likely to be applied in the future. Stay tuned because this is only the beginning. New uses are being created daily and are only limited by imagination and past practices.

Organizations that are on their way to becoming social enterprises are applying Web 2.0 tools in marketing, corporate communications, sales, and customer service to engage customers and potential customers, drive top-line growth, meet customer needs, and improve customer satisfaction. In Chapters 5 and 6, we'll examine how the social web has changed the consumer purchase journey and ways in which these consumer engagement areas can be most effective in reaching their target constituencies.

In Chapter 7, we'll turn to R&D and product development to see how they are being dramatically altered through prosumers, cross-functional collaboration, innovation brokers, and partnerships. There are substantial rewards and some challenges involved with opening up a company's innovation infrastructure, which we will explore.

How is social media changing strategy formation and execution? In Chapter 8, we'll consider how social tools are being harnessed internally to improve employees' ability to collaborate with each other and to better take advantage of the knowledge that is available within an organization, but not always readily accessible. In Chapter 9, we'll explore how social media engagement is changing talent recruitment, training, and retention. We'll consider what it will take to be an employer of choice going forward and the role that social media is having in this transformation. Finally, in Chapter 10, we'll brainstorm about the next steps in social enterprise evolution.

The social web has arrived; passion, creativity, and two thirds of Internet users worldwide are fueling its growth. Social web adoption is happening much more quickly than adoption of radio or television, and its effect will ultimately be larger. In its wake, the social web is causing a revolution in which a new way of doing things is rapidly evolving. Social environments are changing the modus operandi of organizations, challenging the plans and mind-sets of every company, even yours. And they will continue to do so for some time.

Having advised hundreds of companies on a wide spectrum of business challenges and opportunities over the past 30 years, I can unequivocally state that those organizations that get ahead of this change and help define this young communication medium's future will be the successful companies of the future. *Everywhere* will help you maximize the influence of social environments on your entire business, enabling your company to thrive in the new reality.

Questions to Consider

- Are you convinced that social enterprises are a new source of competitive advantage?
- What would your company look like if it had more collaborative relationships with its customers and other important stakeholders?
- What important insights or ideas has your company gleaned from its social media engagement to date? What has it done with those ideas?
- Is your company benefiting from internal communities such as Hello.bah.com or MarkNet? Why or why not?
- What organizations comprise your company's ecosystem? What do they bring to the table? Who else should be sitting at your table of partners?
- What portion of your company's time is spent focusing on long-term strategy?
- Where is there friction in your company's strategy execution? Can social media be useful?
- How robust is your innovation pipeline? What percentage of your new product and service ideas are sourced externally?
- Are your customers acting as brand ambassadors for your company in social environments?
- How is social media engagement changing your industry?
- How social media savvy is your existing employee base? Your new hires?

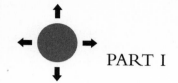

PART I

The Evolving Social Web

CHAPTER ONE

The Social Enterprise

A New Source of Competitive Advantage

Not every organization that is engaged in social media qualifies as a social enterprise—but they all can be. Threadless, Dell, Booz Allen, GE, and ARM are all on their way as are IBM, Procter & Gamble, and Best Buy, whose efforts you will hear more about in the coming chapters.

Today, organizations are at different places on the social enterprise learning curve. While organizations are making their way up the curve in their own unique ways, Figure 1.1 captures some of the stages in which most companies find themselves as they evolve into social enterprises.

At the bottom of the social enterprise learning ladder are what I call "wait-and-seers," those organizations that are watching on the sidelines with senior-level leaders not yet convinced of the effect of social destinations or of how to go about being a part of the new communications landscape. Close by are the "been-there-done-that" types, companies who have jumped off the learning curve altogether, dissatisfied with their early attempts' lack of achievement.

I understand both of these camps. Social media represents a whole new way of doing business, one where, in the early days, none of us

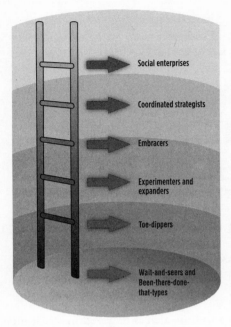

Figure 1.1 Stages in Social Enterprise Evolution

had been trained. Many mistakes were made as people forged ahead without a road map: organizations misrepresented themselves in social environments, employees acted inappropriately, and social tools came and went. Mistakes will continue to happen, but rest assured that new models and processes are emerging that are helping organizations make their way up the social enterprise learning curve—and they can help yours, too.

A rung higher on the ladder are those organizations that are dipping their toes in the social waters, perhaps experimenting with Facebook or Twitter. One step higher are the "experimenters and expanders," who have embraced a fraction of the social web's applications, either as an effective and inexpensive marketing opportunity or a useful internal platform. Higher still are the "embracers," who are putting social tools to work throughout their organizations, each department discovering unique value propositions for how social media can help them meet their goals. Farther out on the curve—but still far from the top because the curve itself continues to advance in this rapidly changing environment—are those organizations that are beginning to coordinate their social media efforts to proactively connect with their most important stakeholder communities and to create an integrated digital presence.

Social enterprises live and breathe at the farthest reach of the curve, a place that is hard for many of us to grasp today, where long-held notions about customers, competition, and commerce may no longer apply. These highly networked entities are building social capabilities seemingly everywhere.

A Closer Look at the Social Enterprise

Social enterprises are still largely theoretical; however, many organizations, across industries and sectors, are well on their way. In the chapters that follow you'll find examples of how various functional areas are enhancing their performance using social media tools today, but here is a glimpse of where they are headed.

Social enterprises are radically transparent entities that engage honestly and openly with their stakeholder communities in a way that other organizations wouldn't dream of or have the capability of doing. They are building long-term relationships with customers and other key constituents, primarily through vibrant digital communities where they connect personally and regularly. Because of these relationships, their communities alert them to problems with their products, services, and operations, share their knowledge, and introduce customers and potential customers to their organizations and their products and services. They assist consumers with purchase decisions and help them derive ongoing satisfaction from their selections. Acting as an ambassador for organizations, causes, and brands, this unpaid and valuable resource contributes directly to social enterprises' bottom lines.

Recognizing that the market demands constant innovation and that this task is often too complex, time-consuming, and expensive to be accomplished alone, social enterprises are cocreating goods and services with customers, employees, innovation brokers, and other business partners be they universities, governments, nonprofits, or other businesses, and sometimes even with die-hard competitors. These partnerships range in complexity from advisors to risk-and-reward sharing peers. Masters at extending the boundaries of their organizations, social enterprises are building access to knowledge and capabilities far beyond what is evidenced by their payrolls.

Social enterprises apply Web 2.0 tools internally, linking employees across functions, business units, geographic boundaries, and partner networks, connecting the dots among their knowledge and expertise and enhancing their collaboration. As they do so, social enterprises are able to more fully capture the collective wisdom, enthusiasm, and commitment of the people comprising their ecosystems.

As they learn to interpret aggregated conversational data from the social web in concert with traditional metrics, social enterprises are becoming highly efficient enterprises, able to reallocate inventory, capital, and talent on a real-time rather than a quarterly basis. This ability, combined with reduced development, distribution, and marketing costs (made possible by going directly to consumers), is transforming the economics of their industries and displacing long-term industry leaders. These porous organizations are proving themselves to be agile and resilient, able to adjust quickly as market opportunities shift. As a result, social enterprises can maintain relevance in environments characterized by constant and disruptive change.

Operating with a broader notion about what contributes to their success in the long run, social enterprises pursue transparency in their actions and a moral purpose along with profits, looking for points of intersection between their value chain and the communities with which they are involved to see where social and economic goals can be achieved simultaneously. This moral commitment improves business results and builds trust with customers and other stakeholder communities in an environment in which the motivations and actions of businesses are largely suspect. It can actually go as far as to put social enterprises and their stakeholders on the same team.

Social enterprises are able to recruit and retain the best and the brightest—and to partner with those that they do not—because of their commitment to innovation, speed, and collaboration. They are building twenty-first century work environments that capture the passion and capabilities of digital natives, those who were seemingly born with a joystick and a smart phone in their hands, as well as more seasoned employees.

Social enterprises outperform their less socially engaged competitors and are enjoying a new source of competitive advantage. Ironically, as they become more porous, social enterprises are actually tightening up organizational inefficiencies. As they broaden their inputs, they are forming clearer and more cohesive strategies. As they pursue a higher moral purpose, they are gaining profitability.

How Are They Doing It?

Managers of social enterprises know enough to let this engagement develop organically to best meet each function's strategic goals and performance indicators and to work seamlessly within their unique business processes. They support each function in determining which of its processes to "socialize" and in selecting the most appropriate vehicles and time frame for that to take place. For some functions this may translate into creating contests and coupons; for others it may mean crowd-sourcing ideas or licensing the organization's intellectual properties.

Social enterprises have integrated marketing departments that act as purveyors of the social landscape, managing the enterprise-wide brand and measuring the organization's overall effectiveness in its community-building efforts. A handful of people in new social media roles, housed internally or with an outside agency, assist individual functions in their social media engagements.

A comprehensive digital strategy, interwoven with a solid operating plan, reflects how these organizations are continually observing their multiple constituencies, engaging effectively in social communities, developing and recruiting relevant and fresh content, and gleaning the most insight currently available through social analytic tools. But social enterprises also know that to reap the real rewards of social engagement and develop sustainable competitive advantage, they must be able to harness the insights captured by each functional area, share those findings across their enterprise, and transform that learning into operational strategy. Toward this end they have developed a cross-functional coordinating team, the social enterprise eforum, that helps build an integrated digital presence, share social media learning, and ensure that insights and knowledge gleaned through each of these touch points with customer communities are cycled through the company and its broader ecosystem to optimize performance.

Managers of social enterprises are actively examining their internal cultures and organizational structures to see what inhibits or promotes collaboration, transparency, and real-time optimization. They are experimenting with flatter structures, new control systems, and more collaborative leadership styles. They are flipping the conventional power paradigm, encouraging insights to flow upward from the trenches to senior management and throughout the enterprise, rather than exclusively in a top-down manner, resulting in smarter, more resourceful, and more self-aware organizations. They are learning to embrace the social web as a way of living.

Facing the Fear

Discussion of social web engagement among executives often elicits excitement, but more often than not, this sense of promise is accompanied by fear. And well it should be. As with any significant change, the new behaviors being ushered in by the expanding reach of the social web are causing plenty of disruption and creative destruction.

What is comfortable about a paradigm shift that brings with it the threat of obsolescence? Social environments have already leveled the playing field of many industries, providing tremendous opportunities to those enterprises, whether they are new entrants or firmly established industry leaders, who understand and are successfully harnessing the power of the social web. Consider how Monster.com reduced the need for classified ads, creating tremendous financial challenges for newspapers, and how LinkedIn, by using a social network to access and recruit talent, is providing a more useful service than Monster's message boards.

How at ease are you with an emerging communication medium that allows anyone and everyone to say what they want about your organization, publicly? Or an internal platform that may create a source of discoverable content that could be used against you in a court of law? Or a vehicle that makes it potentially easier for confidential information to consciously or unconsciously be leaked into the wrong hands?

How do you get your arms around a communications landscape in which a new social destination is constantly going live? It's difficult to get a reliable estimate of just how many social destinations there are presently; however, in January 2009 there were more than 185 million distinct web sites. Although I believe that we will see a shakeout of the social landscape over time with the more influential and reliable social destinations continuing to gain dominance, at the moment it can seem like the Wild West to many who are not regularly engaged in the space.

How challenging is it to find the balance between tried-and-true business processes and structures and what may work better in this networked environment? Will the collaborative culture of the social web translate into fluid work groups, multiple external business partners, and responsibility without authority? If so, how does management make this leap?

Should you move your organization forward into a whole new world when the legal precedent for engagement is evolving and new cyber legal issues are still surfacing? How do you encourage your lawyers and other advisors to help mitigate these risks, to get to "yes," to allow your organization to develop this new source of competitive advantage and harness the substantial rewards?

These fears are very real. However, in my experience, they are also manageable. Once organizations gain even a small amount of successful social media experience, they invariably want more social web engagement, not less. They want to become social enterprises in a way that makes sense for their organization and industry.

Here's what would really scare me: conversations that are taking place about myself or my company throughout the social web without me being aware of what is being said or being available to respond; stakeholders supplying reams of information to my competitors, which is helping them offer better products and services, potentially to my customers, without my taking notice; relying on traditional data to make decisions while my competitors are refining and expanding their abilities to build actionable strategy from real-time data sources; waking up to find out that my long-standing marketing and recruiting efforts are no longer effective, that the conversations and connections that are impacting customers are taking place elsewhere; sticking to my guns while other companies develop the organizational processes and structures that meet the expectations and capabilities of a new breed of employee; failing to develop an emerging source of strategic advantage while waiting for legal foundations to be put in place.

Leaders of social enterprises are proactively addressing these fears while they gain hands-on experience. They are uncovering new issues and challenges along the way and helping to source solutions. With few exceptions, they are discovering that the rewards of social media engagement outweigh the perceived risks.

Keep reading to figure out how you can get ahead of the curve, create a comprehensive digital business strategy, and build a successful social enterprise, regardless of where you are standing today.

Questions to Consider

- Where is your company on the social enterprise learning curve?
- Where are your competitors on this learning curve?
- How is social media engagement changing your industry?
- What characteristics of social enterprises would be most transformative for your organization?
- What fears do you have about social media engagement?
- What questions do you want to have answered?

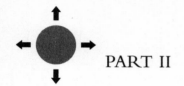

PART II

On Becoming a
Social Enterprise

CHAPTER TWO

Toward a Comprehensive Digital Business Strategy

Imagine having the ability to have real-time information feeds flowing throughout your organization about everything that matters to it. What are your customers talking about today? What concerns are your employees expressing? What factors seem most important to potential hires this week? What new research is on the horizon that will impact your industry? And then imagine employees throughout your organization taking this data and asking themselves, "How does this new knowledge fit into our strategic direction and planning? What needs to be changed and how quickly can we do so?" Seem like science fiction? Actually, it can happen—and is happening—here and now.

To get there, companies are developing a comprehensive digital strategy that informs and builds the kind of community engagement that makes this feedback possible. Although a comprehensive digital business strategy may evoke an image of a several hundred–page document that is bound and updated periodically, it is actually a verb, the nuts and bolts of what it will take to keep a company's multiple social networks humming. And even though the word *comprehensive* makes it sounds like it is a top-down plan that reaches into the cobwebbed corners of an organization, it is actually the inverse. A comprehensive digital strategy is derived in the trenches.

At the risk of being redundant, let me restate these ideas because they run so counter to how strategy has been created for the past 50 years. An organization gets to its comprehensive digital strategy by doing its yeoman's work in digital environments daily, conversation by conversation, not by sitting in a secluded room analyzing numbers and drafting reports. It gets there by listening and thoughtfully engaging, working within broad but essential enterprise-wide guidelines. When it does, it is rewarded with knowledge that is fueled by passionate stakeholder communities that actually care about its business.

A company's comprehensive digital strategy, therefore, is the total of what each function is doing to reach out to its multiple stakeholder communities. But it doesn't end there. It includes the processes that an organization undertakes to funnel the insights that it gathers to the relevant people throughout the organization and to carefully consider the knowledge gathered with an eye to incorporating them into strategy. That means working to digest and transform it from data to information, from information to knowledge, and from knowledge to wisdom. A company's comprehensive digital strategy also includes the way that it closes the loop, letting its stakeholder communities know what it has done with the insight that has been provided. Finally, it incorporates plans for managing any conflicts that may arise with constituent groups.

As such, this all-inclusive strategy is actually highly segmented. It becomes all encompassing only as it spreads throughout an organization. This is not to say that a company's digital efforts are haphazard, however. Social enterprises have goals, protocols, skills, and processes that guide each and every social engagement.

Guidelines Get You There

Having protocols and processes in place to govern and evaluate the success of social media engagement is not the norm in most organizations today. At the moment, the majority of organizations' social media involvement can best be described as haphazard—a program here and a program there, with no protocols or measurement systems in place. A recent study from the marketing firm Digital Brand Expressions found that although 78 percent of corporate respondents say their company is using social media, only 41 percent say they have a strategic plan in place to guide such activity.[1]

This leaves many organizations disillusioned with social media, exposed to the whims of social environments without the necessary tools, and missing out on the real benefits of social engagement. Indeed, a recent study conducted by the marketing firm R2integrated found that 65 percent of marketers surveyed said that their companies have not increased revenue or profited from using social media.[2] A look at the major differences between those organizations that considered their social engagement successful and those that didn't revealed that those who were successful were almost twice as likely to have a formal social media strategy in place.

How do companies ultimately get to the prized comprehensive strategy? Each organization's journey is a bit different—and it should be. However, there are several essential steps that, in my experience, every company must take. They include developing your company's eyes and ears and collective voice; transforming your organization's culture, dominant leadership style, and potentially its organizational structure; and revamping the way strategy is formulated and executed. I'll tackle each of these steps in the pages that follow.

Identify Your Key Communities

Tom Lamb, Senior Vice President of Customer Marketing for Lowe's, gets where the world is going. Almost a decade ago Lamb observed that, "We need to put that entrepreneurial spirit in the middle of our customer interactions to help understand the ongoing story of each customer. Then we can build on the insights that these in-house entrepreneurs provide."[3]

The first step in every organization's comprehensive digital business strategy is understanding who its customers and other key stakeholder communities are, as well as their connections to the business processes and the overall mission of the company. Once this map is in place, companies can begin to develop their social media eyes, ears, and voice, the tools through which these relationships are built. Although this sounds quite basic, in this day and age of highly networked companies, this task can be quite complex.

A company's obvious customers are current or prospective consumers to whom it would like to sell its products and services; however, important communities also include employees, shareholders, franchisees, suppliers, alumni, and policy makers, to name a few. They include everyone who is creating knowledge pertinent to a company's current and future businesses, including business partners, competitors, universities, think tanks, and research organizations. They also include the press and community activists, two groups that have grown significantly more powerful in the last decade.

The Rise of the Citizen Journalists

Before the advent of social media, if consumers had something to say publicly they had to convince a professional media source of their accuracy and newsworthiness to get the word out. Today, you and I—and everyone—can have a voice and the potential to be media. All it takes is access to the Internet. This personal platform combined with the reach of social destinations makes it easy, fast, and free for consumers to be heard.

This new platform is putting organizations' actions center stage, monitored and discussed by growing audiences, whether they have sanctioned it—or are even aware of it—or not. These discussions can be started and spread to customers, other stakeholder communities, and society at large, long before they come to the attention of marketers and media relations experts because they are taking place in multiple social venues, not just where and when a media plan has designated.

Think about Toyota for a moment. Despite years of being known for the quality of its products, within the course of a few weeks that stellar reputation was called into question. Widespread criticism about the company's lack of responsiveness to its customers' concerns posed the threat. These were not just everyday concerns. These were concerns about cars accelerating on their own despite drivers applying the brakes. The company's silence on the issue for what was considered an inordinate amount of time in this day and age chipped away at the core of Toyota's reputation and led to a sizeable civil penalty—the largest ever levied on a car company by the U.S. government.[4] Had Toyota been monitoring the social web, it would have seen these concerns developing sooner. Had it been actively engaging on the social web, it may have been able to avert this financial penalty.

Public companies should be aware of several social venues that focus on retail shareholders and corporate responsibility. Sites like Proxydemocracy.org, Moxyvote.com, Shareowners.org, and AsYou Sow.org enable shareholders to become more informed, empowered, and organized. Each of these groups has several key successes to which they can point. As You Sow, for example, takes credit for getting Best Buy to launch an e-waste recycling program at all of its 1,006 domestic stores. At present, about 25 percent of the shares of publicly held companies are owned by retail investors; of those, only about a quarter are actively involved in shareholder votes.[5] That means there are still many more retail investors that may choose to become involved in these conversations and shareholder initiatives. What risks, developments, and opportunities might your company need to anticipate? What social communities can help your company better understand these issues and trends and engage in proactive dialogue about them?

The bottom line is that you cannot overlook or underestimate the power of bloggers and of community activists. Cultivate relationships and ongoing, authentic exchanges with them because members of these communities may also become your company's greatest advocates.

Developing Company Advocates

The story of "Dell Hell" is well known; what is less well known is how it came full circle. Several years ago, blogger Jeff Jarvis sent an open letter to Dell's Chairman and its chief marketing officer (CMO), in which he took the company to task, publicly, for what he perceived to be shoddy products and lousy customer service. Almost immediately, hundreds of other consumers joined Jarvis's *digital bus*—my term for consumers' digital advocacy movements, harkening back to the days of my youth when busloads of people attended physical protests. But that is not the end of the story.

A few years later Jarvis was blogging about Dell again. This time he was singing their praises. He wrote of how they had been reaching out to bloggers. He acknowledged that Dell employees were blogging and that they were listening to and following the advice of their customers. He noted that the company "that was vilified as the worst at blogs, social media, and customer relations in the broad sense is now, one could argue, the best at this."[6] The ultimate compliment. More important, however, is the fact that Jarvis's original blog helped reorient the company's strategy placing customers firmly at the center. Dell's CMO, Erin Nelson, explained the impact of Dell Hell in an interview with *Adweek*,

> It's been a real blessing for us. It forced us to jump in with both feet. I see a lot of brands talking about experimentation [with social media]. I think you're either in or you're not. When you're in, you better dive in all the way. We weren't overly analytical or conservative about how we engaged in the space. We said we have a brand problem and we need to fix it and make it better. We did what it took to do that. I think it was helpful. It would have been more studied and analytic. The only reason "Dell Hell" existed was because customers weren't happy. Putting the customer at the center is what it taught us.[7]

Competitors as Collaborators

Another important shareholder community for companies is their competitors. Rivals have always had a profound effect on each other; they force organizations to stay on their toes and push industries to their cutting edge. Today they are also important collaborative partners.

Here's an example of how that collaboration plays out. Have you heard of a BlogWell? BlogWells are conferences that are held physically and digitally in which big brands and formidable competitors come together to discuss how they are using social media. Sponsored by GasPedal and the Social Media Business Council, these events create a friendly and productive venue for members to roll up their sleeves and learn from each other about what is working—and what isn't—in this rapidly evolving space. Why do these competitors join forces in an area in which competitive advantage can be found? Quite simply, because they are convinced that it builds better businesses. Even large companies with big budgets, such as Dell, Walmart, P&G, and Coca-Cola, understand the power of collaboration and the gains to be had from sharing their learning in this area. (You can hear many of their presentations on BlogWell's site.[8] To participate in private sessions, membership is required.)

The medical field has long understood the benefits of this type of collaboration. Papers are shared regularly at conferences, even among rivals that compete for hard-won health care dollars. Now that history of collaboration is spreading to the social web. The American College of Cardiology recently brought a new social destination live: Cardio Source.org. A private social network is central to this revamped organizational web site, which connects more than 39,000 cardiovascular professionals. The social destination allows members to discuss issues and research that are important to cardiology.

Even competitive car dealerships are doing it. Jared Hamilton, a third-generation auto dealer, formed DrivingSales.com several years ago. Hamilton originally created the social site as a private automotive business community through which his National Automobiles Dealer Association (NADA) Dealer Candidate Academy class could connect. In 2008, he opened it up nationally, and today it has thousands of members, including dealers, dealer managers, manufacturers, industry experts, and vendors. Members build profiles, collaborate, and share best practices with each other. They also rate and review vendors, and vendors, in turn, have the opportunity to provide feedback on the reviews.

Matt Haiken, General Manager of Prestige Volvo in New Jersey, one of the top 10 dealerships in the United States swears by DrivingSales.com. "I am constantly on DrivingSales, connecting with other people in the industry, sharing and reaffirming best practices or to get a quick pricing opinion. DrivingSales represents the future of dealer collaboration—and perhaps even our survival—because it's a platform where we can share ideas, communicate, see what's working and what's not—far more quickly and effectively than we ever could before."[9]

Once an Employee, Always an Employee

One of the most effective, but often overlooked communities, is a company's own alumni. For many companies that have been around for a while, this can be quite a sizeable group—potentially larger than their current employee base. "Too big of a constituency for companies to ignore," says Anne Berkowitch, founder and CEO of SelectMinds, the largest builder of corporate alumni social network communities. When she founded the company a decade ago, before the days of Facebook, MySpace, and even Friendster, companies didn't always grasp the value of corporate alumni networks. "They often thought good riddance when they thought of former employees," Berkowitch explains. "But with the fluidity of today's job market, it's a great resource for both companies and their alumni."[10] (Today, the average person changes jobs 7 to 10 times in their career.)

Alumni offer several benefits to companies. For starters, they represent a significant referral base for new employees. They know the company and its culture well and can make targeted and vetted recommendations. Sometimes alumni even come back into the fold as "boomerang" hires, or rehires.

Alumni can be beneficial to companies even if they do not return to the payroll. For starters, they are brand ambassadors for a company; their impressions carry a lot of weight because they are considered insiders. What they say about a company and how it engages has had a significant effect on how it is perceived. What's more, in many incidences, former employees join the ranks of a company's clients, suppliers, business partners, or prospective clients, and can open doors for new business development. One of SelectMinds' clients, an accounting firm, found that its alumni network drives up to $180 million in new business per year.

Most companies encourage their current employees to join their digital alumni groups to encourage a free flow of information between current and past employees. These "people-to-people" links keep the network current and useful and, as Berkowitch points out, enable companies to continue to tap the knowledge of alumni and help shape their opinions about the organization.

What's in it for alumni? "Continued access to an amazing portfolio of resources as well as the social satisfaction of staying connected with their former colleagues," explains Berkowitch. A group of former female employees from J.P. Morgan, for example, connect online through the company's alumni network to share advice and thoughts on their corporate board experiences. Members regularly log on for economic insight provided through documents, webinars, and conference calls. It's a gift that keeps on giving, long after the paychecks have stopped coming.

Take a Deep Dive

It is still the case, even within functions outside of marketing, that the more precisely an organization can define its target audiences or communities, the more effective its outreach effort will be. Indeed, if you take an organization's customer taxonomy one level deeper than we have so far, several smaller groups emerge. Human resources, for example, has several constituencies with which is it likely to engage regularly, including current, potential, and former employees. Finance has lenders, investors, and auditors among its customer groups.

What's more, several consumer profiles or personas exist within each of these smaller groups. The social web allows us to identify these groups according to what they do and feel—what is important to them—rather than traditional demographics. At present, there are more than 200 tools out there that can track consumers' behavior—what they are downloading and sharing, who they are friending, and what they are retweeting—as well as their attitudes and interests. Armed with this data, companies can define their target market in terms of personas, that is, the personality of a given group. A client of one of my companies, The Art of Shaving, provides a firsthand example of this persona identification. The company, which is owned by Procter & Gamble/ Gillette, is out to change the experience of shaving for men.

Image Sculptors, Vintage Purists, and Solution Kings

It never ceases to amaze me just how much conversation is taking place in social environments, even when the companies and brands that are being discussed are not actively part of the conversation. When we began listening to the social web to see where The Art of Shaving's customers and potential customers were aggregating and what they were saying about the category and the brand itself, we uncovered quite an active dialog. Over the course of one month of observation, we discovered literally hundreds of conversations about The Art of Shaving brand itself and more than 50,000 conversations about shaving in general. Many of the conversations about shaving were taking place in smaller microsegmented social destinations such as Gear Patrol, Men's Health, and Uncrate, which is not uncommon on the social web.

From these observations we were able to identify three distinct shaving personas: the "image sculptor"—the guy who really cares about what he looks like; the "vintage purist"—someone who is interested in The Art of Shaving products because of their high quality, craftsmanship, and tradition; and the "solution king"—a man who is focused on the end benefit of these high-quality products, whether that be optimal skin health or more confidence because of his improved appearance. We then estimated the size of each of these persona's markets based on quantifiable indicators such as the reach of each of the communities that they frequent as well as their receptivity to the company's message and social presence. From there we prioritized which personas held the most promise for growing The Art of Shaving's business. It's a new wrinkle on an old marketing process.

Personas Outside of Marketing

What might these personas look like for functions other than marketing? Consider human resources. One of their most important constituencies is the company's current employees. Within that group there may be several personas: Employees who have two years of experience and are getting antsy and potentially considering graduate school, as well as employees with two years of experience who are happy as clams, thinking that they may be lifers. There can be clerks and executives. And then there are former employees, who can fall into different camps. There are potential rehires, say after attending business or law school, or at any time in their career really. There can be happy or disgruntled former employees who now work for someone else; the former may be a valuable resource for business development, and the latter may have insights to share that can help a company improve its employees' satisfaction. Even from this cursory glance, it is clear that human resources' map of target personas alone can be quite involved.

Creating these detailed customer maps that identify each function's critical customer communities is important to ensure that an organization's social media efforts are addressing those groups that are most essential to its business goals at any given time. These maps, and the priority ranks that stem from them, should be reviewed periodically to ensure that they remain accurate. Imagine how complex—and insightful—a consolidated map of an enterprise's vital customer communities can be.

It's Payday!

Although these personas may seem challenging to identify initially, there is some good news here. Once you have identified the personas within a given community, you know where to direct your social media efforts. Because the social web is a highly segmented environment and is becoming even more so daily, it allows for fine-tuned marketing.

If you want to find former employees who went through a training program together or men who want a shave just like their dads did, it's quite likely that they have aggregated into a handful of places on the Web where you can find them. If you want to see what potential hires in Dubai and Shanghai are saying about your company, you can do that, too, as long as you have the appropriate skills to conduct your observations in multiple languages.

What's more, now that you have an idea of what is important to your chosen personas, you can develop targeted content that is meaningful to them. Then, as opposed to doing their best to avoid your organization's marketing efforts by fast-forwarding through your commercials, turning the page without reading your ad, shredding your direct-mail piece, or bypassing you all together by listening to their iPods, they will actually welcome hearing from you. The moral of the story: do your work upfront and you will continually reap the benefits.

Look for the Influencers

As you observe the social landscape, you will invariably discover the granularity of digital environments. As in the physical world, in social environments there are people who are more influential than others; they may be bloggers, vloggers, or forum monitors. They are looked upon as authorities because they are often perceived to be on the cutting edge, with up-to-date knowledge of new products and services. Make note of these linchpins as you go about your social web exploration because they can be primary catalysts for future conversations about your products and services—they may already be! A mere 16 percent of online consumers generate 80 percent of consumer online impressions—these are the influencers at work.

Influencers come in all shapes and sizes, ages, genders, and income levels. Because of a life stage, a lifestyle, or a hobby or professional interest, they are passionate about a particular category—a shaving product, mobile phones, or even cleaning products. Because they are influencers, they share that interest with others face-to-face and via the social web.

Some categories have many influencers; others, only a few. Developing a prioritized list of the most relevant influencers for your stakeholder communities goes a long way to ensuring that your social engagement ultimately meets your objectives. Variables to consider include influencers' area of expertise, frequency of postings, size and make up of their audiences, and the format that they use to deliver their messages (e.g., video, podcast, or text).

New companies are coming onto the scene whose very purpose is to create influence indices that can help organizations better identify and prioritize influencers and communities. BlogHer, for example, ranks women's blogs according to crowd-sourced votes. If an organization's target community is breast cancer survivors, for example, BlogHer can identify the three most important breast cancer survivor blogs. This formalization will prove quite helpful to companies' outreach efforts. It's also another sign of the ongoing maturation of the social web. As was the case with traditional media, over time, certain newspapers or columnists proved to have a greater effect than others because they had better sources or were more accurate. They rose to the top and are the ones that are still in business today. The Wild West is being tamed.

Recognizing the importance of these influencers, General Mills is casting a wide net through its web site, MyBlogSpark. In addition to reaching out to bloggers individually, MyBlogSpark allows bloggers to reach in. Member bloggers have access to some of the newest products and thinking at General Mills, as long as they review these products in their blogs. Bloggers do not receive any financial compensation for involvement; what they do receive is social web currency: highly valued content and insider access that helps keep them in an influencing role with their audiences. What does General Mills receive? Social media influence, enhanced relationships with bloggers, and feedback. The company asks its bloggers to contact them if they cannot write a positive review to better understand why. General Mills can also monetize this community by selling access to it to other companies' brands.

Observe the Landscape Continually

Once individual functions have created their customer maps—note that these customer delineations may change over time as organizations refine their understanding—the next step is to observe the social landscape carefully to see where these constituencies are aggregating digitally and what they are saying about the industry, the organization, and its products and services. Acting like the best journalists out there, organizations listen carefully to the social environments in which their constituencies reside.

Starbucks has found that its main Twitter account allows it to take the moment-to-moment pulse of one of its key stakeholder communities: its worldwide customer base.[11] By constantly monitoring its Twitter feed, Starbucks is in touch with thousands of consumers and can essentially use social media as an early warning system. They are so confident that Twitter catches issues early that Matthew Guiste, category manager at Starbucks, said, "If it doesn't matter on Twitter, then it doesn't matter."[12]

White House press secretary Robert Gibbs has found that being on Twitter has helped the White House monitor the responses of one of its important stakeholder groups, the Press Corps, to official messages in real time.[13] By watching what reporters are tweeting about, Gibbs can see what they are reacting to and what questions of theirs remain unanswered. "It's my job to know what is important to reporters," Gibbs explained. "And this is to me a great medium to do that."[14]

By going beyond brand listening to comb the broader social web, Kraft was able to evaluate its potential entry into the mini-burger market. "When Kraft focused in on conversations specifically around 'sliders' or mini burgers, they found some common themes and 'Positive Triggers' across audiences to help focus their thinking," explained Jessica Hogue, Research Director, Online Division, Nielsen, who assisted Kraft in the listening process.[15] This expanded social listening helped the consumer food products company better understand product trends, emerging flavors, and consumer profiles.

Listening for Comments and Insights

A new tool for listening to the social web seems to be launched daily. It could be a full-time job to evaluate these tools as they emerge and to distinguish between their offerings. Fortunately, companies don't have to sort through each and every new product individually as long as they are clear about their overall goals for the tools.

Today's listening products run the spectrum from offering simple monitoring services to providing deeper analytics. How do they differ? Monitoring tools are designed to provide a consolidated list of comments based on brand-related key words. As such, they provide little, if any, analysis of patterns, trends, or insights. Analytic tools, on the other hand, are designed to aggregate data and uncover the bigger underlying picture.

Dan Neeley, chief executive officer (CEO) of Network Analytics, which makes social analytics software, explains that in his experience, companies' early-stage listening often takes the form of crisis management, as well as observing and calculating brand mentions, positive and negative. This is important and highly valuable; however, the real returns come into play when companies can tease out the emerging trends and themes within a customer group or industry.

Building upon similar observations, Jeremiah Owyang of the Altimer Group has divided the universe of corporate social media listening into eight stages.[16] Like Neeley, Owyang has observed that in the early stages of listening, companies often have no specific goal in mind for their listening; however, over time goals are developed and skills are honed. Companies begin to use social listening to identify market risks and opportunities and to respond to customer inquiries. In the most sophisticated stages of listening, companies take advantage of social tools to better understand their customers and potential customers and to develop a social Customer Relationship Management System (sCRM). This sCRM platform takes into account online behaviors, preferred social environments, and other social preferences to better identify, target, and engage prospects and existing customers.

Clearly social observation tools are calibrated for different stages along this progression. Neeley cautions companies that are considering various listening tools to "make sure you're actually getting social-media insights from your service provider, not just a data dump, because few brand teams, or marketers have time to examine thousands of comments to look for patterns or insights." He's absolutely right; in addition to volume, there can be a lot of noise in the information gathered.

As an illustration, imagine a pyramid with four levels. At the base there is "data," and lots of it. The next level is "information" and above it, "knowledge." At each ascending level, more dots are connected and more value gained. The final level—which forms a small triangle at the top—is where "wisdom" can be found. It has the smallest area and requires the most work to get at; however, like a triangle that is the strongest of all the shapes, the wisdom contained at the top is a solid foundation upon which strategy can be built.

Neeley offers several other considerations for companies that are evaluating social observation tools.[17] Timeliness is of the utmost importance. Analysis doesn't have to be provided in real-time, but a tool should be able to provide a daily analysis and synopsis of the strategic insights gleaned. The range of sources that the tools analyze is also critical. Where are the most important conversations about your product, company, and category taking place? Does the tool analyze data from those possibly niche sources? What about its ease of use? Can generalists throughout the organization evaluate the tool's output, or does it still require the expertise of market research gurus? If it requires experts to evaluate or if its reporting is too far after the fact, the goal of near real-time observation will be compromised. Finally, is the tool cost-effective?

Showering Without a Shower Curtain

With all of this listening, what is happening to consumer privacy? It is true that a lot of personal information is being gathered through tracking technology on the social web. As companies become more effective in customer interaction and data analytics, I believe that they will be able to ascertain what they really need to know to best serve their customers without going too far. How is this possible? Companies don't need to know everything about individuals. They can effectively tailor messages to consumers, providing them with the information and deals for which they are looking, based on anonymous aggregated information. If a company knows a group of people's general likes and dislikes, where they like to shop, and what kind of money they like to spend, that is enough. They will be able to make sure that those customers are in the right conversations and receiving the most appropriate offers. They don't have to dig any deeper.

It's clear that companies can benefit from this targeted messaging, but do consumers really want to receive these offers? Many do. Targeted messages and offers are likely to be deemed useful by consumers because they address a current need or interest that consumers have indicated either overtly, by providing a request for information, or inadvertently, by creating a chain of searches or comments that have alerted organizations to their interest.

Eventually the social web will evolve to the point at which consumers will build and manage their own digital marketing profiles, rather than having the multiple organizations with which they interact try to piece their interests and purchase history together. Consumers will be able to request relevant advertising and product and service information when they want it. This information will be enthusiastically received, as opposed to traditional broad brushstroke advertising, because it will be perceived as targeted, relevant, and useful.

Here's an example. Let's say you are looking for an orthodontist for your child whose teeth are coming in every which way but loose. In the future you will be able to indicate the services for which you are looking, along with any necessary qualifications, location parameters, and a preferred price point. Orthodontists who meet those criteria will be able to contact you directly at your convenience. It's likely that you will welcome this information because you will have asked for it, selected the criteria, and will enjoy its convenience. (We'll talk more about this in Chapter 10.) We are not there—yet. In the meantime, companies listen and observe.

Who's on First?

At the moment, corporate-wide observation of the social landscape is being undertaken primarily by marketing, often with the help of outside firms, because they are the most adept at market research—they've been doing it for years in traditional ways with conventional sources of information. However, the listening and observing location is usually determined by where social media activity has been taking place in companies. At the telecommunications company BT, for example, social media strategy was originally led by customer service; as a result, today the BTCare team sits within BT Customer Service, but it works closely with virtual teams across its Online, Product, PR, BT Innovate and Design, Operations, and Media areas.

What do these listening and observation teams look like? Dell has a team of listeners that report to a listening czar. Gatorade, which develops and sells products to enhance athletic performance, has its own Mission Control, a physical room lined with flat-screened monitors where Gatorade staff and their agency partners listen and interact with customers. Live feeds from multiple social platforms are continuously piped into the room, as well as into the hallways of headquarters, so that everyone within the company can be aware of what is being said in the social space about Gatorade, its products and competitors, and about sports and hydration in general. Sporting events involving the company's athletes also appear on the screens of Mission Control, making it easy for Gatorade's social media team to readily tweet or blog about plays and results as they unfold.

In addition to interacting in real-time with Gatorade's stakeholder communities, Mission Control staff generates regular reports for management—disseminated daily, weekly, and monthly—about what is taking place in "the room" and about issues or trends in the marketplace. One of the key kernels gathered through Mission Control came as the company was launching its new product line, the G Series. The company's product launch campaign was in full swing and was successfully increasing consumer awareness of the product. Discussions on Twitter and Facebook revealed, however, that consumers were having difficulty locating where they could actually purchase the new products. As a result of this feedback, the company quickly developed an online and offline product locator that solved the issue until distribution became more widely available.

Consumers have enthusiastically embraced Gatorade's involvement in the social space. "We knew that consumers were craving information," Carla Hassan, senior director-consumer engagement, told

Advertising Age. "But honestly, we didn't really realize that they were going to embrace us being live with them."[18] Although Gatorade is the first brand within the PepsiCo family to establish a Mission Control center, its experience will soon be leveraged as similar nerve centers are established across brands.

Do You Hear What I Hear?

To effectively observe and harness this conversational wisdom, over time this continuous market observation will need to become almost everyone's job. Each functional area will want to develop this listening capability to best capture the nuances of conversations.

Eventually, I envision an engagement manager resident in each corporate function, part of whose job will be to monitor conversations online and to report back to management on key issues. He or she will be charged with continually distributing corporate metrics to the company, in dashboard form. Think of it as being similar to the dashboard on a car that allows you to know in real time just how fast you are going, how much gas you have, how far you have traveled, what the temperature is inside and outside the car, and more. However, instead of car metrics, these dashboards will provide a bird's-eye view of everything of interest to a company that is taking place in social environments as well as real-time measurement of the effectiveness of the organization's engagement efforts.

When that happens, rather than marketing uncovering and addressing the concerns of former employees who are gathering in a Facebook community, human resources will identify their presence and better understand what they liked about the organization and what they would like to see improved. What's more, with a bit of training, human resources personnel will be able to actively engage with them and learn things that I wager marketing personnel and most exit interviews won't begin to uncover.

That's when a company's digital strategy will really take shape. Remember, a digital strategy gets its legs through daily engagement that falls within established enterprise guidelines, not via a predetermined, predescribed road map of what it should be doing in social environments.

What are other critical steps that companies are taking to build their enterprise-wide digital strategy? That's where we are headed in Chapter 3.

Questions to Consider

- On average, how many times a day is your company mentioned in social environments? What is being said?
- Who comprises your company's critical customer communities?
- Who are the primary influencers of the industry (ies) in which your company is involved?
- What areas of your company are actively engaged in social media and how are they benefiting from its use?
- Who is responsible for observing the digital landscape in your company? How sophisticated is your company's listening process?
- What concerns do you have about social media and privacy for your organization?

CHAPTER THREE

Building Enterprise-Wide Engagement Capability

L istening and analysis is not enough. Companies' stakeholder communities want to engage with the organizations with which they are involved. Of course, to do this effectively, employees beyond the marketing department have to be empowered to engage in a variety of digital environments. Given the newness of social destinations and the different rules of engagement that govern them, this requires employees to develop additional skill sets.

For starters, they need to know how to engage successfully and safely and how to do so in what social web users consider a timely manner. To take advantage of the insights gleaned in these conversations, employees throughout the organization also need to know how to funnel their learning back into relevant areas of the organization because customer dialogs don't necessarily follow the delineations of organizational silos. Customer service personnel may end up hearing about new product ideas, just as marketing personnel may learn about the real reason employees left to work for a competitor, and human resources may find itself in discussions about product design flaws.

Finally, employees need to be able to close the loop, explaining to various stakeholder communities what they—and the larger company—have done with the insights that have been provided. This is a critical step. It honors the people within the communities, lets them know that they are appreciated, and keeps them coming back for more conversation.

At the moment, the marketing group is often the engine behind this enterprise-wide expansion. It's the driving force because it has traditionally held the keys to communication with external constituencies and it is where most organizations' social media experience resides. Although marketing employees will remain at the heart of most organizations' social engagement, companies are benefiting from forming cross-functional steering groups, what I call the social enterprise eforum, to broaden their enterprise-wide social capabilities.

Establish a Social Enterprise eForum

The social enterprise eforum acts as a learning center, a living and breathing repository of social media knowledge, experience, and insight. The spirit of establishing this group is not to control social media engagement. Rather, the goals are to foster collaboration, to share knowledge across functions, and to reduce enterprises' processing and reacting times to enhance community engagement and strategy formulation and execution. I envision the social enterprise eforum having responsibility for several major areas:

- Governance: establishing and communicating social media policy guidelines for all employees
- Best practices: identifying and sharing best practices on social media both within one's organization and externally
- Content direction: overseeing content creation for the organization, acting almost like an old-fashioned editorial board
- Training: providing training on safe use of social media
- Technology: staying on top of the latest social media tools and platforms

- Leadership: using and championing social strategies throughout the organization
- Insight dissemination: gathering insights that have strategic implications and making sure that that knowledge gets into the relevant hands and that the customer loop is closed
- Conversation shaping: feeding strategic questions into the hands of frontline engagers so that they can go out to the living laboratory of the Web to source answers
- Conflict resolution: working closely with the corporate communications group to communicate and help resolve any issues that may arise with the company's constituencies

Social media–savvy organizations have established similar groups in a variety of shapes and forms. Several are designed as self-organizing entities that function on their own without executive direction. Others operate at the other end of the spectrum, using a top-down approach in which the chief executive officer (CEO) handpicks the members and they serve on a more conventional-style committee. Either of these models can work, as can variations on the themes, depending on the organization's culture, leadership, organizational structure, and business goals.

Some companies have established more than one entity. Coca-Cola, for example, has established two Social Media Councils, one for its national and one for its global business. Linda Cronin, director of media and interactive integrated communications, described the effect that these councils are having on Coke's business:

> Once people are on a council, they start working together. Not only do they talk about best practices, ideas, and programs they are struggling with, these groups become informal sounding boards where people feel comfortable working together and looking at things together. It's more than the actual council itself—it's about connections made across disciplines.[1]

Who comprises this cross-functional group? Members of the eforum should be socially-savvy doers and respected opinion

Figure 3.1   The Social Enterprise eForum

leaders drawn from each area of an organization that will touch or be touched by social media engagement. Think marketing, corporate communications, sales, customer service, operations, human resources, innovation, information technology (IT), legal, and government relations. Ideally there is some C-level representation in the group. (See Figure 3.1.) Although no one particular function owns this assemblage, a marketing representative, or whoever is leading the social media charge in an organization, may be the best initial moderator. This responsibility can be rotated over time as an organization's expertise grows. Humana's cross-functional "uncommittee" is an example of how this social enterprise eforum can take root.

Humana's Town Square

Greg Matthews, former director of consumer innovations at Humana, created the company's cross-functional "uncommittee" after successfully kicking off the organization's first social media engagement. Reflecting the health plan's commitment to fitness and wellness, at the 2008 Democratic and Republican conventions, Humana's innovation center launched the largest bike-sharing program in the United States. Matthew's team was charged using social media to increase awareness, participation, and excitement about the events. The "free-wheeling" campaign, which went on to win a PRSA Silver Anvil award, proved to Humana's senior management that there were ways for big companies, even in highly regulated industries, to harness the power of the social web. This "quick win" also got Matthews the go-ahead to develop a framework for the company's future social media engagement. Over the course of the next year, Humana moved forward rather quickly, executing more than 30 social media projects across 10 different functions and organizations.

The framework that Matthews created for Humana's social media expansion was an "uncommittee," modeled after a Chamber of Commerce, rather than a typical corporate committee. Matthews also envisioned an Electronic Commons Area, or town square, that was surrounded by a series of empty—but highly desirable—lots upon which every department could build whatever type of social media structure that they thought would best serve their business function. The commons was the place where each function or business unit would come out of their individual buildings to share what they were doing with the Chamber. As such, the uncommittee was designed to serve, and continues to serve, a coordinating function, not a controlling function.

The 19 members of the uncommittee were handpicked by Matthews and a handful of other social media–intrigued people at the company and came from all parts of Humana's business. There was no official leader, or executive sponsor, nor were minutes taken from meetings. Instead, the group shared ideas, invited in experts with which to consult, and brainstormed programs that were in the works. They live tweeted all their meetings and shared their findings on an internal blog and externally on www.crumpleitup.com.[2] This unconventional process was quite inspiring to Humana's employees. One participant shared the following in a post on Crumple It Up shortly after their first gathering:

> An amazing thing happened to me at work the other day . . .
> I got to sit in a large boardroom with leaders from around our
> little Fortune 100 company to take part in a discussion about
> shaping the social media policy for Humana, and a record
> of the event can be found on Twitter. That's right; it's been
> captured in the public domain. Seriously. Now, as a project

manager I've facilitated and sat in my share of project kick-off meetings. Most of them have been tremendous wastes of time. . . .

When the team meeting got under way, everyone was expecting more of the same and that's when one of the team members threw the room a giant curve ball: Let's do a live tweet stream of the meeting's high points and use this record for our meeting notes. My hand was giddy at the thought of not having to feverishly scribble down notes, so I was obviously in favor of the Twitter option. We went around the room to get consensus, and there were some legitimate concerns about being too transparent, but we ended up agreeing to a basic KISS guideline: when in doubt, don't Tweet it . . .

After sitting through this particular kick-off meeting, I think that we're on the right track. There was a genuine exchange of ideas. Viewpoints were clarified and understood with the high points going out on Twitter. People were smiling. It was amazing.[3]

Despite this enthusiasm, Matthews cautions that, "This organic model may not be right for every organization. I knew that at Humana, if we tried to be too controlling, it would be easy for people to run for the hills." Matthews also feels strongly that a safe space for experimentation is critical to really discover the possibilities of something new like social media. "If you try too soon to build a strategy, it can be limiting. Start building the capacity and then see what can happen."

Now that the company has an extensive portfolio of social experience upon which to draw, Matthew believes that the need for a more coherent strategy is emerging. Toward this end, the uncommittee has established core principles that govern social web participation—"they give us flexibility as well as something to hold on to"—and is beginning to develop processes that provide a solid way of quantifying and reporting on their learning and results.

Matthews hopes that Humana's social engagement efforts will continue to grow and that eventually every employee across Humana will act as the organization's eyes, ears, and voice:

When you think about 30,000 employees each doing a little bit in their own space, all of a sudden you have this incredibly active and vibrant set of conversations going on. If you do it right, that information can be continuously measured and reported to your senior strategy team for them to be able to take action on.

Broaden Your Base of Engagers over Time

Who should comprise the company's voice? Companies' choices run the full spectrum from having only one Twitter handle to, as Matthews envisions, empowering every professional within their organization to engage. Of course, the answer to this question depends on what kind of engagement you are looking for. If you are asking your employees to only forward special offers or job openings through their personal networks, that is quite different than asking them to be the eyes, ears, and voice of your organization.

To build broader institutional capability, some organizations prefer to build their organization's voice internally first. This was the tactic that General Mills took. An internal portal enabled employees to form communities and discussion groups early on. Over time, best practices emerged and leadership began to recognize and embrace further possibilities. Today the company is actively applying social tools both internally and externally.

Other companies, recognizing that much of the knowledge they are after is located outside of their organizations, jump right in, using social tools to engage with their external constituencies. If you have chosen the latter route, don't neglect the internal applications. There are sizeable dividends to be had from tapping into the full capacity of the minds within your own organization.

Whatever the case, in every organization, building an institution's voice is an evolutionary process. Initially most companies start with a few voices. As their comfort and capability grow, more and more people become involved and discover new and varied ways to achieve their functions' goals.

Dell, for example, has realized that, given the enormous daily volume of commentary about the company in social environments, keeping its social media effort centralized is limiting the company's overall effectiveness. Although its social media group has expanded over time to keep pace with the number of venues and business objectives being addressed, Lionel Menchaca, the company's chief blogger, believes that Dell can't grow the group large enough to address each of these mentions individually. Instead, the company is looking to tap "responders" and subject matter experts in functions throughout the company to assist the social media group in engaging in many of these conversations. Areas of the organization that are being corralled to help connect, act, and close the loop with customers include Customer Service & Tech Support, Product Group & Professional Services, Communications, Marketing & Online, and Sales. To help better scale its efforts, Dell is also investigating a semi-automated approach to customer engagement. By formalizing some of their responses, redirecting customer requests to venues where the answers to frequently asked questions can be readily found, Dell hopes to be able to realize some gains in efficiency while still connecting with its key communities.

IBM's Progression

IBM has taken a "full-on" approach to its enterprise-wide engagement from the beginning. As a result, Big Blue is one of the most socially engaged organizations out there. The company doesn't have its own corporate blog or Twitter account; instead, it calls upon "IBMers" in aggregate to be the company's voice. "We represent our brand online the way it always has been, which is employees first," explained Adam Christensen, who shepherds social media efforts across the company and globally. "Our brand is largely shaped by the interactions that they have with customers."[4]

A few statistics provide a fuller picture. The company has more than 200,000 current IBMers on LinkedIn. That is, according to Christensen, the largest single community of corporate employees on any social network platform, anywhere. More than 1,000 current IBMers blog externally; the majority represent the company off domain. Three thousand IBMers are active on Twitter; 75,000 are active on Facebook; and approximately 100,000 current and former IBMers are involved with IBM's Alumni Social Network. That equates to a lot of voices talking about the company and listening for insights. The company recently launched its IBM Expert Network on Slide-Share to help consolidate some of the thinking of several of its thought leaders. Although only 50 experts are currently represented on the network, the company plans to work with SlideShare to grow its global presence over time.[5]

IBM did not get here overnight. The roots of its widespread employee engagement began in its now famous 2003 company "jam." This online collaborative event, which has since been repeated annually and has served as a model for many other organizations, set the stage. Christensen remembers the first few hours of the multiple-day experience as being quite negative but says that tone soon gave way to constructive discussion.[6] As a result of that social engagement, IBM learned that it could trust employees to engage. Similarly, employees realized that if they acted within reason, they were going to be trusted. Shortly thereafter the company created internal blogging platforms for their employees to continue talking. With this experience in hand, employees later began blogging externally.

IBM makes it a practice to launch in-house versions of social media tools that are proving themselves in the broader marketplace. Today, about a quarter of its employees are registered on the company's internal blogging platform, where they rate and comment on 17,000 internal blogs. More than a million page views are tracked on the company's internal wiki daily, and downloads from the jukebox, the company's media library, exceed 11 million. Employees share information about themselves on the company's social network, tweet internally through Blue Twit, and bookmark information on Dogear, a tool similar to Delicious. (A public site has come out of the latter, DogearNation. Written by three IBMers, it offers a humorous take on technology and Web 2.0.)

This in-house experience not only builds corporate capability for external engagement but helps the organization collaborate more efficiently and effectively internally. Furthermore, this internal learning lab provides firsthand knowledge about what works and what doesn't when it comes to collaborative systems, information that IBM Research's Collaborative User Division funnels directly into the company's product line—think Lotus.

Are There Downsides to Multiple Voices?

There are downsides to everything in life; the trick is to mitigate these risks as best we can. I like the idea of multiple voices representing a company. It creates a richer, fuller, and more accurate market presence than any centralized communications staff could ever hope to achieve on its own. Is it confusing in the marketplace to have so many voices, platforms, and perspectives? Not if employees identify themselves, state where they are from, and make it clear that they are speaking on their own behalf, and not necessarily representing the company's official point of view. More often than not, multiple voices are more effective at getting customers the information for which they are looking. For example, if you had a question about your new Dell Netbook, wouldn't you appreciate being able to converse with a Netbook expert rather than a social media or marketing guru? Of course, employees throughout multiple departments must be well trained in how to communicate transparently, prudently, and effectively with social tools.

What if an employee makes a mistake publicly? It has happened multiple times in the past and will in the future. However, the social web is great about self-editing. Jon Iwata, senior vice president of communications at IBM, told the story of how one blogger at the company spread a false rumor that IBM was about to lay off 130,000 employees. (To put this number in context, that is more than a third of its workforce.) "All kinds of IBMers showed up on this person's blog" to refute the rumor, which, according to Iwata, "carried much more credibility than any official company response and helped dampen any media backlash from the incident."[7]

What if one or several voices become very well known and quite influential in and of themselves? Does this detract from the corporate voice? I don't think so. Does quarterback Tom Brady's notoriety detract from that of the Patriots football team, or does it add to it? What if a significant voice leaves the company? Hopefully the company has taken steps to build out the enterprise's social engagement ability and has put a sustainable process in place that will live beyond the tenure of a single individual. If it has, then the company can move on with its multiple other voices keeping the conversation going. Perhaps the former employee will continue to use his or her voice to support the company in other social destinations.

Pursue a Strategic Approach to Social Engagement

The applications of social media to business challenges are just beginning to unfold and are limitless. To ensure their success in your organization, however, you have to fight what marketing strategist and blogger B.L. Ochman calls the urge to GMOOT—"get me one of those"—in favor of a more strategic approach.

At my companies, we use a four-step approach to social engagement that has proved itself countless times. The process is both linear and iterative. It starts with setting strategic goals for social engagement programs and continues sequentially through design, activation, and sustainment, followed by measurement and analytics (see Figure 3.2). Insights gleaned through the process allow organizations to optimize their engagement for the next iteration of the cycle.

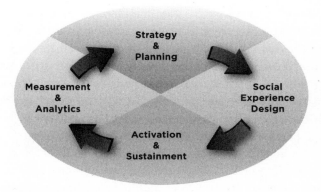

Figure 3.2 A Strategic Approach to Social Engagement

Although discussion of this process could warrant a chapter in and of itself, let me hit some of the highlights here. I'll illustrate each step with a brief explanation of how one of our clients, Sony, went about designing a program to set the stage for the relaunch of its eBook Readers.

Step 1: Social Media Engagement Begins with Business Goals

Although Sony was first to the United States market in 2006, Amazon's Kindle's marketing muscle had stolen the limelight in the digital reader category. This was a David and Goliath situation in which, ironically, technology giant Sony was actually in David's role. A tremendous market opportunity was on the horizon as the e-reader category was growing; its appeal was spreading beyond early adopters and niche customers to a broader mass audience. A dramatic shift in marketing was needed to fuel this growth and to ensure that Sony captured a good portion of the growing market share. With the imminent launch of a new line of Readers in the summer of 2009, Sony's goals were to drive brand preference and sales of Sony Readers and to accomplish this by creating a strong emotional connection around the product with customers through social media.

As this Sony snippet illustrates, successful social engagement is rooted in business objectives—not in a desire to "be on Twitter" or to "build a microsite." Twitter and microsites are tools, and tools only, with which organizations address business opportunities and challenges. Before undertaking any social media initiative, companies need to make sure that it is clear how the proposed activity will touch their consumers and other key communities. This may sound obvious, but it's a discipline every organization has to develop.

Examples of clear goals include increasing awareness, driving sales, providing industry thought leadership, soliciting input into product development, improving customer service, or increasing employee retention. Note that as multiple functions begin to engage in social media, new business objectives should develop.

Step 2: Align Social Programs with Business Objectives

The cornerstone of the social media program that we worked with Sony to build was an important insight: people love connecting around books. Readers love to share their favorite literary moments—those quotes and poems that have impacted them, those characters and authors that they have hated or admired. Think Holden Caulfield, *Huckleberry Finn*, Ayn Rand, and the *Little Engine That Could*. Using this insight as a launching pad, we created a social media program that encouraged people to connect and share the literary moments they love with others. This program took the form of a community-focused microsite experience in which users were able to share and search for book and poetry suggestions by title, author, topic, or even emotion; a distributable blogger widget program; and several features to share across platforms like Twitter and Facebook. Through this multi-pronged program we were able to introduce a broader audience—skewing older and more female—to Sony's Reader products.

As you can see from Sony's experience, the second step in the social media strategic process is designing the social experience. This is where strategic insights and business objectives are carefully aligned with social media tools. In addition to understanding how customers connect emotionally around a product or service, at this stage it is vital to have a handle on their purchase behavior surrounding the product or service and the role social media plays in influencing those decisions. (We will talk more about this in Chapter 5.) What online and offline channels do consumers utilize at different stages of their purchase journey? Is it enough to be present in existing communities, or does the company need to create its own digital destinations? The answers to these questions will fall out naturally from the original research that was done on the target market, its influencers, and personas.

For example, with The Art of Shaving, we decided that, given the richness of the dialog that is already taking place about their brand and the category on the social web, its social media engagement would initially take the form of reaching out to customers in these existing social environments. In addition, like Threadless, we would work with them to both mirror and augment the digital experience in The Art of Shaving's physical retail stores. On the other hand, for Sony, we reached out to existing communities through a blogger widget program, Facebook, and Twitter and we also created a new digital destination, a social community through which literature lovers could connect.

Step 3: Activate Your Program

This site or application is built and launched. Everyone can sit back and watch the results roll in, right? Wrong. This is when the work really begins because, contrary to Ray Kinsella's conviction in the movie *Field of Dreams,* if you build it, they won't necessarily come. Indeed, many companies, having invested time and money in social media pilots have become frustrated by the lack of business. They may have tried to build a community, a blog, or a Facebook page, and despite great content, have not seen results. The conversation is not taking place.

Often the culprit is a failure to really engage consumers. It's not enough to just create the tool; the tool has to be activated so that the real value of social engagement—dialog—can take place. Building a social experience for targeted communities without a plan to reach them and stimulate their involvement is like building a luxury resort on an undiscovered island without any infrastructure to get people there.

In my companies we talk about *social activation,* which is our term for energizing a social initiative. It involves both reaching out to customers in the environments in which they are already active and guiding customers into an organization's own social destinations. How does activation work? It involves creating an outreach strategy for each key influencer. This personalization is important. To be effective, organizations should understand each potential influencer's voice, focus, opinions, and biases. What are their hot buttons? What other brands or companies have they been involved with? What is their preferred way to be contacted?

The problem that follows is how to engage influencers. A variety of roles exist for them to play; what is essential is making the right match. What are some of the ways influencers can be involved? Have them advise you on your social media plans before a launch. Ask them to serve as a program expert by writing or commenting on specific issues. Engage them in promotions such as a contest, product giveaway, or special offers. Invite them to test a new program or product. Or simply ask them to mention your product or service in posts on their blogs.

What Would Sony Do?   For Sony, activation meant reaching out to bloggers who were actively engaged in the world of books. Sony wanted to get these bloggers and their followers involved in the program with the goal of driving awareness and consideration of Sony's Reader products. To accomplish this, Sony provided 24 bloggers with a widget that they could embed in their own blog that captured the blogger's contributions to Sony's literary site. Their favorite quotes, characters, and literary moments were right there, front and center, for all of their readers to enjoy. They also offered bloggers a giveaway, a Sony Reader Pocket Edition, to, you guessed it, give away on their sites in whatever way they chose.

One blogger, Booking Mama,[8] asked her readers to comment on a book they had read when they were growing up that had stayed with them. Her plan was to select the five "best" answers and then randomly select the grand-prize winner who would receive the Reader. Little did she know how hard that task would be when her challenge was more than enthusiastically received. She wrote:

> I was blown away by all of your responses, and I could definitely relate to many of your feelings. The responses were just amazing—some made me laugh and some even made me cry. Many of your comments brought back wonderful memories about books that I read and loved as a child. Quite a few of your comments made me write down books that I definitely need to read and even reread. I have to say that narrowing the list down to five was next to impossible for me.[9]

Develop a Sustainment Plan   True activation builds an audience over time not just at the launch of a social media program. What are the day-to-day activities that ultimately drive success? Once again, it's quite different from traditional marketing. What I call *social* *sustainment* involves daily and weekly review of program results and identification of new ways to improve the experience.

Creating and sustaining an active presence over the long term takes active planning. Recognize that whatever business you are in, if you are active in the social web, you are now also a publisher. Content is what drives engagement. It is the motivator, the reason that customers continue to engage with you over time. Content can take all sorts of forms—blog posts, tweets, Facebook comments, SlideShare, short videos, webinars, white papers, interviews with experts, contests, gaming, physical events, and more. Don't forget user-generated content; it is often the best and most widely viewed by consumers. (We'll talk more specifically about content generation in Chapters 5 and 6.)

Step 4: Measurement and Analytics

The final step in the four-step strategy process is measuring and analyzing, or understanding the effect of your program.[10] As social media becomes an integral part of organization's outreach, companies need to be able to effectively measure the success of their programs. Questions to ask include: Did the program meet the goals outlined in Step 1? What worked, and what didn't? Were we able to capture the desired data and insights? How should the program be modified to achieve better results? What was the return on investment (ROI)?

Whereas companies have gotten traditional marketing channel measurement down to a science, they are less comfortable with measuring their social media programs. According to a recent study conducted by Babson Executive Education and Mzinga, 80 percent of marketers surveyed are not currently measuring the effectiveness of their social media programs.[11]

In my discussions with companies, I've uncovered several reasons for this lack of analysis, including an incomplete integration of social and traditional marketing programs, a lack of standard metrics and easy-to-use and affordable measurement tools, and the absence of a strategic approach to creating sustained ROI. The good news is that much progress is being made in all of these areas and companies can increasingly measure social media ROI with confidence.

At present, there are two basic categories of metrics that can be used for ongoing optimization and sustainment: activation and business metrics. Whereas activation metrics tell you how effectively you are aggregating and engaging an audience, business metrics measure ROI. These metrics, combined with anecdotal experience, can help companies evaluate the overall effectiveness of their social media engagements.

Data regarding reach, engagement, and sentiment are the fuel for social activation metrics. These metrics can be captured by popular and specialty search engines, social media platform analytics, and Web analytics.

Reach describes how well social tools are reaching your target audience. Metrics for measuring reach include:

- Number of users reached
- Number of visits
- Number of unique visitors
- Number of page views
- Content viewed

Engagement metrics address the question of how customers are engaging with the brand. Did they spend 20 seconds or 10 minutes on the site? Did they comment on the content, rate it, share it, or download it? Engagement metrics include:

- Time spent
- Repeat visits
- Choosing to follow on Twitter; retweets
- Facebook fan page additions
- Registrations
- Contest entries
- Reviews
- Downloads, viral forwards

Business metrics reflect changes in attitude and behavior. Specifically, attitudinal measures consist of:

- Brand/product awareness
- Brand affinity
- Brand perception
- Purchase intent

Several companies are developing technology that will allow data to become increasingly portable and sharable across programs and campaigns, making it possible for companies to significantly broaden their understanding of users. As this technology continues to evolve, companies will be able to use an integrated measurement dashboard to view performance of their social media initiatives across a whole slew of channels—the company web site, Facebook, Twitter, Yahoo!, and other social environments, and link this information to behaviors such as registrations and purchases.

Now we look back to the Sony tale. How did their social engagement fare? In less than 90 days, Sony recorded a 247 percent increase in dialog volume about its Readers and a 7-percentage point shift in positive sentiment. In terms of the blogger widget program, the 24 widgets led to 7,362 comments, 49,110 page views, and 1,726 "literary moments" posted. Did it affect readers' interest in Sony Readers? It turns out that many of the visitors who browsed the literary moments on the site also sought further information about Sony's products: 38 percent viewed product content and 23 percent clicked through to the Sony Store for greater product details.

Create New Social Media Roles

As social media engagement spreads throughout an organization, several new roles must be developed and woven into its organizational structure to support each function's efforts.[12] A summary diagram of these roles and their major responsibilities can be found in Figure 3.3. Although many specifics about these job descriptions and qualifications follow, let me also say that there is a lot of flexibility around these roles. They can exist centrally and

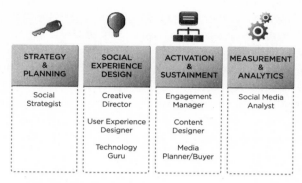

Figure 3.3 New Social Media Roles

be shared across an organization; they can be provided by an outside agency; or they can be housed in specific business groups. For smaller companies, they may be merged into fewer roles. What matters most is that they are woven into the four-part strategic process previously described.

The Social Strategist

This new role helps kick off any function's social media engagement. Social strategists work with each function to articulate the business goals that their proposed social media program is designed to meet and to translate these goals into achievable and measurable objectives (Step 1). After helping to articulate these goals, the social strategist then designs and executes a research plan that addresses key areas of investigation and measurement:

- Listening: scanning and analyzing conversations on blogs, social networks, and other communities to learn what is being said about the brand, product, service, or issue
- Behavioral research: observing the target audience's social behavior to see what people are downloading, what they are sharing, who they are friending, what they are retweeting

- Competitive analysis: tracking how the competition is using social media to engage with customers and influencers
- Audience insights: coming to a deep understanding of the persona of the target audience and determining their needs and likely behaviors
- Actionable recommendations: converting insights into actionable recommendations for how the company can deliver on those needs and behaviors through the social experience

Based on this comprehensive research and insights, the social strategist develops the following types of strategies:

- Integration: ensure the integration of traditional and social media strategies and programming
- Measurement: establish metrics to measure the success of the marketing plan and evaluate the contribution of social media
- Resource allocation: identify the budget and other resources required to implement the strategy
- Internal champion: get buy-in from other internal executives and socialize the plan with other functional areas

Given the nature of the responsibilities and functions previously discussed, it is apparent that the social strategist is not a junior-level position. It should be filled by someone who is not only social media savvy but who also has solid experience in strategy development, business planning, research, measurement, and analytics and who can play a leadership role in championing social strategies. This position does not have to be filled in-house, however. Many companies look to agencies for strategic input and guidance.

Creative Director, User Experience Designer, and Technology Guru

Three additional roles are critical to creating an effective social experience: creative director, user experience designer, and technology guru. Depending on the size and complexity of the programs and the technology platforms that need to be developed in support of them, these roles can exist internally or be outsourced. Here again, there can be some benefits to hiring an agency that has extensive capability and dedicated design and technology experts. When working with agencies, companies will achieve the greatest results when the agency team is integrated into all of the planning, input, and feedback sessions.

The creative director is responsible for the overarching creative idea that drives the entire social program and supports the original strategy. It goes without saying, but I am going to say it anyway, that the creative idea must be engaging, articulate the type of experience the user should have, and in the end, realize business results. Creative directors drive ideation and concretize big ideas, oversee all creative work through strong program management skills, and understand the technologies required to support the creative vision.

The depth and breadth of skill level necessary for the creative director varies according to the strategies developed. If the strategy calls for developing a rich community-oriented site that requires extensive creative input to ensure a consistent branded experience and complex technology platform—as in the case of Sony—companies will need a creative director with a more extensive skill set. Or they may look for an agency to fulfill this role. If the strategy is based on existing virtual communities, such as Facebook or Twitter, then there is less of a requirement for extensive design and development skills (think: The Art of Shaving).

The user experience designer (UX designer) translates the high-level user experience into functionality, features, and look and feel across all social channels. UX designers must be deeply experienced in information architecture, usability, user interface design, heuristics, and human factors and behaviors.

The technology guru is just what it sounds like. Someone who understands the underlying technology required to support the creative idea and design. This is a challenging role because the online environment is heterogeneous, open, and constantly changing as technologies evolve. Online performance affects the user experience and engagement. If the site doesn't work, the links are broken, or download of content is too slow, the user experience will be poor and the user will disengage. If it's done well, the technology will be almost transparent and, as one of my colleagues says, somewhat magical.

Engagement Manager, Content Manager, and Media Planner/Buyer

As you now know, social activation brings social experiences out to target audiences and draws target audiences to companies' social destinations. Although most companies focus on the design stage of this process (Step 2), this third step is critical to the ongoing success of the program, to driving business outcomes, and to maximizing ROI. The three key roles in this third stage include engagement manager, content manager, and media planner/buyer.

The engagement manager identifies key influencers and then engages them in discussions about a brand, product, service, or issue. This role is referred to as community manager in many companies, but I have expanded it to engagement manager because this person's responsibilities are not limited to communities. Engagement managers should have excellent listening skills, know how to use listening tools to monitor conversations online, and be able to find the right tone to use with each influencer. They should also be able to report back to management on key issues and respond quickly to requests and feedback. Public relations (PR) professionals are generally good candidates for this role.

The content manager is responsible for the materials presented to this group across all social channels. This integration is important; it considers your customers' entire virtual experience with your organization. A soup-to-nuts approach works best, including integrating everything from a Google search to a corporate web site and microsites, from a web site to a YouTube channel, from a Facebook page to a Twitter handle.

The content manager must continually provide something of value to engage people in conversations. This person should be able to conduct content audits throughout an organization, keep a content calendar, create original content in many formats—SlideShare, webinars, podcasts, video shorts, blog posts, tweets, Facebook comments, and so on—and repackage existing content for different communities across the social web. Content managers need to have strong editorial skills and be experienced in packaging content in different formats. This position is often filled by former magazine or newspaper editors or broadcast producers who know how to create large amounts of content efficiently and effectively.

The main function of a media planner/buyer is to recommend the best possible mix of media to reach, engage, and sustain target audiences. Media planners/buyers develop media strategy for paid and unpaid media, negotiate rates and copy deadlines, and arrange terms for merchandising deals with the media. This role is often outsourced to an agency that has expertise in negotiating media buys and can take advantage of volume purchases to obtain better pricing.

Social Media Analyst

The last new role, social media analyst, is responsible for assessing whether programs meet marketing and business goals and for providing recommendations on how to optimize programs to achieve better results. This role analyzes both activation metrics (reach, engagement, and sentiment) and business outcomes (attitudinal and behavioral).

As the title suggests, this person must have strong analytical skills and be able to parse through mountains of data and metrics to extract the insights that are most important to evaluating the success of social media programs. He or she must have excellent communication and business skills to measure ROI and present findings and recommendations to executives. Frequently this role can be integrated into other online analytics activities, but regardless of where it resides, knowledge and the ability to understand social media measurement and tools are key.

Engage, Engage, and Engage Some More

You can read books, blogs, and case studies about social media engagement until you are blue in the face, but it isn't until an organization starts to experiment more broadly that it will begin to gain traction. Encourage every area of your organization to find a piece of their business that may gain results from social media. Human resources can start with posting a job opening on Facebook and sales can prospect in LinkedIn or Twitter. (See Chapter 9 for how to do this.) Eventually, the social enterprise eforum should collect findings from each function's engagement (both anecdotal and hardcore metrics in the form of page views, conversions, hires, sales, etc.) to build a central repository of a company's learning. This record will be important in making the case for taking additional steps toward social enterprise development.

Where does the money come from for social engagement? Once again, there is some good news. Depending upon the size of your program, social engagement can be relatively less expensive than mass media and more effective. (We'll examine the reasons for this more closely in Chapter 6.) By reallocating marketing dollars to social destinations, many companies are able to spend less on marketing while still improving their performance. Sound too good to be true? It's not. Social engagement can take time, however. Once again, resources can be shifted from one area to another. In marketing, for example, there will be less of a need for an exclusive direct-mail or advertising person; these resources can be refocused to include social media engagement.

Proactively Manage the Enterprise-Wide Brand

There are some things that social media engagement has not changed. Marketing continues to have responsibility for oversight of the enterprise-wide brand. What has changed is that marketing is no longer the exclusive voice of the company. Professionals across the enterprise will eventually comprise the company's voice and, together, with the multiplicity of other stakeholder voices, shape the enterprise's brand. Managing the enterprise-wide brand has become a broader and more complex responsibility because there are so many moving parts.

As a result, marketing's role is morphing into becoming a purveyor of the environment and an overseer of an organization's Web 2.0 activities. Working with senior management and the social enterprise eforum, the marketing group ensures that there is a consistency in vision across an enterprise and a demonstrated link between each function's or business unit's social media programs and overall corporate strategy. It measures the organization's effectiveness in its social engagements. Are we making progress? Are there more positive comments than negative comments? Are our customers getting our messaging? Do they understand what we stand for? Are we charging the right prices? Are our employees learning what they need to know to effectively engage and learn in social environments? Reflecting the evolution of this department's role, the chief marketing officer's role will eventually morph into a chief social officer.

Close Up with Threadless's Social Strategist

Jake Nickell is Threadless's chief strategic officer (CSO). As a leader of a small and fast-growing company, he has his hands in many pots, including helping to code the company's web site and even submitting his own T-shirt designs for consideration to the Threadless communities. A handful of marketers assist him in maintaining the company's design and customer communities by monitoring the discussions, keeping the conversation going, and determining when to make a community-based initiative—a contest, for example— officially sponsored by the company. The team helps plan physical events—content in the flesh—such as the Threadless Everywhere Tour across the country, to further engage and put faces on the community.

Another of Nickell's primary roles as CSO is maintaining the culture of the company as it grows. This turns out to be a challenge because the company is growing rapidly and people hired from the outside often don't understand how a community-centric organization like Threadless operates. The company tries to home-grow its leadership to provide a growth path for employees and to ensure that its leadership understands the company from the bottom up. A prime example is the head of warehouse operations; he started as a temp with the company several years ago.

Sometimes an outside hire is necessary. When Nickell hired a CEO, the new hire's task for the first four months was to "not do any work—just build friendships and an understanding of how the company works." In this same spirit, every new employee spends his or her first week on the job working in the warehouse, filling orders, and getting to know the ins and outs of Threadless's operations. Monthly "awesome parties" that often have a community service angle help foster a sense of connectedness internally.

Nickell is also in charge of the company's physical space—they've had to move several times in the last decade to accommodate their growth—to make sure that it is conducive to community building. (He has found that creating an environment that is akin to a boys' and girls' club works well.) To bring the digital community into the space along with them, he regularly tweets about their headquarters' renovations and posts pictures of progress on Flickr. Nickell's role as a CSO clearly includes but extends beyond the use of social media tools. As he says, "It's all about building community."

A View from the Yellow Arches

Rick Wion is the first director of social media for McDonald's. As the world's largest hamburger chain—it serves more than 58 million customers daily—and one of the most talked about brands in social environments, Wion has a fabulous opportunity for social media engagement. As a director of social media, Wion is responsible for understanding how the company can best use social media externally, the tools that are involved, and the communities with which McDonald's wants to engage. Wion connects closely with a working group comprised of constituencies inside of McDonald's, such as the internal social media team, corporate communications, and the sustainability team, to make sure that their social media efforts are aligned. "We want to make sure that we are all singing from the same song book," Wion told me.

Wion works closely with each of the local McDonald's regions in the country; there are more than 20 and each has its own marketing teams, PR agencies, and ad agencies. How does corporate coordinate social marketing efforts with each of these regions? "It's all about alignment; alignment with a capital 'A,'" Wion explained.

Corporate creates the framework through which the local groups operate. For example, McDonald's has a national Twitter page as do the local regions. The local regions distinguish themselves by their geography; Atlanta is "MCD Atl," and Philadelphia is "MCD Phili." Consumers can choose to follow the company at the national level, the local level, or both depending on their interests. McDonald's corporate Facebook page has a similar capability. Consumers can input their zip codes and receive customized, local information. This feature is important because although many people think of McDonald's as a global brand, a lot of folks identify with the local restaurant down the street.

Wion spends a lot of time getting to know bloggers—mommy bloggers, nutrition bloggers, online game influencers, regional bloggers, and more. His job is also all about relationship building. Often Wion helps locally focused bloggers get to know the resident owners of the neighborhood franchises in the hopes that they can work together. This community outreach is what keeps Wion tweeting from his phone on the train home from work in the evening. As he told me, "Last night I was having a Twitter conversation with a mommy blogger who was opening up for the first time. It is super having the ability to connect with people like that. We were swapping stories about kids . . . these conversations just give you a lift in your job."

Get Senior Leadership Involved

An organization can't develop the comprehensive digital strategy that transforms it into a social enterprise without the help of senior management. In the experimental stage of the social web, it often was the case that social media efforts sprung up organically and were conducted without executive direction and even sponsorship. Software developers and engineers launched a wiki for product collaboration; human resources began to reach out to candidates via LinkedIn and Facebook; customer service monitored complaints and sent updates via Twitter; marketing hired an intern or a recent college graduate to set up a Facebook page or Twitter account to promote new products and services. Although this organic approach worked fine for limited pilots, it doesn't scale as companies' use of social media takes off and becomes mission-critical.

Setting the tone for the organization, asking the strategic questions that can help front-liners best learn from social media conversations, integrating strategy that bubbles up from below, being a source of content for the organization's thought leadership, influencing and implementing a community conflict resolution plan, and reworking an organization's culture, structure, and incentive systems are all work of an organization's leadership team. These are topics we'll address in the following chapter.

Questions to Consider

- Does your company have an entity like the social enterprise eforum? If so, is it working? Why or why not? If not, why not?
- Who currently comprises your company's voice in the social space? Does it make sense to expand this presence? If so, what needs to be done?
- Does your company pursue a strategic approach to social engagement?
- Are there any aspects of my proposed strategic approach to social engagement that may be useful to emphasize in your company?
- Is there a need for any of the new social media roles I have outlined for your company?
- How involved is your company's leadership in social media? Do they view it as mission critical?

CHAPTER FOUR

Developing a Digitally Driven Company

Culture, Structure, and Leadership

I t is often the case that a company will observe the social media success of other companies and try to replicate their programs hoping
for similar outcomes. What's going on when, at the end of the day,
their results are completely different? Sometimes it is as simple as the
"me too" company not having developed the requisite social media
engagement skills. But more often than not, the difference is cultural.

"Culture is, in my view, the most overlooked, underestimated
factor determining whether social media succeeds or fails in a company," explained Andy Piper, social bridge builder and a consulting
information technology (IT) specialist working for IBM Software
Group in the United Kingdom. "And when corporate culture and
social media are pitted against each other, social media will always fail.
Always."[1]

To develop a social enterprise, management has to be intentional
about creating a culture that values openness, transparency,

collaboration, and innovation. Although many social forces are making this directional move inevitable, it often goes against the grain of how companies have traditionally been run, not to mention with what they have been familiar and have valued, and with how they have evaluated their people. That doesn't mean that it cannot be done. In fact, hopefully I have convinced you that it has to be done for companies to thrive in the social media age. Although I am by no means an expert in organizational change, I can suggest a few things that management can do to enhance their organizations' success in becoming a social enterprise.

Create the Vision

At the heart of any social enterprise is a vision of what it would look like to be a truly customer-centric organization. This goes beyond mere customer focus to actually shifting the center of gravity of an organization toward its stakeholders. It means getting to know what stakeholders really want from a company, the context of their demand, and the kind of communities in which they want to be a part. It means designing processes and systems to make that type of customer experience possible. It means rethinking consumer touch points to see how new social technologies, particularly mobile, can augment their experience. In essence it is creating more porous boundaries between a company and the outside world.

Selected organizations and industries have been moving toward this openness for several years. Technology companies led the way in the 1980s as they formed user groups for their software products. Customers, often competitors, would gather in the same rooms for days at a time, sharing information about how they used a company's products, how products and processes could be improved, and what additional features would be useful. Eventually, as the enabling technology became available, online communities supplemented these physical gatherings.

From Technology to Shoes and Housewares

Today many companies operating in and across multiple industries are learning to be more customer-centric, even Internet-based shoe companies. Zappos, for example, is consistently held up as an example of a company that gets customer orientation. Indeed, Zappos's chief executive officer (CEO), Tony Hsieh, will tell you that the company's goal is to provide the best customer experience possible. What they are selling is secondary—although they are expanding quite nicely these days into apparel, accessories, and housewares. "We think we're just at the tip of the iceberg of what's possible as we continue to build the Zappos brand to be about the very best customer service and the very best customer experience," Hsieh wrote in a recent update that he posted on his blog.[2]

How does Zappos do it? It starts at the very foundation: whom it hires. Hsieh talks of the importance of hiring people who embody what the company values. Toward this end, each potential hire goes through two sets of interviews, one to ascertain relevant experience and technical ability and the second to determine whether there is a cultural fit. Recruits have to pass both sets of interviews to be hired.

The next step in culture building is training. Everyone who is hired goes through the same four weeks as a call center representative, regardless of the position for which they are hired. This training includes indoctrination in Zappos's culture, core values, customer service, and how the warehouse works. It also includes two weeks of fielding phone calls from customers, a practice that reflects the company's belief that customer service is everyone's job, not just that of the function that bears its name. At the end of the first week of training, the company offers new recruits a quitting bonus of $2,000 to help weed out the people who are there only for the paycheck—it saves them the cost of putting them though the rest of the training sessions. Less than 1 percent of new hires take them up on the offer, which stands through the end of the training period.

The company uses social media to provide its stakeholder communities with a broader glimpse into the company's culture. "We don't really think of them as marketing channels so much as ways to develop a more personal connection with people, whether they are other employees or our customers," Hsieh explains.[3] Of course, Hsieh knows that culture is tantamount to a company's brand, so indirectly all of these efforts are, on some level, marketing. Hsieh blogs, but not excessively. Other employees blog on topics such as family, the outdoors, and health and fitness. Employees are not required to use Twitter, but more than 400 employees currently do—with substantial followings. Every employee also reads and contributes to Zappos's culture book, which is unedited and provides a comprehensive, life-in-the-trenches snapshot of what makes the company tick.

Empowerment and purpose, rather than high salaries and bonuses, ignite employees' motivation. They are entrusted to represent the Zappos brand and to do whatever they can to meet—and exceed—customer expectations. They can help customers find the shoe or bag they want, return the items, and even tell them where they can get any items if they are not available at Zappos. Recently they walked a friend of mine through the steps of reporting credit card fraud after she had received a package from Zappos that she had not ordered. They arranged for UPS to pick up the package and even called to see if they could be of further assistance the next day.

Zappos's customer service is always on and available by phone, web site, or Twitter, although 95 percent of transactions take place through their web site. The web site is chock full of video product descriptions and contains customer comments and videos describing individual items and their experience with the company as a whole. Free shipping, both ways, combined with a 365-day return policy, reduces the risk associated with online purchases for consumers. Its warehouse is open 24/7, and the company keeps an inventory of all of the products it sells so that items are readily available—most often in customers' hands within 24 hours.

Here's an example of how far Zappos will take customer service. One unfortunate day in 2010, the company's computer system had a glitch, and for several hours, everything on its sister web site, 6pm.com, was priced at $49.95 or less. This included items that would normally be priced at several thousands of dollars. What did Zappos do? They honored the purchases. The mistake cost the company more than $1.6 million; however, it won them at least that much in enhanced reputation equity.

The upshot of this extraordinary customer centricity: customers are the primary driver of the company's growth. Zappos has thousands of brand ambassadors worldwide and is enjoying long-term relationships with a bounty of satisfied customers. The company is recognized as a leader in customer centricity and shares its manage-ment tips for a fee via zapposinsights.com, in management seminars, and in Hsieh's recent book. Since its founding in 1999, Zappos has grown to more than 400 employees and is regularly listed on *Fortune*'s "100 Best Companies to Work For." In 2009, Amazon purchased it for shares worth $1.2 billion. Customer centricity creates value.

Extending Customer Centricity Throughout the Value Chain

To really be successful, a company's commitment to customer centricity cannot end at its official organizational boundary, however. Instead, a company's entire value chain must share this commitment. Social media can provide a vehicle for every member of the value chain to be in touch with its own customers, with the ultimate end user of the product or service, and with every other business that is a part of the supply chain. This dialog can reduce the problem of asymmetric information, which often leads to an individual partner's optimization at the expense of the whole supply chain. A more communicative ecosystem can take advan-tage of multidirectional information flows to help individual members create better demand forecasts for their products and for the supply chain as a whole, which can reduce costs and provide better customer service at every step along the way. Closer collaboration can help solve problems and design better products, services, and policies.

Embrace Transparency

Transparency and integrity are the foundations of the social enter-prise. They have to be. Companies cannot be this connected and not be honest with their constituencies. Yochai Benkler, professor for entrepreneurial legal studies at Harvard and faculty codirector of the Berkman Center for Internet and Society, describes the emergence of a new social contract between businesses and their stakeholders:

> Over the course of modern economic history, markets be-came evermore separated from social relations; people spe-cialized and segmented their moral outlook. Some actions

were fine in the market, even if we would never dream of taking advantage of people in similar ways in social relations. People behave differently when they understand themselves to be acting in the market, as opposed to acting is social relationships. Peer production and other forms of collaboration reverse that by breaking down the barrier between the market self and the social self.[4]

Given this new social contract, consumers expect that companies will be transparent and authentic in their interactions and in the way they conduct their overall business. If they are not, consumers will blog, tweet, comment, and vote with their feet. This genuineness is becoming a fact of life; indeed, I believe the great brands of the next generation will be those that are the most transparent. Why? When consumers find a brand that they trust, they own it. They build it into their digital identity; they associate themselves with it through posts on their Facebook page, blogs, or in other social environments. They tell their friends and the community at large. Remember the influence of the peer network. This is powerful stuff.

Take BP, for example. Here's a company that didn't get it. Rather than being open and upfront about the oil spill in the Gulf, the company misread the social environment in which it operates and took a "less is more" approach. When its representatives did speak, they placed ads rather than shared knowledge. They didn't reach out to ask for help when it became clear that BP didn't know how to fix the situation—despite the fact that thousands of people would have jumped in with assistance.

Actually, a number of people did try to help BP by submitting solutions. In fact, days after the oil spill, InnoCentive launched an oil spill challenge to source solutions to help BP solve the problem. Dwayne Spradlin, president and CEO of InnoCentive, recalled:

This was the fastest we've ever seen a challenge go from zero to thousands of solvers. Over a thousand solutions ultimately were submitted by experts—oil spill recovery experts, chemists, and construction engineers. The kind of public good inside [people's] brains, the outpouring of passion and engagement in solving these kinds of problems, will absolutely blow you away.

Thankfully, the spill has been stopped. Now, BP should be actively involved in honest conversation about what the company is going to do over the course of the next 30 years to restore the environments that have been affected by the oil spill. BP should pick the 10 most salient issues that the disaster has caused and go deep into what it is going to do to change them. Forming a broad ecosystem from which BP can actively solicit input from anyone and everyone who has knowledge about oil spills and their clean up should be at the top of BP's priorities. In my opinion, this is the only way that they may be able to change public opinion of them. It is not going to happen overnight.

Manage from Your Moral Purpose

In addition to transparency, social enterprises need to have a pervasive and driving sense of moral purpose. What do I mean by moral purpose? It's the underlying principles that define and shape an organization. It's the motivation for creating your products and services in the first place. It is what makes a company great and encourages its stakeholder communities to want to be a part of the company and the contribution that it is making in the world.

We've all seen people who are on fire, filled with seemingly boundless and contagious energy about what they do. Human behavior experts will tell you that this is because they are being true to themselves; that is, they are living out of their deepest values. Providing employees, customers, and other stakeholders with the opportunity to live from their deepest values through your organization is a winning strategy.

Southwest Airline's underlying moral purpose is: "We democratize the skies and give people the freedom to fly." ING Direct's fundamental vision is: "We lead Americans back to savings." Twitter's is to "be a force for good." Part of the way that principle is played out for Twitter involves focusing on emerging markets, those countries where a mobile phone is a person's only ticket to information networks, which are essential to rising up and out of poverty. Twitter's cofounder, Evan Williams, describes Twitter's focus as targeting the base of the pyramid, that is, striving to give the most disadvantaged and marginalized a voice.[5] Already Twitter access has played a substantial role in protests in Iran, China, and Moldova and has helped to harness substantial support for Haiti.

What's the difference between a company with a moral purpose and a not-for-profit humanitarian organization? The market opportunity. After all, the bottom of the pyramid represents about 20 percent of the world's population. The World Bank estimates that by 2030, 1.2 billion people in developing countries will comprise the "global middle class." (That's 93 percent of the world's total middle class—in 2000, people within developing countries comprised 56 percent.) With their purchasing power projected as being between $4,000 and $17,000 per capita, this represents a huge opportunity for Twitter to advance social conditions while still pursuing a profitable business strategy.

Harvard University professor and business strategist, Michael Porter, firmly believes that companies can reinforce their corporate strategy by advancing social conditions. In an article that he coauthored with Mark Kramer for *Harvard Business Review,* Porter wrote: "The mutual interdependence upon corporations and society implies that both business decisions and social policies must follow the principle of shared values, choices must benefit both sides . . . a temporary gain to one will undermine the long-term prosperity of both."[6]

Porter encourages companies to look for points of intersection between their value chain and communities with which they are involved to see where social and economic goals can be achieved simultaneously. This includes how the company is affecting the environment in its ordinary course of business (e.g., hiring practices and waste disposal) and how the environment is affecting the company's long-term competitiveness (e.g., shortage of skilled workers and unstable supply of inputs).

Porter is optimistic, "When a well-run business applies its vast resources, expertise, and management talent to problems that it understands and in which it has a stake, it can have a greater effect on social good than any other institution or philanthropic organization."[7] It can also make a difference to a company's stakeholders. How do you want your stakeholder communities to feel when they do business with or for you?

Realize It Doesn't Have to Be Made in Your Shop

Here's a truism: Not all smart people work for your company. Here's another: taking advantage of the knowledge and capabilities contained within other companies can be a winning innovation and economic model.

Endo Pharmaceuticals' business model, for example, is predicated upon creating new alliances to bring innovative products to health care providers more efficiently. Under the direction of Dave Holveck, who joined Endo as chief executive officer (CEO) in 2008, the company is building upon its traditional strength in pain management to develop a solutions-oriented approach to healthcare. This approach provides providers with multiple therapeutic options for a given condition, the goal of which is to improve patient outcomes. This approach also provides Endo with the opportunity to grow through carefully selected pathways, even as the U.S. health care industry experiences changes in significant areas (e.g., patient demographics, treatment economics, reimbursement, and the demand for more innovation solutions). By diversifying in this way, Endo has retooled itself for rapidity and agility—two qualities needed to thrive as the economic and health care landscapes continue to shift.

A business model that champions partnering with others in critical parts of a highly segmented pharmaceutical industry supports this strategic vision. How is Endo tapping the best minds globally to provide breakthrough drugs, devices, and treatments to its customers? First, they have concentrated their research and development dollars on the most promising treatments available within their areas of focus. To accomplish this, in addition to their own research and development staff, Endo works virtually on discovery projects with several high-tech, multinational partners; it is investigating new biological pathways in pain management with researchers at Harvard University and collaborating on novel drugs across multiple therapeutic areas with Jubilant Biosys, Aurigene, and Sungene International. Strategic acquisitions in 2009 and 2010 augmented the company's portfolio of treatments and provided Endo with additional manufacturing capabilities and advanced drug delivery systems, which will introduce new types of treatment for patients across therapeutic areas.

Endo's partnerships go beyond research and development, however. The company works with its customers to explore how patient
care is provided to identify gaps in the delivery process that Endo may
be able to address. Further, the company collaborates with physicians,
payers, managed care experts, and policy makers to help improve patient outcomes.

In short, Endo is working to deliver products and services more
effectively, with higher quality and greater efficiency, to ultimately
produce better patient outcomes. Holveck was not afraid to think big
and shake things up a bit, to reach this end goal. Endo's commitment
is reflected in the innovative drugs, devices, and services the company
is developing, the people they are hiring, the partnerships they are
establishing, and the value they are creating for their stakeholders.

Commit to Working Collaboratively

Social tools are allowing people to work differently. Collaboration is
the name of the game; its ultimate goal is to bring forth organizations' best thinking and to apply it to improve products, services, and
the way business is conducted. Social media tools are allowing companies to collaborate internally as well as with customers, suppliers,
business partners, and whoever else is important to their businesses.
These broad innovation networks make it possible for companies
to tap into the knowledge base and capability of others, creating
resource-rich and remarkably efficient extended enterprises. This
wide-ranging partnership is essential for organizational success in the
complex and constantly changing environment in which companies
compete today.

Some companies are revamping their organization structures to
better facilitate collaboration. John Chambers, CEO of Cisco Systems, for example, is convinced that "The future is going to be all
around collaboration and teamwork, with a structured process behind
it."[8] As a result, Chambers has put aside the traditional management
style that has served the company well in the past in favor of decentralized internal collaborative teams or communities. Cross-functional
leaders from sales, finance, engineering, and legal, among others,

comprise these councils, boards, and working groups, which are empowered to respond quickly to market developments.

"I might be involved in only two to three of the councils and boards and working groups," Chambers explained. "Each of our key executives will do the same; and instead of 10 people running the company, with a very heavy leaning toward the command, the top 500 people are running it today." Now that the new organizational structure is in place, Chambers believes that it is more replicable than the company's former command-and-control model because it "gains the power of the human network to really move on decisions and directions."

Other companies are experimenting with social network analysis (SNA) to determine how their companies should best organize work and select leaders. SNA maps knowledge relationships between people and departments. These maps can be used for leadership selection by observing who are the most trusted and respected "go-to" people within the informal organization. (It is surprising how often these informal maps differ from the formal organizational chart.) Humana has been exploring the use of SNA to help create teams that are optimally "connected" throughout its multiple organizations for the given task or opportunity at hand.

You Get What You Ask For

Reward systems work every time. They always get the result for which they are designed. The problem is that often companies inadvertently choose the wrong behaviors to reward. For example, most companies today do not reward people for collaboration. People are still promoted and paid primarily on an individual basis.

To really take advantage of the power of collaboration, companies have to rethink their reward systems to encourage people to share knowledge. Companies do not have a chance at building effective engagement with outside communities if they don't have an effective community inside their organization with which stakeholders can interact. Visibility, enhanced responsibility, and the opportunity to contribute to rewarding and purposeful initiatives should all be explored in addition to financial compensation. A consistent framework for evaluating the effectiveness of employees who work collaboratively across functions and constituent groups is also critical.

Rethinking Your Leadership Style

If organizations choose to go down the social enterprise path, their tried and true leadership styles are likely to be challenged, just as it was for John Chambers. For Chambers, moving away from a command and control leadership model goes against how he was trained in law school and what has worked for him and the company in the past. But Chambers is quick to say that the change was inevitable, "I had to change. And I had to realize that I would either be part of the future success, or I would be the one that would slow us down. . . . If you think that you cannot be left behind, you're wrong—regardless of what position you're in."[9]

Many leaders are finding it necessary to reconsider "command-and-control" leadership styles in favor of a more "inspire-and-enable" style. Stated differently, it's a transformation from being a general to becoming a provocateur.

Provocateurs are learners and listeners. They don't have to be the smartest people in the room, and they certainly don't want to be in a room with everyone who thinks like they do. Rather, they surround themselves, and their companies, with multiple and diverse communities from which they can learn and improve constantly.

Provocateurs shepherd their organizations, not through coercion and tightly wound control systems, but through shared purpose and vision. Provocateurs motivate others to help them accomplish their company's mission whether they work "for" them or not. They are systems thinkers, able to envision, realize, and manage networks beyond their own institutions' borders. The most successful are relationship-oriented, willing to work with partners and help nurture their success. Although they are formidable competitors, they don't see business as a war, or even as a zero-sum game, in which only one entity can win. Rather, they believe that great things can be realized when everyone shares in the rewards—including society in general.

It's Murder on Middle Management

Make no mistake; some degree of leadership transformation is likely to be necessary, but not necessarily easy. Brad Anderson, Best Buy's vice chair and chief executive officer (CEO), describes the organizational changes his company is adopting as a result of social web engagement as "murder on middle management—actually the more senior the management is, the worse it is."[10] Why is this the case? As Anderson said, "This absolutely flips the role of the leader. We weren't built to do this." But there is a good reason to make the change. More often than not, employees can see situations clearly and intuitively and, according to Anderson, their advice has been dead on." Social media is allowing companies to gain "insight from within the system that is not captured by hierarchy."

Jeff Severts, executive vice president at Best Buy puts it this way, "Big companies are like communist countries—we all know how well communist countries worked. At some point they fell apart, not because the leaders were dumb, but because nobody would tell the leaders at the top, who had to make decisions, what decisions to make."[11]

Sometimes the feedback received can be hard to swallow. Anderson tells the story of how one vice president of his company thought that the system was not working because he had put out a proposal to the community to which no one, literally, had responded. "He later realized that he did get an answer, in fact he got a very profound answer to his recommendation," Anderson said.[12]

Ten Other Essential Leadership Skills

In addition to rethinking leadership styles, the Institute for the Future outlined 10 new skills that are essential for leaders to master given the complexity of the anticipated operating environment and the tasks for which they will be increasingly responsible. That future is now. Think for a moment of how vital these 10 skills are to leadership, even today:

Ping Quotient: Excellent responsiveness to other people's requests for engagement; strong propensity and ability to reach out to others in a network

Longbroading: Seeing a much bigger picture; thinking in terms of higher level systems, bigger networks, longer cycles

Open Authorship: Creating content for public modification; the ability to work with massively multiple contributors

Cooperation Radar: The ability to sense, almost intuitively, who would make the best collaborators on a particular task or mission

Multicapitalism: Fluency in working and trading simultaneously with different hybrid capitals, e.g., natural, intellectual, social, financial, virtual

Mobbability: The ability to do real-time work in very large groups; a talent for coordinating with many people simultaneously; extreme-scale collaboration

Protovation: Fearless innovation in rapid, iterative cycles; the ability to lower the costs and increase the speed of failure

Influency: Knowing how to be persuasive and tell compelling stories in multiple social media spaces (each space requires a different persuasive strategy and technique)

Signal/Noise Management: Filtering meaningful info, patterns, and commonalities from the massively multiple streams of data and advice

Emergensight: The ability to prepare for and handle surprising results and complexity that come with coordination, cooperation and collaboration on extreme scales[13]

And, of course, leaders have to be committed to building social media–enabled capabilities for their companies to tap into their multiple constituencies, manage the knowledge gained effectively, and translate that knowledge into actionable strategy.

Enourage a Culture of Controlled Risk Taking

Big ideas are essential to companies' growth. What does it take to think outside of the box? Many things, but at the top of the list is freedom from fear and reprisal. If innovation is important to your industry, you can't afford to stifle your employees' thoughts and suggestions. Whereas this makes intuitive sense, it does run counter to the risk aversion common in many businesses.

Charlene Li, author of *Open Leadership,* talks about the failure imperative, a necessity when companies are trying to become more open. In an article for *The Strategist,* she wrote, "even with the best structures and planning in place, things go wrong. By mastering failure, you create an environment in which risk taking is encouraged and recovery from failure becomes a skill that everyone in the organization possesses."[14] This attitude is not an excuse for overlooking rigorous analysis, thoughtful and strategic planning, and dogged persistence, however. Rather, it is a "both/and" mandate: establish appropriate processes and protocols, train employees in what is possible and trustworthy, and reward new thinking and initiatives. When failure happens, pick up, clean up, move on, and learn from it. And remember to reward people, despite failure.

One of the great things about the social web is that it lowers the cost of failure for organizations. Clay Shirky, an adjunct professor at NYU's graduate Interactive Telecommunications Program and author of *Here Comes Everybody: The Power of Organizing Without Organizations* and *Cognitive Surplus: Creativity and Generosity in a Connected Age,* told me that he sees the social web changing businesses' "experimental tempo" because it reduces the cost of failure. It affords companies the opportunity to experiment in smaller, faster, and less expensive ways and it provides them with immediate feedback so that they can readily change course. "But to take advantage of that you have to have a culture that understands how to fail fast and to fail informatively," explained Shirky. And, I might add, an organizational structure that allows that information to be acted on—thoughtfully and quickly.

Technology companies like Google and Facebook understand this. Rather than following a formalized and lengthy process of producing a product, testing it, revamping it, retesting it, and ultimately releasing it, they truncate the process and release products in beta form, perpetually optimizing them as a result of consumer feedback and patterns of use. Technologies that allow for collaboration, real-time interaction, and user-generated content and involvement are central to this ability.

Microsoft's Dana Boyd discussed this product development strategy at the company's 2009 Research Tech Fest:

We saw half-baked ideas hit the marketplace and get transformed by the users in an elegant dance with the developers.

This was a critical disruption to the way in which technology was historically produced, one that rattled big companies, even those whose agile software development cycles couldn't cope with including all consumers as active participants in their process.[15]

If you want to see this process in action, spend some time on Google Labs. Here's the company's description of what goes on there:

Google Labs is a playground where our more adventurous users can play around with prototypes of some of our wild and crazy ideas and offer feedback directly to the engineers who develop them. Please note that the Labs is the first phase in a lengthy product development process and none of this stuff is guaranteed to make it onto Google.com. While some of our crazy ideas might grow into the next Gmail or iGoogle, others might turn out to be, well, just plain crazy.[16]

From Bold Moves to Real Dialog

When Ford first entered the social media space, it blundered. It created its Bold Moves social site to "present Ford as a company coming to its senses, open to new ideas, and ready to learn from its mistakes." Content on the site included good and bad news, lots of video, and a section for comments and questions. Sounds good, but it was only skin deep. It was faux transparency.

Rather than having its employees write blog entries, it hired journalists to tell a story. Videos were professionally created and captured beautiful women happily driving their Fords by the ocean's edge. And rather than actually being interested in readers' comments and questions, it simply ignored them. I know, because I posted several myself and they never showed up.

Things are different today. The company has become quite adept with social media. It engages in real, ongoing conversation with multiple stakeholders. As Ford's CEO, Alan Mulally, explained to *PR Week:*

It's [social media] changed all of our lives because it's moved the whole communications and PR process to a conversation.

It's a daily conversation; it's a thoughtful conversation; it's an individual conversation—in addition to being a broad conversation. People want to know exactly what your brand stands for. Having this conversation with all stakeholders, beginning with consumers, is a very powerful part of the Ford plan.[17]

Putting the Product in Bloggers' Hands

Ford's Ford Fiesta Movement is a social media case study from which to learn. A year and a half before the company planned to launch its new and improved Ford Fiesta in the United States—a different version of the model had previously been launched in Europe—the company decided to put the brand in the hands of a hundred digital influencers. Ford gave each influencer a European spec car and said, "Do what you normally do with social media; talk freely and openly about your experience with the car." And they did.

Ford took all of the 100 bloggers' unedited content streams and aggregated them onto one site, www.fiestamovement.com, so that the public could view them in real time. (Take a look; some of the content is wonderfully creative and downright clever.) This Ford Fiesta Movement captured the public's attention, generating more than 6 million YouTube views, nearly 740,000 Flickr views, and more than 3.7 million Twitter views. That translated to a 58 percent level of awareness about the car before it even got to market. As Scott Monty, global digital multimedia communications manager for Ford said, "[that is] higher than some of our vehicles that have been in the market for two to three years."

In addition to building brand awareness, this open strategy communicated how confident Ford was with its new product and how comfortable the company had become in letting people talk unedited about Ford in public spheres. "It's a symptom of the larger transparency that is going on at Ford Motor Company," said Monty. "It's a culture change that is, fundamentally at the root of our success." What's more, this transparency gave Ford's engineering team the opportunity to gather and incorporate real-time feedback from these North American Fiesta agents into the design of the American model prior to its release.

Rethink Your Notions of Speed and Professionalism

Several years ago, just in time was all the rage for companies. Now it's real time. Social media conversations and feedback are immediate. Customers have come to expect 24/7 engagement with brands. As a result, companies' reaction time has to be quicker. Companies—and any agencies with which they work—have to let go of the annual planning cycles and get comfortable with an ongoing optimization process. For most companies this requires adjustments to their organizational DNA and that of their extended ecosystem.

Another area for organizational revamp is the notion of professionalism. Social media requires an openness that many companies may have considered to be unprofessional in the past. David Weinberger, senior researcher at Harvard's Berkman Center for Internet and Society and the coauthor of *The Cluetrain Manifesto,* cautions that:

> If you take somebody, who, twenty years ago was the exemplar of professionalism, and you put her on the Web, unaltered, to engage in conversations today, that person is quite likely going to come across as a stick in the mud. What may be considered unprofessional, embarrassing, and dragging down the good name of the company in the past, today is probably accomplishing the exact opposite.

Here are a couple of examples to consider. JetBlue's Founder, David Neeleman, went on YouTube to explain what the company was doing to avoid future delays and stranding of passengers after what he said was "the most difficult time in the company's history"; was that dragging down the good name of the company or elevating it in customers' eyes?[18] Conversely, Tony Hayward, the former CEO of BP, played his cards close to his chest and was not forthcoming initially about the extent of the challenge associated with the oil spill in the Gulf and his company's ability to resolve it; was he protecting the good name of the company, or dragging it down—along with its market value?

There is also a new merging of personal and professional lives in social environments that can be seen as unprofessional. Not long ago the distinction between public and private activities was quite clear because their contexts differed: work took place largely at work, and personal life took place outside of work. Today those contexts have blurred. Smart phones and flexible working arrangements have perforated the line between work and play both physically and temporally, ushering in a blended "weisure" time. As a result, sacrosanct social rules are being called into question.

Is it fitting to post photos of oneself and one's family on a company's internal social network? Is it appropriate to use one's Facebook profile to solicit business or list job postings? Does the fact that Adam Christensen, who is responsible for IBM's global social engagement and the editor of the company's Smarter Planet blog, includes his Empanada Lover's Guide to Westchester county and the State of the Taco in White Plains on his web site render him less professional? Or does it make him more personable and approachable? (It goes without saying that it shows how much he misses the food of his native Southern California.)

Walk the Walk

Tom Peters once cautioned corporate leaders, "They watch your feet not your lips." It's true for leadership in general and for social media engagement specifically. It's not that every senior executive needs to be outwardly engaging in social media, although in some cases this can be quite helpful for firms, but it does mean that they have to model and champion its use. This doesn't have to be hard. It can amount to sharing their thoughts on a couple of external sites that are relevant to their firm's business and on an internal blog with employees. And it doesn't have to be all or nothing—it's not necessary to make social engagement another 24-hour-a-day job on top of the one that executives already have.

But it may be habit forming. John Chambers will tell you that blogging—mostly video—has become his primary way of communicating with his employees. He also makes use of Cisco's TelePresence product, which in essence creates a virtual presence between people regardless of where they are located physically. Using TelePresence,

Chambers meets "regularly with nine or ten people around the world at 9 or 10 different locations, and it's as though you're at the same table."[19]

Chambers's adoption of social media tools has provided a vision of what is possible for his employees; since he began using them it has been "like a virus that grows." The company's use of TelePresence has cut its travel budget from $750 million a year to a sustainable $350 million a year. Cisco's use of discussion forms has also grown— 1,600 percent over the course of one year. Similarly, the company's use of CiscoVision, its internal YouTube capability, grew 3,100 percent in that same period with 54,000 of 66,000 employees making use of it. Use of WebEx, which allows for internal and external collaboration, was up 3,900 percent. As Chambers said, "These are clearly numbers that indicate a new market transition."[20]

Benefits of Senior-Level External Social Engagement

Many executives understand the possibilities created by the social web. More than half of C-level executives under the age of 40 maintain a work-related blog, tweet, and use RSS feeds and a Web-enabled mobile device.[21] Social media engagement allows them to provide thought leadership, establish credibility, magnify public relations efforts, and develop a firsthand read on what their customers and other stakeholder communities are saying. If done correctly, this engagement gives them a prominent seat at the social media table.

Bruce Bullen, president and interim CEO of Harvard Pilgrim Health Plan, and his predecessor, Charlie Baker, made extensive use of their blog, letstalkhealthcare.org, to express their views about health care reform during the country-wide debate. Paul Levy, CEO of Beth Israel Hospital in Boston, chronicles the daily issues that arise in running one of the largest hospitals in the United States, in his blog, runningahospital.blogspot.com. As it turns out, one of the most active constituency groups on the blog is the hospital's own employees.

Jeff Leach, one of the Founders of Naked Pizza, a New Orleans– based pizzeria that you will read more about in Chapter 5, uses the company's blog, LIVNAKED, to talk about health and wellness, food, and food politics. The *New York Times* ranks Naked Pizza the number two company to follow on Twitter, a testament to its leadership's ability to build and connect with an active and passionate social community. So central is social media to the company's business success that Leach will tell you that they aren't really running a pizza business—they're running a social media operation that happens to sell pizza.[22]

Ted Leonsis, owner of the Washington Capitals and former group president and vice chairman of AOL, connects regularly with the hockey team's fans through his blog, Twitter, e-mail, message boards, and forums. Leonsis explains:

> I am a fan! I want to participate in discussing the team's prospects with my fellow fans—who happen to also be our customers. . . . The 18,000 people all dressed in red shouting their lungs out in favor of the Caps . . . they're not just customers, they're my community.[23]

What if Senior Management Doesn't Get It?

This is not uncommon. To address this very issue, several companies have created reverse mentoring programs in which employees experienced in social media coach senior executives as to how best to use social tools. But the cultural change being ushered by the social web requires leaders to think differently beyond how to use social media tools. It requires leaders to be able to think openly, transparently, and across departmental, functional, and organizational silos because it's in the mashup that real discoveries can be found.

Cisco knows that its leaders have to be able to think broadly and across organizational silos. They nurture bridge thinkers at the top by having senior leaders from one area cross over to run another organizational area. For example, "a Sales leader will run Engineering; a lawyer will run Business Development; and a Business Development leader will run Consumer Operations."[24] In this way, the company is training a group of "generalist leaders"—not generals—who know how to learn and operate in a collaborative environment.

There are some cases in which management either can't grasp this collaborative paradigm shift or chooses not to. This is also not uncommon. Chambers will tell you that about 20 percent of his leaders didn't survive Cisco's transition. Why didn't they make it? Chambers explained,

> They were command-and-control; wonderful leaders but [they] wanted to stay command-and-control and couldn't transition over. And I had nothing against that. It's like a basketball player who can score 30 points a game. But if you're going to go into a real, unique style of team offense and team defense, if a person can't adjust, it's probably better that they get traded to another team. And so, all of us have to change. And the leader has to not only say the talk, she or he has to walk the talk. Got to be the best example.[25]

The flip side is that new internal leaders can emerge as an organization embraces social tools. These leaders may come from the periphery of an organization; they gain their following not through formal titles but through their digital prominence. These are the people who participate regularly in online discussions and whose contributions are consistently tagged, retweeted, or rated as valuable by their peers. Through their influence they become trusted authorities. It is in traditional manager's best interest to identify and nurture these emergent leaders and to develop their own digital eminence so that the formal and informal leadership of a company are one and the same—or at least close.

In the chapter that follows, we'll consider how social media is changing the role of marketing, sales, corporate communications, and customer service.

Questions to Consider

- How customer-centric is your organization?
- How transparent is your company in its interactions with stakeholders?
- What is your organization's moral purpose?
- What internal changes might be necessary for your organization to truly become a social enterprise?

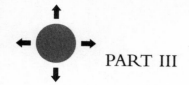

PART III

Across the
Business Universe

CHAPTER FIVE

Marketing, Sales, and Service, Step 1

Organize Around Customer Engagement

S ome of life's most influential moments startle you, capturing your attention; others are subtler, perhaps noticed only with the benefit of hindsight.

A cultural appreciation class in middle school provided a startling moment for me. On our first day of school, we clever boys thought we would play a prank on our teacher, a proper and elegantly dressed French woman who could not have been taller than 4 foot 11 inches. Having borrowed a live frog from the biology lab, we tucked it inside a boy's athletic supporter and placed it on her wooden desk at the front of the classroom. Confident that we were in control and setting the tone for the class, we sat back, giggling, waiting for the bell to ring. When madame entered the room, carrying something discretely behind her back, she glanced at her desk, completely ignoring the frog and the strap. Surprising us all, she pulled a knife from behind her, and thrust it, forcefully, into the surface of her desk, just missing the frog. Wood chips flew. The frog went jumping. Madame never missed a beat.

"Today's lesson, boys," she said, "is about time. You cannot cut it with a knife. People did not go to sleep in the Renaissance knowing that they would wake up in the Baroque Era. It is not always clear when one era is ending and another beginning—it's not like the precise slice of a knife. D'accord?"

Needless to say, she got our attention. Through her atypical pedagogy, we learned several things that I would wager none of us have forgotten: whether the context is planning a class prank or the ushering in of a new historic age, change happens, regardless of your plans, and seismic shifts may not always be obvious at the time.

Anyone who is involved with marketing, corporate communications, sales, or customer service knows that a seismic change has happened, regardless of our plans. We have gone to bed in the broadcast era, when marketers used television, radio, and print ads, along with direct mail, to push customers through the sales funnel, and have awoken in the social media era, in which customers are now embarking on a more circular purchase journey and looking to the social web, rather than traditional channels, as their primary source of information, news, and entertainment. As we rub the sleep from our eyes, we are realizing that the Web has transformed from a place to find information to a place to share information and from a place to consume content to a place where everyone can create value. These changes are turning marketing, corporate communications, sales, and customer service upside down.

Say Goodbye to the Funnel

It used to be fairly straightforward. Marketers and sales folks had one dominant model to describe the customer purchase journey: the funnel. Like a physical funnel that is wide at the top and narrow at the bottom, marketers assumed that consumers began their purchase journey with a large set of products and services to consider and they narrowed their choices along the way (see Figure 5.1). Operating under this paradigm, marketers spent a lot of time and money working the top of the funnel, trying to build consumers' brand awareness and

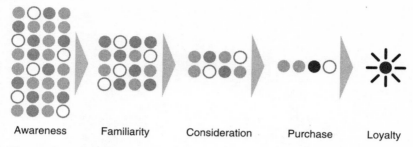

| Awareness | Familiarity | Consideration | Purchase | Loyalty |

Figure 5.1   The Traditional Funnel

Source: "The Customer Decision Journey," June 2009, *McKinsey Quarterly,* www
.McKinseyQuarterly.com. Copyright © 2010 McKinsey & Company. All rights
reserved. Reprinted with Permission.

consideration using traditional broadcast tools and techniques. These
marketing messages were one-way and were designed to be memorable in hopes of keeping brands at the top of consumers' minds. The
idea was that by "pushing" customers through the funnel, they would
eventually wind up in the store, or in the case of a business-to-business company, in the arms of their salesperson, where they would
make a purchase decision in the company's favor. Promotions at the
point of sale were offered to provide the final "push."

The social web has changed the game. For starters, it has given consumers a plethora of new media choices, rendering traditional marketing
channels much less effective. Today, it has become virtually impossible to
gather together mass audiences for any event except for perhaps the
World Cup finals, the Olympics, the Academy Awards, or the Super
Bowl. Furthermore, the social web has provided customers with the opportunity to engage directly with each other about products and services,
bypassing the need—and the desire—for traditional corporate messaging.
Consumers can even read user-generated reviews and compare features
and prices on their smart phones or send photos of potential purchases to
friends and family while they are shopping. It's a whole new world.

A recent study of the purchase decisions of almost 20,000 consumers across multiple industries and continents by McKinsey & Company
documented that the consumer decision journey has changed as a result
of these developments.[1] It turns out that in the social media era the consumer decision journey is actually more circular than linear (see Figure
5.2). Customers start out with a smaller consideration set and enlarge

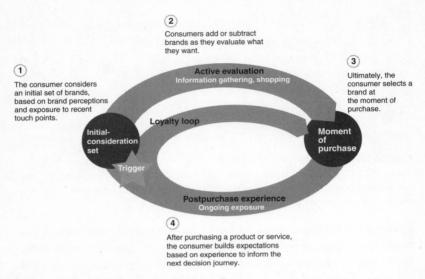

Figure 5.2   The Consumer Decision Journey

Source: "The Customer Decision Journey," June 2009, *McKinsey Quarterly,* www .McKinseyQuarterly.com. Copyright © 2010 McKinsey & Company. All rights reserved. Reprinted with Permission.

this set, rather than narrow it down, as they embark on their purchase journey. This enlargement happens not because consumers are being pushed by marketing messages but because they are actively "pulling" information from a variety of sources to assist them in their decision making. Two thirds of the information that is "pulled" comes from social web reviews and peer recommendations, in-store interactions, and past experiences. These same sources help consumers pare down their choices to ultimately arrive at a decision.

There is one further twist in today's customer purchase journey: Many consumers are looking to be engaged with companies even when they are not actively looking to purchase a product or service. Why is this the case? People like to stay in touch, at varying levels of intensity, with businesses with which they are involved. This desire can be driven by a love of a company's products, an interest in the industry, or an interest with the company's leadership. Consumers like to collaborate with companies on product design, development, and packaging. They enjoy providing feedback about products, services, and the competitive environment.

Consumers also want to know what really motivates the companies with which they interact. They want to know what companies stand for in addition to making money and whether companies are interested in their customers beyond the prospect of an imminent sale. Consumers today want to interact with companies in their everyday state, not just when they are on their best behavior.

Take Apple for example. The company has a following that is akin to the Red Sox or Yankees. Think of how many people hang out at Apple stores, eagerly await the company's new product announcements, and monitor the health status of Steve Jobs. It's fairly safe to say that most of Apple's followers are not continually in the market for a new product—and the company knows that. When you enter an Apple store, it is not a hard-sell experience. It's fun and informative. It encourages you to hang out and play. And when you are ready to purchase, the company has already done the lion's share of its work. You know where to go, what to purchase, and why.

Resetting the Game Plan

What do these new behaviors mean for marketers? They mean that the rules of the game have changed. The game has not: marketing's role is still largely about defining target markets, communicating with prospective customers and other stakeholders, and building loyalty. But as Figure 5.3 captures, most of the plays in the well-worn playbook are no longer working.

For starters, marketers have had to learn a new way of communicating to be effective in social environments. Gone is the one-way mass messaging delivered through television, radio, magazines, and direct mail. In its place marketers are engaging in dialog—highly democratic, multidirectional conversations with customers, potential customers, and potentially every other company stakeholder. (These stakeholders are all talking with each other, too.) The nature of these conversations is quite different from traditional broadcast messaging: more social and informative than transactional, more open-sourced than controlled. And any topic is fair game.

Components	Old Marketing	New Marketing
Customer purchase journey	The Funnel: customers begin their purchase journey with a large consideration set and narrow their choices along the way with the "push" advertising.	Multiple Channel Pathways: Customer purchase journey is more circular and consideration set grows along the way as they "pull" information from a variety of sources, many of which are social.
Marketing mind-set	Use one-way, one-sided communication to tell brand story.	Nurture dialogue and relationships; be transparent, earn trust, build credibility.
Brand equity	Brand recall is holy grail.	Brand value is determined by customers: How likely are customers to highly recommend the good or service?
Segmentation	Group customers by demographics.	Group customers by behavior, attitudes, and interests—what's important to them.
Targeting	Target by demographics, especially for media buying.	Target according to personas based upon customer behavior.
Communication	Broadcast style: create and push message out for customer to absorb.	Digital environment for interactive communication through search and query, customer comments, personal reviews, or dialogue.

Figure 5.3   Old Marketing versus New Marketing

Components	Old Marketing	New Marketing
Content	Professional content created and controlled by marketers.	Mix of professional and user-generated content, increasingly video-based.
Virality	A nice feature but popularity too often driven by flashy presentation rather than content.	Virality based on solid content about remarkable products or features that will get people talking and sharing.
Reviews	Think Michelin Guide: the experts weigh in.	Think Amazon: users review and vote on everything.
Advertiser/Publisher role	Publisher established channel and controls content to gather an audience for the advertisers who sponsor channels of programs.	Build relationships by sponsoring (not controlling) content and interaction when, where, and how customers want it.
Strategy	Top-down strategy imposed by senior management drives tactics.	Bottom-up strategy builds on winning ideas culled from constant testing and multiple customer community's input.
Hierarchy	Information is organized into channels, folders, and categories to suit advertisers.	Information is available on demand by keyword, to suit users.
Payment	Cost per Thousand (CPM); Emphasis on cost; advertisers buy with the idea that share of voice=share of mind=share of market.	Return on Investment (ROI): Invest in marketing for future growth and profitability based on measurable return.

Figure 5.3 Old Marketing versus New Marketing (*continued*)

These new behaviors mean that marketers have had to stop pursuing brand recall as the Holy Grail, recognizing that dialog is now what drives purchases. Brands have become living, breathing entities that are shaped by the conversations that take place about them. The stronger the dialog, the stronger the brand.

Marketing has also had to realize that it is no longer controlling the message; it shares that job. As consumers blog, write product reviews, and discuss products and services in social environments, they are shaping brands. Through their reviews, recommendations, and sharing of content, customers have become brand and company ambassadors. To encourage this free and influential advocacy, marketers are providing consumers with the tools to comment, share, download, and embed content across the social web.

This new customer behavior also means that marketing is learning to put connection before commerce. (In Chapter 6, we'll explore these new rules of engagement more closely.) Successful companies are thinking more broadly about their customer interactions, nurturing these relationships throughout the entire customer life cycle, from first impressions to sharing and advocacy—not just focusing on the sale.

Say Hello to Multiple Channel Pathways

People are multifaceted and engage with multiple online and offline media channels as they go about their daily lives. Their purchase journeys—from beginning to end—reflect this constant shifting. Monitor's Channel Pathway's Framework (Figure 5.4) captures the variety of pathways that customers can take as they move through the buying process. Notice the variety of customer interfaces with companies and their products and services—third-party sites, company web sites, physical stores, family and friends, radio and television—and at what steps they may be used. By understanding the pathways that your customers generally follow, companies can more effectively help consumers through the purchase cycle so that they can become loyal brand and company sharers and advocates.

Monitor's Channel Pathways™ Framework

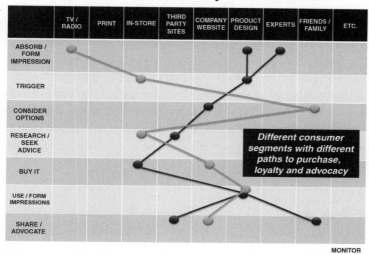

Figure 5.4 Customer's Use Multiple Channel Pathways
Source: Monitor, www.monitor.com. Copyright © 2010 Monitor Company Group
L.P. All rights reserved. Reprinted with permission.

What do these multiple pathways and interfaces mean for marketing, corporate communications, sales, and customer service? They suggest that companies need to reexamine their marketing activities to determine whether they are in alignment with how customers go about researching and buying products and with their preferred communication interfaces. These multiple pathways also offer the promise that if companies can understand their customers' purchase journey—where they are getting their information, through what media, and at which stage of the buying process—they can more effectively tailor their marketing, sales, and customer service efforts to be in the right place at the right time, offering the content for which their consumers are looking.

The multiple channel pathways also suggest that if companies want to correlate their communication dollars with the influence that tools have on consumers, a fair amount of money is going to shift away from mass-marketing campaigns toward online content development—with some money left over. Let me say that again. By reallocating marketing dollars to social destinations, many companies can spend less on marketing, while still improving their performance.

You Can Get There from Here

How effective is social media at various stages of the consumer purchase journey? Can it effectively build brand awareness? Absolutely.

Remember the 58 percent level of awareness that the new Ford Fiesta enjoyed before the car even came to market? Here's another example. General Mills recently launched a new Progresso broth through its own Pssst . . . online community, with almost no support from traditional media. (Members of this self-selected group of consumers are interested in connecting with General Mills about new products, special offers, and what goes on "behind the scenes" at the packaged goods company.) The company sent samples of the new soup to thousands of its 170,000-plus members in a package labeled, "Pssst . . . special delivery included" along with a coupon offer. Interaction with the Pssst . . . online community helped build awareness and involvement with the new Progresso product and facilitated a powerful buzz when it was ultimately launched.

Cisco's launch of its Aggregation Service Router ASR 1000 product series provides an example of a business-to-business product introduction that used the social web. It offered "über user" testimonial videos with a tell-a-friend function for viral distribution; the Edge Quest 3D game to highlight product innovation and encourage widespread sharing; a Second Life launch event that enabled attendees to experience the new platform in the virtual world; a tongue-in-cheek "Cisco Support Group for Uber User Internet Addicts" on Facebook; a social media web widget; online, live product introduction broadcasts with Q&A in 19 languages; and worldwide TelePresence for international coverage. It works.

Right Here, Right Now

How effective is social media in driving purchases? According to a recent study from Chadwick Martin Bailey, 67 percent of consumers who follow brands on Twitter are more likely to buy those brands after becoming a follower.[2] The same is true for Facebook fans, which are 51 percent more likely to buy after becoming a fan. Research shows that consumers spend more after receiving recommendations from their online community of friends.[3] Furthermore, adding social commentary to packaging and displays legitimizes brands, improving sales and conversion rates for coupons.[4]

Smart phone applications like aisle411 take it one step further. In addition to providing UPC barcode scanning that allows users to pull up customer-generated product reviews at the point of sale, aisle411 helps people locate products in specific aisles at retail stores. Participating stores can choose to add coupons and other offers.

Location-based social networks (LSBNs) like Foursquare, Gowalla, Loopt, Stickybits, and Facebook Places, can also facilitate this buying behavior. These tools offer companies the possibility of the holy grail: "right-time, right-place" marketing because they reach consumers when they are out and about, perhaps even on the sidewalk in front of a company's own retail store. Utilizing GPS technology embedded in smart phones, LSBNs connect people with friends and places that are located nearby; these connections are updated as a person's location changes.

Here's an example of how LBSNs work. Imagine sitting at a weekend-long soccer tournament in which your child's team is participating. It's hot and they are playing on turf, which increases the temperature by several degrees for both the players and their parents. In a moment of attention lapse, instead of following the game, you look down at the Foursquare application on your smart phone. You click on "place" and scroll down the list of stores, restaurants, and even historical sites that are located near the tournament. Much to your delight you discover that there is a Starbucks and a Dunkin' Donuts, both of which serve delicious and refreshing iced coffees, located less than a mile from where you are sitting, and did I mention, sweating? A smile comes over your face as you click on Dunkin' Donuts and a map pops up showing you just how close it really is located. So close that you can almost taste it. What's more, a coupon then pops up, offering you $1.00 off of your next beverage because you are a frequent customer. It's almost too much to take at this point—if only they delivered!

Here's another example. *Lucky* magazine is making use of Foursquare to share its curated shopping directory of the best boutiques in cities across the country. Women look to *Lucky* for fashion advice and tips about where to find the best local deals and designers. By checking-in at a Lucky recommended store, users have access to editors' insider tips and deals. *Lucky*'s Web director, Mary Gail Pezzimenti is convinced that "Foursquare adds enormous service to our readers," because, "we want women who are out shopping to think of *Lucky*, connect with *Lucky*, engage with *Lucky*. . . . This is the perfect forum to deliver insider info instantly."[5] Can't you envision *Lucky* sponsored "boutique crawls?"

LSBNs connect people and places, creating that powerful combination of online and offline interaction. They can quench thirst and direct women to fabulous boutiques, and yes, they can sell products. They can also be fun. Many LSBNs have gaming features that reward customers for frequent visits (you can become a mayor of certain establishments on Foursquare) or can enhance users' experiences at places or events. (The next time you are in Chicago, take some time to learn about some of the 77 different neighborhoods, 552 parks, and more than 7,000 restaurants on the city of Chicago's Foursquare site, ExploreChicago.) LSBNs are also tapping into an emerging itch that people are feeling for tools to help them self-monitor—just how many times are you getting a latte? Going to the gym?

At the moment LSBNs are growing rapidly but they still do not yet enjoy widespread adoption. According to a recent study by Forrester, only 4 percent of online adults in the United States have ever used location-based social networks on their mobile phones, with only 1 percent using them more than once a week.[6] Despite these current usage numbers, LSBNs are a development to watch. Several companies, including Starbucks, have already experienced success by connecting their existing loyalty programs to a LSBN.

At Your Service—Everywhere

How effective is social media at improving customer experience? Here are a couple of interesting examples from the medical community in Miami. Dr. Carlos Wolf of Miami Plastic Surgery uses social

tools to provide updates to patients' families during surgery. (He identifies patients by their initials and is careful not to disclose the type of
procedure that he is conducting.) "At this point, it's really to make
those patients, family, and friends feel comfortable," Wolf told the
Miami Herald. "We don't have a two-way conversation. The most important thing is for me to concentrate on what I am doing."[7] (Bad
news is still delivered face-to-face.)

Dr. Redmond Burke, director of the Congenital Heart Institute
at Miami Children's Hospital, posts many of his surgeries on YouTube
to ease parents' fears about the procedures that he will be conducting
on their children. "They have no idea what's happening inside their
baby's chest during the scariest time of their life," Burke says. "I want
a family to be able to see precisely how I operate."[8] A majority of
families opt to have their child's surgery recorded. "As a parent, you
really want to get video of all those critical moments in your child's
life—their first step, first soccer game," Burke says. "With this video,
they can tell their child, 'Here's what happened to you. Here's what
you survived.' "[9]

What about improving customer experience during a product recall? Nobody wants one, but they can be a part of customers' purchase
journey. In fact, recalls can be an opportunity to build customer loyalty and ambassadorship. Graco, a manufacturer of infant and children's products, utilized social media as part of its communication plan
surrounding a recent recall of 1.5 million strollers.

Here's how they did it. Having previously developed social
engagement skills as well as strong relationships with customer communities and influencers, when the recall became necessary, Graco
was able to get ahead of the news. Prior to the official announcement,
Graco alerted its brand ambassadors and influencers about the details
of the recall so that they could clearly and accurately blog about the
issue and the company's plan for resolution. These advocates helped
to calm down many understandably nervous parents and provided a
platform for Graco customers to continue to support the company
publicly. Senior executives, the legal department, and customer service personnel were continually kept abreast of developments so that
the company could respond quickly to resolve issues identified
via Twitter, Facebook, YouTube, and the company's own blog.

Employees across functions at Graco that are active in the social space were harnessed to be the eyes and ears of the organization—even if their job had nothing to do with the recall. A dedicated page on the company's web site allowed customers to order replacement parts directly and easily.

As a result of these efforts, the company was able to continue to build good customer experiences even in the midst of a product recall. One of the most negative and vocal customers did a public turnaround, ultimately telling social media audiences that, "I'll always continue to buy and use Graco products because of the way this was handled."[10] It doesn't get much better than that.

Integrating Social and Traditional Channels

Given the interconnectedness of social and traditional channels in consumers' lives, it makes sense to try to link these efforts to better reflect how people actually live their lives. In my experience, when companies begin to connect the dots between all of their consumer interfaces, they invariably realize greater value.

As Figure 5.5 illustrates, many businesses use social and traditional channels initially to create a presence. In this early stage, the social channels (communities, blogs, Facebook, and so on) are often not linked to one another or to a corporate web site, direct mail, events, public relations efforts, or even product packaging. As a result, businesses are missing the opportunity to fully connect with their potential customers in the medium they want, when they want it.

As companies become more knowledgeable about social media and the multiple channel pathways that their customers use, they begin making some initial linking between channels. The Facebook page, for example, becomes linked to the web site, where visitors can access more information and purchase the product or service. Eventually, the integration is complete and all social media channels are fully integrated with traditional channels. Television advertising sends people to a socially integrated web site, and the web site is linked to a Twitter page, which is also linked to a Facebook page. As the channels become interconnected, value steadily increases.

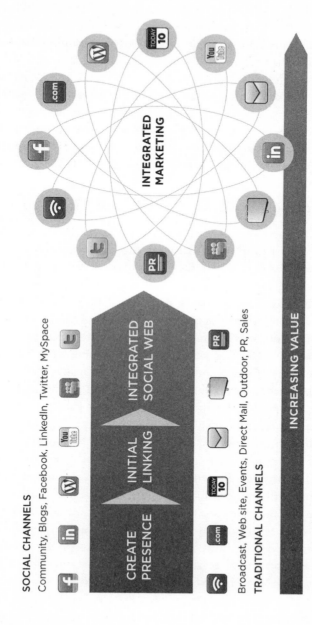

Figure 5.5 Integrated Marketing Is the Most Effective

A word of caution: I am not encouraging you to have automatic feeds across all channels, just to link them. Why? Each social channel has a different tone and culture. When you blindly link your feed across the channels, you are essentially saying that you don't really care about these nuances, that efficiency is more important than connecting. LinkedIn users really don't want to hear about what kind of coffee you happen to be drinking; they'd much rather receive a Slide-Share from you on a topic that is important to them. Information dumping across channels defeats the purpose of being engaged in social media in the first place.

Everything but Anchovies and Link Them, Please!

Naked Pizza, a New Orleans–based pizzeria, does a terrific job of linking almost everything. Early on, the company replaced the traditional "call for delivery" sign on its storefront with a sign that displays its Twitter handle, front and center, and an invitation to follow "NAKEDpizza" for special deals. iPads in the store allow customers to sign up for a Twitter account right then and there so that they can follow the company's tweets. Their Twitter feed runs constantly on the company's web-based ordering site, providing customers with details about the products and the company that makes them. The company's leadership writes about nutrition, food politics, and health on its blog, LIVNAKED, which is linked to their Facebook pages, Twitter, Foursquare, and Flickr. Their pizza box says it all as well.

Through this ongoing and linked dialog, Naked Pizza has built a vibrant community of brand-loyal customers. They love the company's 100 percent all-natural pizza—it even contains probiotics and has significantly fewer calories—as well as the conversation and community that the company fosters. Has social media helped drive Naked Pizza's business? Yes, indeed. The company tracks Twitter promotions via a custom Twitter button in its point-of-sale system. Sixty-eight percent of total dollar sales one day came from customers who indicated that they were calling from Twitter.[11]

"Our social media strategy has also helped to land two billionaire investors, more than 5,000 franchising inquiries, and has generated international press attention all of which has been beneficial in leveraging favorable agreements with suppliers helping to contribute to very competitive prices," explains Robbie Vitrano, the company's Chief Branding/Design Officer. Jeff Leach, one of the company's cofounders, sums up the impact social media has had on Naked Pizza's business as follows, "If your business doesn't have anything to tweet about, you'd better shift into a business that does have something to tweet about."[12]

What About Paid Media?

Is there still a role for advertising, the founding father, so to speak, of broadcast-age marketing? General Mills's launch of its new Progresso broth certainly raises this question.

Let's be clear on the distinctions because they are relatively new. *Owned media* refers to a company's own domains, such as their Web and mobile sites, blogs, and Twitter handles. These are distinct from, although increasingly connected to, *earned media,* which is the dialog that takes place in social environments. Owned media reflects the company's voice; earned media captures the thoughts and perceptions of its customers. As company's sites become more interactive and inclusive of customer comments, this line is blurring. Paid media, on the other hand, includes activities in which companies pay for exposure, which includes traditional advertising, display ads, paid search, and sponsorships.

I have never been a huge advocate of paid media. It is the easy way out and much less effective compared to the challenge—and fun—of participating openly and honestly with one's constituencies in social environments. Earned media is far more credible than paid media and more useful in influencing customers as they take steps along the purchase journey. Earned media is authentic; it reflects how a company actually operates, the quality of its products, and how it values its customers—not just a statement or slogan as to what it aspires to be.

That having been said, there is evidence that at this time integrating limited paid media with social engagement can be effective. Why? Because paid media can act as a catalyst, driving people to digital destinations where the real influence and connection takes place. At the same time, social media has been found to enhance the results of advertising. It provides listening platforms for marketers about products and services. It provides content as well as a platform for restricted paid media dissemination. And it can enhance consumer recall of advertising. A recent study by Nielsen and Facebook found that Facebook users who viewed an ad in conjunction with a news feed mention of the brand by a friend were three times as likely to remember the ad.[13]

The upshot is that there is no substitute for earned media but there can be some room for paid media when it is used as a bell ringer. I think sponsorships are a good way to go in the paid realm, particularly if it is companies sponsoring discussions on Facebook or LinkedIn about subjects that are in line with their purpose. Mutual of Omaha got it right years ago when they underwrote *Wild Kingdom*. They thrilled viewers by taking them to the far corners of the globe to see animals in their natural habitats, while simultaneously expressing their commitment to environmental conservation and protecting families' health and financial resources. That fact that they are still at it speaks to its success.

Integrating the Marketing Department

As we have seen, today's customer purchase journey involves multiple marketing functions—search, events, promotions, and even some advertising—and they are all interwoven with social media. As a result, marketing can no longer afford to be broken down by channel or even by distinctions like paid and unpaid media. Instead of having the search person, the events person, the direct-mail person, and the promotions person, marketing departments have to become less tool-focused and more customer-centric. Every member of the marketing team has to be able to see and operate beyond his or her individual silo to engage in a broader, and more effective, communication plan.

Unfortunately, despite job titles that would suggest otherwise, this is not what is happening in most marketing organizations today. Rather than observing, targeting, and integrating, most marketing departments are playing a variation on the arcade game Whack-a-Mole, trying to activate every possible marketing vehicle in hopes of reaching customers somewhere, somehow. The result is fragmentation, when what we are looking for is integration.

Even when companies realize that integration is what is now called for, it is not that easy for marketing departments to accomplish right off the bat. Steve Goldbach, a partner at Monitor who has worked extensively with consumer products goods companies to help them better integrate their marketing efforts, offers three reasons why:

1. Processes and systems are designed around the requirements of the old marketing mix.
2. Inappropriate metrics and measurements are being used to evaluate new media.
3. Resources are overly specialized and, therefore, not especially helpful to the new marketing mix.

As companies go forward, Goldbach and I agree that every effort needs to be made to break down the silos that exist in marketing departments. We are not saying that we don't need specialists, but we certainly don't need new silos in the form of Twitter or Foursquare specialists. Rather, companies can benefit from generalists who can communicate well and advocate for the consumer rather than for individual tools. A native Canadian, Goldbach likes to think of hockey players comprising the new marketing department rather than football players. Hockey players are more versatile than their very specifically trained counterparts on the football field.[14] Like hockey players, going forward marketers have to function more as communication integrators rather than specialists in order to effectively and seamlessly accompany the consumer through their purchase journey.

Coordinating the End-to-End Customer Experience

The need to integrate reaches beyond marketing silos, however, because the roles of marketing, sales, corporate communications, and customer service also overlap in social environments. Is this overlap problematic? No and yes. As I have said before, I have no problem with multiple voices representing a company. What I don't like is having artificial separations between functions that are all involved with customer engagement, especially when they need to be working together. Accenture's recent survey of 400 senior marketing executives at large companies found that the majority feel that "their teams need to learn how to work more closely with other front-line organizations including sales (70 percent) and customer service (55 percent)."[15] Rather than having these organizations remain as separate entities, I favor the idea of having these functions seamlessly connected, as they are in consumers' eyes.

Where Does Marketing End and Corporate Communications Begin?

It's clear that the distinction between marketing and corporate communications is blurring in the social media age. Traditionally, corporate communications has been responsible for reputation management, investor relations, and public relations, and it has used unpaid or earned media. Marketing, on the other hand, has focused on promoting companies' products and services through paid media—television, radio, and print. Today's social web is primarily earned media. Successful engagement is rooted in building relationships and trust—corporate communications' traditional areas of expertise.

However, because we are living in a recommendation economy that reflects a significant change in how consumers actually search and buy in today's world, marketing is also involved. Wise marketers who have grasped the paradigm shift realize that social web engagement is a vitally important way to reach potential customers. They are using their budgets, which are generally much larger than that of corporate communications, to develop venues for consumers to talk with each other and engaging in social environments where people are already actively researching and buying products. They know that if their company isn't part of that dialog, it is quite likely that they will not be considered at all. In this environment, where does corporate communications' job end and marketing's begin?

What About Sales?

Sales is part of the social media mix now, too. In the early days, social dialog primarily took place in microsites or social networks, far away from e-commerce sites. Today that practice is changing as companies realize the benefits of linking social commentary and consumer ratings and impressions to their sales environments.

Dell is integrating some of the content from its social communities into its e-commerce site, Dell.com. Lionel Menchaca, the company's chief blogger, explains the reason for the integration: traffic.[16] Dell's social communities have 600,000 visitors per quarter, whereas the Dell.com web site has closer to 100 million. The company is convinced that the wealth of information contained within the social communities would be useful to the 100 million people, who, by virtue of having visited its corporate web site, have expressed interest in Dell and its products but don't necessarily frequent its social destinations.

Here's the supporting evidence: ongoing dialog with consumers via Twitter has dramatically increased Dell Outlet's sales. Within the first year of using Twitter to announce deals, the company realized $2 million in revenue on its Twitter page. It was able to attribute another $1 million in sales of other products on Dell.com to dialogs that were initiated via Dell Outlet's Twitter handle.[17] Dell wants to capture that same success by syndicating content across its corporate and social sites and wants to use a single user-identification process to make it easy for visitors to move between sites. Customers won't know, or care, where sales' responsibility ends and marketing's begins. Why should they?

Retailers like Levis and Urban Outfitters are integrating their customers' "likes" directly into their e-commerce sites utilizing Facebook's social plugins.[18] Levi's site allows consumers to shop with friends at the Friends Store; its tagline is: like-minded shopping starts here. Consumers can sign into their Facebook accounts via the site and see what Levis merchandise their Facebook friends and other Facebook users have "liked." They can also e-mail or share photos of items that have caught their eye with friends, asking them, "What do you think?" (The site will also quite conveniently alert consumers to friend's birthdays.) Urban Outfitters allows shoppers to view items by brand and price as well as by items that have received the most reviews or the highest rating. Visit these sites and explore for yourself. It's very interesting to experience the power of others' suggestions on a retail site first-hand.

Providing Better Customer Service

Customer service is also part of the engagement blend. Social tools can enhance cohesive customer service because they allow for the fast resolution of issues and mutual learning.

Delta Airlines, for example, is using a Twitter account to help resolve travel problems—you know, the missed flights, weather delays, and lost baggage moments. Customer service agents are available to respond to all sorts of issues for limited periods of time. (Late-night and weekend travelers have to fend for themselves.)

"The whole idea is to address issues so that they don't escalate," said Susan Elliot, spokesperson for Delta. "It is ideal for us to have these agents at the customers' disposal to offer guidance in resolving issues even during their travel experience."[19] One traveler who tweeted Delta after missing a connection ended up being rebooked on another flight with the help of one of the tweeting customer service agents. "Having that immediate attention from Delta on Twitter is one of the reasons I select them," he later posted.[20]

McDonald's also has a Twitter team that actively monitors social conversations. When issues arise, they contact the tweeter to help resolve the situation. The team also thanks each tweeter for his or her feedback with a physical thank-you note and a coupon for a free meal. "It gives us a really nice outcome from something that initially started out as a negative experience for customers," explained Rick Wion, director of social media at McDonald's.

When Lenovo purchased IBM's PC Computing Division, it took a different tack and decided to launch its own customer service community. At the time, customer dialog about the newly acquired products was actively taking place in other third-party forums, and Lenovo wanted to be more involved in the conversation. The company revamped many of its internal processes as a result of these conversations, including making collaboration between marketing, customer service, and other departments "the way we do business around here."[21] This collaboration led to alterations to the company's manufacturing process that enhanced product quality, reduced warranty and customer service costs, and improved customer loyalty.[22] Sounds good to me.

The bottom line is that companies should organize themselves in a way that will yield excellent experiences for their customers. According to Forrester data, 91 percent of executives believe that customer experiences are critical or very important to their businesses.[23] Customers confirm these executives' assertion; Forrester found that nearly 5,000 customers surveyed said that they prefer better customer service to lower prices. What's more, companies with good customer experiences are more profitable and enjoy positive word of mouth and customer loyalty.

Introducing the Customer Engagement Department

I recommend that companies consider merging marketing, corporate communications, sales, and customer service into one customer engagement department whose sole reason for existence is to make sure that customers and potential customers have the information they need to make decisions and resolve issues, when they want it. This department's vision will be broad because they will try to satisfy the content needs for customers at all stages of the purchase journey—from developing brand awareness to becoming brand sharers and advocates.

Some companies are well on their way. Best Buy, for example, created @twelpforce to provide real-time interaction with customers about whatever they want to know. The company knows that customer questions can span the range from product features and benefits to customer service challenges. As a result, any Best Buy employee working on company time can provide answers to customers' posts. Because the tweets are all tagged (#twelpforce), interested customers can search the questions and answers that are posted. This is just one of many social media initiatives Best Buy undertakes to offer seamless and positive customer experiences.

In addition to making organizational changes, successful companies are mastering the new communication paradigm and its rules of engagement. They are realizing that whatever business they are in, if they are active in social environments, they are also in the publishing business. We'll tackle this new reality in Chapter 6.

Questions to Consider

- What is your typical customer's purchase journey? Has the prevalence of social media introduced other paths that warrant attention?
- Given what you know about channel pathways, what may need to be reset in your company's game plan?
- How else can social media improve your customers' experience?
- How integrated are your traditional and social channels?
- How much paid media do you need? What is working?
- Does integration of your marketing department make sense?
- Can you envision a Customer Engagement Department in your company? Why or why not?

CHAPTER SIX

Marketing, Sales, and Service, Step 2

Converse with Your Customers

Social media tools have changed the way that we communicate. The seemingly innocuous chatting, creating, sharing, and collaboration made possible by the social web has ushered in a new communication paradigm that is dramatically different from the broadcast paradigm that has dominated the communications landscape since the advent of radio and television. The widespread adoption of this new communication paradigm has important ramifications; as NYU professor Clay Shirky observed, "When we change the way we communicate, we change society."[1] And he is absolutely right.

Social destinations are the new town greens, playgrounds, and neighborhoods. Whether they are accessed via computers, smart phones, or other portable devices, social environments are rapidly becoming primary centers of activity for people, *the* place that they shop, plan, learn, work, communicate, and hang out.

Without stepping outside a door, consumers can meet up with friends, find a spouse, secure a job, go to work, earn a degree, or participate in a virtual hajj if they are so inclined. They can share their views and record their experiences with text, video, audio, and photos. Consumers with GPS–enabled phones can tap into location–based social environments like Foursquare and Gowalla to find a Chinese restaurant, McDonald's, or an obscure history site wherever they happen to be. They can even receive mobile coupons from retailers at the point of sale.

Increasingly, technology is erasing the distinction between the physical and digital worlds. Telephony systems like Skype and video conferencing platforms make it possible for people to stay in touch with friends and family all over the world and to attend meetings held remotely with customers and business partners. As one user said, "It's almost like sitting across the table." With the dawn of augmented reality technology, consumers can interact with objects virtually. For example, Best Buy recently made it possible for consumers to interact virtually with a new Toshiba laptop by simply focusing their web cam on some of the company's recent newspaper print ads.[2] Recognizing that consumers move back and forth between the physical and digital worlds, companies like Threadless and The Art of Shaving are creating complementary physical and digital outreach efforts to reach customers where they are and through the medium that they prefer at any given time or place.

Social Destinations Are Satisfying

In addition to offering utility, social destinations are becoming readily available sources of fun, satisfaction, entertainment, comfort, collaboration, information, and relationship for young and old, *everywhere*. Sound far-fetched? Consider the following example:

Just over 10 years ago, Stephen Heywood was diagnosed with ALS (amyotrophic lateral sclerosis; also known as Lou Gehrig's disease) at the age of 29. Inspired by Stephen's experiences with the disease, his brothers and long-time family friends envisioned an online social community of patients, doctors, researchers, and companies all dialoguing about his—and eventually others'—life-threatening diseases. Today that vision is a reality and communities have developed around several diseases on PatientsLikeMe.com. By sharing information in this social environment, patient members find answers to the questions they have, learn about treatments that work, and have the ability to gain additional insight from other patients facing similar challenges. As a member of the Parkinson's community wrote, "When I read a posting, even questions, I find it very helpful to look at the poster's profile . . . it boosts my confidence in what I'm reading when I see how long they have been at it, what they have tried, what else they have said." That's satisfaction, collaboration, and comfort.

Social tools are also unleashing a tremendous amount of creativity and passion. Under the broadcast communication paradigm, the general public was primarily a consumer of information; in this new world, it is also a creator of experiences. An amazing proliferation of folk art is taking place. Some of it is quite good; some of it is not. Regardless of what we may think of the quality of an individual contribution, we can all agree that the passion behind it is remarkable.

The social web has also created new vehicles through which people can work together. As Shirky explained, "We now have communications tools that are flexible enough to match our social capabilities, and we are witnessing the rise of new ways of coordinating action that take advantage of that change."[3]

Wikis are a great illustration of this collaboration in action. Ward Cunningham, the developer of the first wiki software, WikiWikiWeb, named the social tool after the Hawaiian word *wiki,* meaning "fast," because it allowed for quick, easy, and efficient online interaction. Although we refer to wikis as nouns, they are actually more of a verb because they are constantly being updated by whoever is interested. Wikipedia, the free online encyclopedia, is perhaps the most familiar example. Since 2001, people from all over the world have contributed to this wiki, which is currently available in 273 languages with more than 3.4 million articles in the English Wikipedia (and enjoys nearly 9.9 million views per hour).[4] That's extraordinary collaboration, especially when you consider that it has been accomplished entirely by volunteers.

Delicious.com and other bookmarking sites facilitate people working together to organize and create meaning in the digital world.

Here's an example that's close to home. For many months I have been scouring articles, blogs, videos—searching *everywhere*—for stories and examples to include in this book. One way to save my findings is to download them to my computer and then organize them into a browser-based system of folders. Another way to do this is to bookmark and tag my findings on a social site such as Delicious.com. When I find a Web resource that I would like to keep or share, I save the links to my Delicious site and tag them with several words that describe what the article is about. Later, when I return, I can pull up all articles that are related to a particular topic. I also have access to all the other articles, podcasts, and videos that others may have posted and tagged similarly. Some sites have incorporated features that allow users to rate and comment on bookmarks. Several companies have brought this capability in-house, creating internal bookmarking platforms that allow employees to tag and share relevant documents with their colleagues.

What is it that motivates people to bookmark and rate Web resources, share parenting tips, blog about the latest technology start-up, produce and share videos on YouTube, or contribute to an article on Wikipedia? Unbridled passion. People don't hang out in or contribute to social destinations for any other reason than because they want to. It has taken companies time to understand that people's primary purpose in being on the Web is not commerce. Social web users are there to inform and entertain themselves and others, to connect with each other, and in many cases, to help address some of the largest challenges facing the communities around them—together.

A Preferred Way of Researching and Staying Informed

Before the advent of social web destinations, people relied on established media outlets for news and entertainment. When I was growing up, for example, my mother would turn the television on in the morning and it would stay on until we all went to bed. We gathered around the television for Disney movies, football games, and the nightly news. We had limited choices; broadcasters determined what we would watch and when. Every few minutes our programs would be interrupted for a commercial message from sponsors. We all had the sense of being connected to the world "out there" all day long until the signal faded late at night.

Fast-forward to our home today. If everyone is home and we are enjoying "quality" time together in the family room, it is likely that each person is tuning into his or her own medium—or even several media sources. My daughters are likely to be catching up on the last episode of their favorite shows that have been downloaded to their iPads or TiVo'ed while simultaneously writing on friends' Facebook walls; my son is probably video chatting with several of his friends; my wife is checking her e-mail and RSS feeds; and I am probably surfing the Web, reading my favorite blogs and maybe posting a tweet or two, and asking myself why we purchased a big screen television for us all to enjoy together. Our family is a microcosm of the country; media choice is providing consumers with access to the information that they want, when they want it, 24 hours a day. And they—we—are loving it.

The social web is also changing how consumers search for information about products and services. Since the advent of the social web, it has become quite simple for consumers to bypass the advertising of companies and the opinions of experts in favor of consulting their peers for their ideas, opinions, and experiences. With a few keystrokes, people can survey others—people they know well or don't know at all—via Twitter, Facebook, or even e-mail, about hotels in South Africa, potential curfew times for teenagers, or which companies may be hiring. While shopping for clothes, my daughters often text photos of shirts and shoes to their friends to get their opinions on whether they should purchase them.

The term *lazyweb* has been used to describe this outsourcing of questions to one's network. Although it may be true that people are too lazy to answer these questions for themselves, more often than not, searches are conducted to take advantage of the experience of others. People can be more confident in their decisions by connecting with others through their social networks.

So valuable is this resource, that the search engine Bing and Facebook have formed a partnership in which Bing will bring the searcher's Facebook friends into the traditional search experience. For example, utilizing Bing's new feature, "Liked Results," while querying for restaurants in a given city, you can see which of the restaurants your friends have previously "liked" on Facebook. Where available, these personalized responses will appear at the top of the search results based upon this *social signal*. This way of sourcing answers through one's peer network is known as *social search*. It is distinct from standard search results resulting from search engines like Google and Yahoo!. Social search is an important trend to watch. How much more impact might results confirmed by friends have on you?

Being Welcome at the Social Table

It's easy to see why consumers love the social web: it's empowering, entertaining, resourceful, and satisfying. It's also easy to see how attractive the promise of these social destinations is to companies. It puts them in touch with their stakeholders with the possibility of more meaningful, creative, and potentially profitable long-term relationships. It holds the promise of a new source of competitive advantage. However, social web success is not just a case of putting the right technology in place. The value of social environments is in the dialogs that take place, not the underlying technology itself. Companies have much unlearning and reinventing to do to be welcome at the highly prized social table.

New rules of engagement are emerging as the social web continues to mature. These rules are bubbling up from Web users, not dictated by some authority. If companies violate them, they can count on being called out. Here's a summary of the rules today:

1. *It's a conversation.* Social destinations are about interacting, not just sending a one-way message. (That's why they're called social!) The social web is not a venue for sales pitches. People connect on the social web around interests and passions, not to be sold. Successful organizations are learning to talk *with* their customers rather than *at* them. Exchanges are characterized by a softer, more educational tone, rather than a hard-sell or transaction-oriented approach.

2. *Connection before commerce*. A good rule of thumb is to follow the model of connect first and allow customers, if they choose, to further investigate the possibility of a sale. Recognize the value in the communication itself and the relationship it builds, rather than being micro-focused on its potential transaction value. I realize that most of us are in the business to make money; however, in the social media age, this goal has to be balanced with creating a positive emotional connection with your customers. Trust me, in the long run, this is the most profitable strategy.

3. *Be relevant*. The social web is a highly personalized world. In this marketplace consumers want news and information about the things *they* care about, not what corporations necessarily want them to care about. They want to be able to find these things easily and yesterday. Successful companies are learning how to "smarten" their social destinations to engage with consumers personally and to reflect knowledge gained in earlier interactions.

   Amazon is fabulous at this. After author John Updike's death, I received an e-mail from Amazon inviting me to view a video about the author's life. (A previous purchase of one of Updike's books had alerted them to my interest.) I clicked though and watched a terrific video—in its entirety. But it didn't stop there. I then followed several links to other books and events related to Updike. Prompted by Amazon's book suggestions—readers who liked this book also liked these books—I then moved beyond Updike to read and post several more reviews and even bought some books. All in all, I spent 1.5 hours on their site. Although it is astonishing that I spent that much time on an e-commerce site, the more astonishing thing is that during that whole time, I never once felt as if Amazon were marketing to me. I felt resourceful and in control; no one was telling me what to do or directing my experience. As a result, I bought more and probably will in the future. That's how it's done.

4. *Be approachable*. Companies and brands are highly personified in this new environment. Betty Crocker, General Mills' baker

extraordinaire, has cared about your chocolate chip cookies for generations, but now she acts even more like family by posting photos and recipes on Flickr, providing access to her entire cookbook of recipes through a free mobile application, and "making you hungry, one tweet at a time."

Successful companies are putting a face on their brands. This doesn't necessarily mean that they are associating themselves with a character like Betty Crocker, but they are interacting with their stakeholders in a more personal way. They let their customers talk to a person, not an entity. They tell their brand's and organization's story—a story that doesn't come just from the marketing department. More often than not, consumers add to that story themselves.

5. *Be authentic.* As a result of this enhanced personification, consumers expect brands and companies to follow the social rules of acquaintances, rather than those of an impersonal marketplace. Organizations are expected to listen and be highly responsive to their customers' and other stakeholders' concerns. If they are not, consumers will blog, tweet, comment, and vote with their feet. Successful companies listen without fear and respond rapidly, honestly, and humbly, taking full responsibility for any errors they have caused. Their responses are as fast, direct, and informal as the conversations consumers have with friends.

6. *Stand for something.* There is a trust gap today that transparency is helping to fill. Consumers are looking for more from the companies with which they interact, however. They want companies to be multidimensional, to be pursuing a moral purpose in addition to profitability. Talk with your customers about who you are, your expertise, and the contributions your company has made to its field. Show them the types of people who work with you, what you care about, and the way your company is making a difference.

7. *Be generous.* Reward your customers for their loyalty. A recent six-country study by the advertising firm DDB, found that people's most important reasons for following brands on Facebook is for the promotional benefits, followed by liking

the brand, wanting to know about new products, gaining access to exclusive information, and being able to provide opinions about the brand.[5] Importantly, the study also showed that after following a brand on Facebook, more than a third of the respondents "want to buy this brand's product more." Give them what they are asking for!

The rock band Chester French, for example, has a VIP application for its fans. The more fans promote the band, the more points they get. Prizes include free music and T-shirts. JetBlue offers specials deals for its customers that follow it in digital destinations. Dunkin' Donuts rewards fans who post photos of themselves with Dunkin' products by selecting a "Fan of the Week." This practice recognizes customers; provides Dunkin' Donuts fans with social currency, in the form of recognition; and generates visual, customer-generated content for the company's official Facebook Page. Clorox rewards customers, employees, and suppliers that are active on its CloroxConnects site with personal blogs, guest appearances, access to insiders, and even increased internal responsibility. These are all win–win situations.

8. *Make it easy*. If you want customers to find you, make it easy for them. Fully integrate your marketing channels so that if consumers find you in one spot, they will be able to easily find you in another. For example, if television spots are still effective for your business, make sure that they direct viewers to your web site, and that your web site, in turn, is linked to your Facebook page and Twitter. Furthermore, make sure that your content allows for sharing, downloading, and embedding so that your fans can share it across channels and thereby speak on your behalf.

9. *Be brief*. Almost 150 years ago Mark Twain said, "Anybody can have ideas—the difficulty is to express them without squandering a quire of paper on an idea that ought to be reduced to one glittering paragraph."[6] Twitter could not agree more; it forces users to get their message across in 140 characters or less. A rule of thumb for bloggers is no more than a page per entry. White papers don't have to be longer than 4

to 6 pages. Really effective videos can be 30 seconds long. People want to feel like they have completed something when they have finished reading or viewing a post. Make this possible.

10. *Be portable.* Here's a sign of the times: more people in India have access to mobile phones than they do toilets.[7] According to the consulting firm Yankee Group, 1.6 million new mobile phones are added every day and more than 5 billion people are expected to connect through mobile devices by 2015.[8] Morgan Stanley's recent *Mobile Internet Report* forecasts that, within the next five years, more users will connect with the Internet via mobile devices than with desktop computers.[9] It's already happening in Japan, where 95 percent of the mobile market has 3G capability and 85 percent subscribe to a data plan as part of their wireless contract.[10]

    To be really useful to consumers, content must be able to be enjoyed on the devices that consumers are using. Content also has to be customized to reflect how these devices are being used. For example, according to the Mobile Intent Index, newly created by the public relations firm Ruder Finn, mobile phone users take advantage of their phones to connect socially with others, manage their personal finances, and advocate for causes.[11] What they are not doing is using them for educational or creative purposes.

11. *Keep it simple.* Most customers don't know the difference between blogs, forums, and wikis, and why should they? Social technology should be a nonevent, the messenger, not the message. Indeed, if technology is cumbersome, unreliable, or even noticeable, rest assured, it will be abandoned with no second chances—digital natives are a lot less forgiving of technology than those of us who grew up rebooting.

    Over time I predict that the words that we use to describe social web technology, like *online* or even *social web,* will completely disappear. As our collective *predigital accent* fades, we'll talk about social destinations and environments themselves instead of the technology that gets us there.[12]

When was the last time you talked about turning on your kitchen lights in terms of electricity and circuits?

12. *Take a long-term view.* The old marketing model—struggle to get a campaign out the door, launch it, and watch the results stream in (or not)—does not apply to social environments. What works is creating connections and relationships with a core group of stakeholders that can be sustained and grown over time. Contests and campaigns can be used to build these relationships, but with social engagement, the horizon goes beyond short-term offers and quarterly budgets and reviews. So does the value of social media efforts. Remember, effective social engagement increases in value over time as communities and dialog grow. As a result, marketing efforts that were formerly viewed as expenditures are being transformed into long-term assets. Start early and be patient.

13. *Be committed.* A commitment to full-body immersion, rather than getting one's feet wet, is also critical. I am not saying that companies have to tackle internal and external applications of every social tool in hopes of cultivating relationships with all stakeholders in every marketplace at the same time. What I am saying is that they should pick an important goal and build a comprehensive strategy around that goal so the opportunity for success is greater.

14. *Be remarkable.* That's good advice from consumers and marketing guru Seth Godin; if you're not remarkable, you'll be eaten alive. There is nowhere to hide product or service failures in this new communication landscape. There is room for gradations in quality, but not for overstating what you have to offer. If what you have is really good, you're golden. Rest assured, remarkable or not, they'll talk about it. In fact, they already are.

15. *Keep it interesting.* For consumers, it's a case of so many inputs, so little time. For organizations, it's a question of how to get consumers' attention. The solution: recognize that every company, no matter the nature of its primary business, has to become a publisher and get to work creating and sourcing great content. Use rich media—a picture or video is still

worth a thousand words. Genzyme, a biotechnology company focused on rare inherited disorders, posts videos of clinical trials of their experimental drugs so that interested consumers can observe results firsthand. I can guarantee you that for families, friends, and medical providers of someone with one of these diseases, these videos are riveting. Be thought provoking, have a sense of humor, and create social experiences that remind you of your favorite places to hang out. Most of all, work to build a genuine sense of community.

Don't forget offline opportunities for connection, too. Another chapter in the Ford Fiesta Movement story illustrates why this integration really hits home. In addition to all of the online connection that the Fiesta movement generated—6 million YouTube views, nearly 740,000 on Flickr, and more than on 3.7 Twitter—Ford also set the Guinness World Record for the most attendees at a tweetup. A *tweetup* is a gathering of two or more people who are brought together via Twitter. Ford's tweetup brought together 1,149 people to honor their favorite Fiesta agent and get a sneak preview of the new Fiesta at their Ford Fiesta Awards Celebration. Agents and social media followers had the chance to meet each other after interacting via the social web for months. The offline event created a lot of buzz, fun, and connection.

Here's another example. The Hershey Company used a combination of online and offline connections to introduce its Chocolate Bliss product line. Over the course of one weekend, fans hosted 10,000 parties where the product was introduced to about 129,000 people. Participants blogged and uploaded photos of the fun, which ultimately reached an audience of more than 7 million people. Almost a year and a half later, one of the participants wrote, "I am still buying Bliss chocolates and loving them."[13]

You're a Publisher Now, Too

As you can see, delivering a compelling customer experience is critical in this new environment. Content is at the heart of this task. It's valuable because it leads to conversation, which leads to connection. It is the basis for how customers build relationships with companies and ultimately make purchase decisions. It's also the basis for how companies retain customers and transform them into brand sharers and ambassadors.

What do I mean by *content*? Content can come in a variety of forms, including video, games, white papers, blogs, short commentary, expert opinions, and even physical events. Good content can demonstrate a company's expertise or it can entertain or educate consumers—or do all three.

The best content is highly targeted, designed to readily connect with its designated customer. Think back to the customer identification process that we talked about in Chapter 2. Who are your target stakeholder communities and what characterizes their personas? What do they want from you? Information, entertainment, discounts? What are their likes and dislikes? What tone and style makes them comfortable? Where are they congregating—on Twitter, Facebook, blogs, social bookmarking sites, or LinkedIn? Does there need to be a physical component to your content? The answers to these questions will provide a framework for your ongoing content development. The most interesting digital content is increasingly visual, customized to each user, up to date, and available when people want it.

Creating Content to Fuel Connection

How do companies fulfill the expectations for content? Once again, I recommend taking a more strategic approach. Conducting an asset review or audit to see what content you already have is a good place to start. As you review this content, consider its relevance and value to your target market. If the content that you have available is not a direct hit, see if there is any way that it can be modified to be appropriate and useful. If it is a direct hit, then consider what format the content is in and in which channels it can best be used. Finally, make sure that these channels are in sync with the channels that your target consumer uses. I can't emphasize the importance of matching the tool with the audience enough. A mismatch can completely backfire. It is tantamount to saying: we are not really listening to you.

One of the outcomes of this asset review is a good sense of where there are content gaps that require new content to sustain a high level of engagement with your target constituency. Bear in mind that content doesn't always have to be proprietary. It can come from your customers and from third parties. By making it easy for customers and other parties to add to any and all of your content, you can easily multiply the quantity of relevant content on your social sites and add to your credibility at the same time. This feedback will also prompt future topics and ideas for content.

Are consumers really creating that much content? In a word, yes. A recent study by Forrester found that almost one quarter of online adults in the United States are creating content.[14] More than one third of online Americans take part in activities like posting reviews and commenting on blogs and one in five categorize Web content via tags, RSS feeds, and "voting" sites like Digg and Reddit. When you look at engagement by age group, you can see shades of things to come: more than half of young adults between the ages of 18 and 24 currently create content. I expect that data will keep doubling every 24 months on the Web—welcome this "Weber's Law" of data creation. Make it easy for consumers to leave their mark.

Are people really interested in consumer-generated content? You bet. The same Forrester study found that three out of every four online Americans consume social content. Here is a really interesting fact: user-generated video viewing, blogs, and online reviews are driving the growth of social content consumption. That means that people are very much interested in what their peers are saying, showing, and sharing online.

Develop a Content Calendar

Developing a content publishing calendar that outlines what new content will be produced, when it will be delivered, and who owns the development of new content is critical to effective ongoing social engagement. Some companies use formulas for their content. On certain days of the week they do product reviews, on others they talk about industry trends or host guest bloggers. Some designate themes for a given period of time. As this new content is being created, identify the channels where it will be used and develop it in a way that is easily converted for use on the social web.

Be disciplined about content generation because it can get expensive. Don't fall prey to the content bug and create everything from sales support materials to instruction manuals for every product, every audience, and every channel. It is likely to become obsolete before you even post it. Evaluate the effectiveness of your content regularly to see what is working and what isn't. Disseminate the good stuff; see how it can be repackaged and reused with different communities. Consider using RSS feeds to provide product updates to employees and customers. Make sure that there is consistency among online content and that it is well tagged. Finally, don't get bogged down in perfection. In an environment like this that is driven so much by user-generated content and timeliness, content does not have to be museum quality. Relevance, accuracy, and timeliness are far more important than the highest quality.

What is the right amount of content? Find the rhythm of posts that suits your audience. Too many posts and it's too much work for both you and your customer. Too few and you are not really a part of the conversation. Don't ask your customers to jump through hoops, because they won't.

Sampling, Applications, Contests, and More

There are many ways to get customers creating and engaging with your content. Couponing combined with online commenting can be effective. Procter & Gamble (P&G) created a sampling program for its dish soap, Dawn, and asked those who tried it to rate the product. The company received more than 500 ratings. As Stan Joosten, innovation manager of holistic consumer communication at P&G, said, "the best part is that we're not saying it [comments about the brand], they are."[15] P&G magnified the effectiveness of this initiative by bringing the online experience offline, incorporating these comments back into store displays.

Applications can also be effective. For their IMS brand of dog food, Eukanuba created its OFF LEASH iPhone application, which pinpoints the five closest off-leash dog parks for a given zip code. It allows users to rate the walks and add their personal favorites. Speaking of which, one of my favorite applications is SitOrSquat, sponsored by Charmin. It locates public restrooms wherever you are and allows you to "add a toilet" as well. Discussion forums tackle health issues such as Crohn's disease, irritable bowl syndrome, and pregnancy; parenting challenges; and application support. As you can imagine, there is a lot of bathroom humor on the site as well.

Contests can be a good way to solicit user input as well. When P&G requested consumer stories about the Mr. Clean Magic Eraser, it received 25,000 stories in one month—that's a lot of content. Remember the 2010 Super Bowl? Not the game—the ads. Two of the best spots—"House Rules" and "Snack Attack"—were consumer-made videos that had been submitted to Doritos for their Crash the Super Bowl contest. This crowd-sourced ad strategy has worked well for the company and played well with Super Bowl audiences. If you haven't seen some of the consumer-generated videos from Ford's Fiesta Movement, take a peak. There is some great consumer-generated content there.

Life Is a Game

To capture some of the growing enthusiasm surrounding gaming, as evidenced from the popularity of simple pastimes like FarmVille to elaborate all-consuming activities like World of Warcraft, companies are adding gaming mechanics to their digital properties. Sometimes these games have retail tie-ins. Zynga, which owns FarmVille, Mafia Wars, and YoVille, for example, recently linked up with 7-Eleven (and 7,000 of its retail stores) to offer limited-edition virtual goods, redeemable in one of their three hit games, to customers who purchased specially marked products. To put the magnitude of this opportunity in context, consider that 70 million people per month play FarmVille. (In 2009 the population of the United States was estimated to be just north of 307 million.)

McDonald's has years of experience with gaming. One of the most successful is a sweepstakes game that mimics Monopoly and has been running annually since 1987. Briefly, customers receive game stamps when they purchase certain menu items that correspond to property spaces on the Monopoly board. (Monopoly purists will quickly note the addition of the "Golden Avenue" and "Arches Avenue" properties to the board.) There are instant win stamps and stamps that, when combined into color-matched properties, can be redeemed for money— even up to $1 million. An online counterpart to the original game was introduced in 2004. The fun is not reserved only for adults. Kids can explore the virtual world of McLand on www.happymeal.com and play the McDonald's Sims Game and several others on popular gaming sites.

Gaming is not only fun, it can be educational. In fact, a whole new field of study, immersive learning, is developing, predicated on early theoretical and experienced-based research that suggests that games provide powerful learning experiences. Here's an example of how one microfinance organization is using gaming to introduce young children to the world of microlending.

Katie Smith Milway thought that she was writing a book. As it turns out, she was starting a movement. Since her book's publication in the spring of 2008, *One Hen* has evolved from an award-winning children's book to a provider of enrichment curriculum that teaches elementary school children in over 150 countries about world issues and how they can make a difference. The book's web site, www.onehen.org, provides kids with gaming opportunities to learn more about microfinance.

Here's how it works. Kids play games on the One Hen site, where they also learn the story of Kojo, a highly successful Ghanaian poultry farmer, who started his business by purchasing a single hen with a small loan. As his business grows, so does the welfare of his community and ultimately his country. He is able to lift himself, his family, and several communities out of poverty through the growing success of his poultry business. As kids play games, they accumulate beads, which they can then allocate to various virtual entrepreneurs, whose profiles and stories are shared on the site. But that's not all. One Hen has partnered with Opportunity International, which provides microfinance loans, savings plans, insurance, and training to more than two million people working their way our of poverty in the developing world. Following the players' designation of beads, Opportunity International directs real investment funds to the entrepreneurs that are represented by the virtual images. Kids love it. Not only are they having fun, but they are also learning and making an impact on the world around them.

How can your company use gaming mechanics to reward and educate your stakeholders?

Moral Purpose Makes for Great Interactions

We've talked about how many stakeholder communities are looking for companies to be more involved with making a difference in the world. Showing your constituencies how you are doing that, in fun and useful ways, makes for good content—and for good stakeholder relations.

Ed Nicholson, director of community and public relations for Tyson Foods, says that in his experience, sharing information about his company's hunger-relief efforts with consumers has helped humanize their brand. It establishes the company as a thought leader and committed partner in the cause of hunger. What's more, the company's social engagement helps link existing players—people and organizations that have been actively involved with hunger for years— in an online community. This helps further the cause and generates a host of credible brand ambassadors for Tyson.

Tyson donates 8 to 10 million pounds of food annually as part of its hunger-relief efforts. Its social media engagement helps them "leverage [these] in-kind donations toward more than publicity," Nicholson explains.[16] Creating events around their donations that "point to the need," and tweeting and blogging about them, helps generate broader awareness of hunger and the organizations that are working to alleviate it.

For example, Tyson blogged from the University of Arkansas's stadium, where they were partnering with the Arkansas Razorbacks and Lift Up America to distribute a truckload of Tyson products to agencies of the Northwest Arkansas Food Bank. Partnering with these organizations helped raise the public's awareness of hunger within their own community. Tyson regularly tells the stories of Hunger All-Stars, people who are working in hunger relief in multiple social venues around the world. The company archives these profiles on their microsite, tweets about them on the Tyson handle,[17] and uploads related photos and videos to Flickr and YouTube.

Consumers respect what Tyson is doing and enjoy the content it creates. One consumer commented, "Tyson's commitment to the basic core value that 'Hunger is Unacceptable' shows outstanding leadership—I challenge others in the food industry to follow."[18] Another wrote, "Thank you Tyson for using social media to create something productive and to contribute value and attention to others instead of merely grabbing it up for yourselves."[19]

Tyson has also found its efforts to be appreciated by the company's internal constituencies. As Nicholson said, "Everyone wants to work for a company that gives back. [It] makes you feel good about the company that you work for."[20]

Chatting About Fish, Coffee, Soft Drinks, and Burritos

What are some other examples of companies connecting with consumers about what makes them tick? The next time you are ordering fish in a restaurant, pull out your phone and text 30644 with the message "FISH" along with the variety of fish that you are considering ordering. You'll receive a text message back from the Blue Ocean Institute that will tell you whether your potential entrée is sustainable, and, if it isn't, it will send you a list of ecofriendly alternatives. What a great way for the Institute to keep their sustainability message front and center.[21]

As a part of the Haitian earthquake relief effort, Starbucks stores in the United States and Canada made it possible for customers to make monetary donations directly to the American Red Cross while they were paying for their java—customers could even apply funds from their Starbucks cards. Haitian American musician Wyclef Jean collaborated with Starbucks to bring the needs of the Haitian community into the public arena, a combined effort that created buzz and good will. As one customer commented on the Starbucks' blog:

> Once again Starbucks lives up to its social responsibility statement and is reaching out to help our global neighbors . . .

great going . . . my hope is this will truly inspire others to give . . . even if it is only a single dollar . . . if all of us who frequent SB did . . . WOW what an impact. Again, thanks.[22]

Companies such as Pepsi, American Express, and Boloco have had success in asking customers to help them decide to which causes they should make financial contributions. Boloco, a regional burrito chain in the Northeast, is committed to being green. As a reflection of this goal, the company created a green fund to which it donated a portion of all customer purchases made over a given period of time. The ultimate goal was to engage Boloco customers in identifying "deserving green causes" and selecting the top three local green charities to which the company would make a donation.

Boloco fans were asked to nominate their favorite charities through the company's Facebook page and to encourage others to "like" their causes. As the results came in, fans were then directed to a poll on the company's web site where they could vote on the finalists. Eventually, the three highest-ranking organizations received a check from Boloco, on the same day that Boston's mayor presented the company with the Boston Green Business Award.

Inviting customers into the innovation process can yield both content and new product ideas. We'll talk about how companies are using social media to put their stakeholders, business partners, and innovation brokers at the center of their ideation process in Chapter 7.

Questions to Consider

- What can your company do to be welcome and successful at the social media table?
- What content has worked best for your organization? Why?
- What content ideas do you want to further explore?

CHAPTER SEVEN

Innovation

Commit to Openness, Speed, and Crowds

When the movie rental company, Netflix, decided that it needed better software to more accurately predict the movies its customers would like, it decided to look beyond its own backyard to tap into the wisdom of a broader community. The company offered a $1 million reward to the company, group, or person that would be the first to create a solution that was at least 10 percent better than its in-house software, Cinematch.

A total of 41,000 teams from 186 countries worked on the challenge for three years before two groups submitted successful solutions within 24 minutes of each other. A seven-person team of computer engineers, statisticians, and machine-learning experts from the United States, Austria, Canada, and Israel comprised the winning team, which came to be known as BellKor's Pragmatic Chaos.

When asked about the secret of BellKor's success, Chris Volinsky, who served as the leader of the BellKor team and whose day job is running the statistics research department at AT&T Labs Research, said, "All of the top teams had many discussions with many of the other top teams. We realized we needed to get in on that game in order to stay on top."[1]

In the end, they did exactly that. In fact, it was only after Volinsky's original three-person team expanded to include additional minds and disciplines that a solution was reached. The team combined the individuals' several hundred algorithms to come up with the winner. That's the power of effective collaboration. It brings together people who see the world differently to move ideas forward. Here's a sign of the times: BellKor never gathered together, in person, until the awards ceremony. That's the power of social media.

Innovation Is the Trump Card

Operational improvement alone is no longer enough to ensure success. The long-term viability of any company depends on its ability to reinvent its products, services, and itself. Traditionally, innovation in organizations has been primarily an insular activity, a closed loop. It followed a trajectory from in-house idea generation, to testing, and eventually to new product or service launch. Today that model is broken. We've learned that isolation is the greatest obstacle to innovation. It takes interaction with others, people who see the world differently, to solve challenges and birth new ideas. With few exceptions, the insular company model is no longer fast enough, nor does it have the depth and breadth to generate the kinds of ideas that keep organizations growing in a competitive global marketplace.

Netflix knows this; that's why they looked outside of their company to a broader assortment of minds to develop better prediction software. Although it took the winning team three years to find a solution that was 10 percent better than Cinematch, Netflix chief executive officer (CEO), Reed Hastings, told the audience at the awards ceremony that it took the first team only three weeks to beat the internal Netflix team's results, which they had been working on for five years.[2]

Today, many companies are thinking very differently about the innovation process. Rather than looking exclusively to their research and development (R&D) departments for new product and service ideas, companies like Netflix are reaching outward to tap into the insight and creativity of broader communities. They are probing their customers, employees, business partners, and competitors as well as think tanks, universities, and Web-based innovation brokers to help them source and broker intellectual property that can fuel their growth. They have buried the notion that "it has to be made here" in favor of "letting a thousand flowers bloom."

The social web's connectivity helps make this open innovation possible. As in the case of BellKor, it brings together people from a variety of places and backgrounds easily and for very little cost. It also taps the wisdom of the crowds to sort through the ideas gathered allowing what the market views as the best ideas to rise to the top.

"The Net is the greatest medium for innovation ever in the human history with a possible exception of writing," said David Weinberger, senior researcher at the Harvard Berkman Center for Internet and Society and coauthor of *The Cluetrain Manifesto*. "Never before have we had a medium that combines information, communication, and that ability to be social." And we are still in the early stages of its development.

By the People and for the People

It's black cherry–lime flavored and is fortified with eight key nutrients and caffeine. Its package design includes a Facebook logo and a paragraph about untagging and friend requests. It's called Connect, and it's VitaminWater's newest flavor. Why the connection to Facebook? It's where the product came from. The company conducted a contest on its Facebook page that invited fans to design their own flavors, packaging, and ingredients and then vote on the results.

To launch the product, VitaminWater gave away 100,000 bottles of Connect to its Facebook fans. To try the new flavor, intrigued customers went to the company's Facebook page and requested a coupon for a free bottle. They were also asked to share the offer with their other Facebook friends. Think about it: that's product and package design and launch combined, and all undertaken by customers via Facebook. That's successful use of the social web.

Going direct and talking with your rank-and-file consumers, with the goal of developing new uses for products or product line extensions, is perhaps the most well known and widely used of the collaborative innovation models. Decades ago futurist Alvin Toffler coined the phrase *prosumer* to reflect this fusion of producers and consumers. Today, this is not earth-shattering news; companies have been surveying their customers and running focus groups to gather their insight for years. The difference that the social web makes is in the scope and frequency of these interactions, the depth and breadth of the discussion that it evokes, and the way it makes a broad base of consumers feel to be asked for their input if they know that they have truly been heard.

Volkswagen knows that the discussion of ideas can be as important as the ideas themselves. That's why participants in their App My Ride contest are rewarded for winning submissions as well as for discussing and evaluating the apps and ideas of other contestants in the community.[3] Here's how it works. The company hopes to tap into the wisdom of interested users, coders, and developers to develop innovative applications for their new infotainment system. Participants can submit creative ideas and/or compiled apps to the company. Although Volkswagen reserves the right to make all final decisions, this community input is invaluable. By studying the points that the community raises about proposed ideas and applications, Volkswagen can better understand the underlying need that consumers are trying to meet and the pros and cons of the various solutions offered. This understanding is the basis for both evolutionary product development—new variations on an existing product—as well as disruptive innovation, those game-changing ideas from which competitive advantage is born.

Exercise, Eat Right, and Innovate Daily

Some companies, rather than running a one-off contest, have set up web sites to tap into the wisdom of customers, employees, and anyone else for that matter, on an ongoing basis. I've previously mentioned Dell's IdeaStorm; Huggies has another interesting e-innovation vehicle.

The diaper brand is branching out into the early-stage venture capital business through its MomInspired grant program. Huggies' parent company, Kimberly-Clark, is offering grant money to fund mothers' ideas for "a unique baby or childcare product that addresses an unmet parenting need."[4] Through the ongoing program, the company hopes to foster its own innovation and to encourage and inspire entrepreneurial moms.

The company has two submission periods a year. Their judging panel evaluates all submissions and gives notice to "mompreneurs" several weeks later. Successful submissions and their visionaries are highlighted on their web site along with helpful business resources, such as information about how to write a business plan, secure financing, evaluate distribution methods, and even manage one's time. Moms chat with each other on Huggies' Facebook page—a highly valued resource. As one of the grant recipients said, "Receiving great feedback is the best reward."[5] Having its fingers on the pulse of mothers and the product and service needs they are uncovering is a substantial prize in and of itself for Kimberly-Clark.

Closing the Decaf-Grande-Nonfat-Latte Loop

Starbucks was one of the first companies to form a consumer ideation site. Today, myStarbucksIdea, or MSI as it's known to the community, is quite well known.[6] Anyone can post ideas on MSI. In addition to posting suggestions, the site lets you see what other people have contributed, discuss ideas with other community members, and ultimately vote on the submissions. These features bring the ideation process full circle by tapping the community to help evaluate and prioritize new ideas.

Forty Starbucks Idea Partners from various departments are available to answer questions and provide insights to the conversation. Starbucks knows that creating a listening initiative requires action. Providing feedback and implementing suggestions, where appropriate, is essential because it shows that a company really is listening and builds accountability into the listening process. To close the loop, the company has an "Ideas in Action" blog where it announces what actions have been taken. (The reason that they don't have coffee ice cubes for drinks, by the way, is because "only a small percentage of our retail stores have freezers."[7])

Connecting and Developing at Procter & Gamble

Head & Shoulders, Pampers, Old Spice, Tide, Oil of Olay . . . this may sound like items on a shopping list, but they are actually some of the many products that make Procter & Gamble (P&G) such a formidable consumer products company. For all but the last decade of its 175-year history, the company has relied on its internal R&D department to keep its pipeline filled with new products. That strategy has worked well; how many other companies have enjoyed 175 years of market leadership and staying power?

In 2000, its then newly appointed CEO, A. G. Lafley, challenged the company to think differently, and openly, about innovation. Although the company had been experimenting with outside innovation well before that time, Lafley gave the company a specific goal: 50 percent of all innovation should come from external sources. As a result, the company's Connect + Develop program was established. Through Connect + Develop, P&G began to collaborate with individuals, companies, academia, research institutions, suppliers, and e-innovation networks (we'll talk more about those shortly) to discover new product ideas. The company's philosophy began to morph from relying on "our know how" to "who we know."

The Connect + Develop program remains central to P&G's innovation engine today. The company's current chairman, president, and CEO, Bob McDonald, described his vision for the company: "P&G's purpose and growth strategy is to improve more lives in more parts of the world more completely—with an unrelenting focus on innovation. We want to partner with the best innovators everywhere, which is why Connect + Develop is at the heart of how P&G innovates."[8]

Every year, P&G's leadership prioritizes its top 10 challenges. These needs are then articulated and sourced through both the company's proprietary and open networks. Today, more than 1,000 outside business partners are part of P&G's extended ecosystem. Lafley's goal has been realized: approximately 50 percent of product initiatives at the company involve significant collaboration with these outside innovators.

The Connect + Develop web site allows anyone to browse P&G's current needs and assets as well as to submit their own ideas for consideration. A broad range of ideas is sought after including new products, technology, package design, and even business models, as well as opportunities to expand existing product lines. In 2009, about 4,000 ideas were submitted through the site, of which 8 percent were "substantial things we need to look into," said Chris Theon, managing director of Global Open Innovation Office. "Every business unit is looking into one opportunity—some of them are things we didn't even know we needed to figure out."[9]

The Mr. Clean Car Wash franchise system, which leverages the brand equity of P&G's Mr. Clean and the broad reach of the car wash industry, is an example of a successful submission. The company also has an entrepreneurial new-business generator, its FutureWorks program, which "transforms fledgling businesses currently serving new markets into businesses that can scale to serve the mass market."[10]

Although open innovation is clearly essential to the company, P&G's own R&D department is still robust and vitally important. A strong R&D department helps to further develop or customize external technologies to make them appropriate for the market opportunity. It also generates intellectual property that can be licensed, yielding incremental revenue for the company.

Here's an example. Several years ago P&G developed a calcium formulation that was superior to what was previously available. The calcium was both ingestible and more absorbable than existing formulations. P&G successfully licensed the calcium technology to Tropicana, helping it to become the best-selling orange juice in the country. The associated licensing fee feeds straight into P&G's revenue stream.

In an interview with IdeaConnection.com, Jeff Weedman, vice president for external development, explained how P&G makes use of both internal and external R&D, "Our philosophy is how to continue to do what we are best at, and very systematically and aggressively reach out to literally the entire world. It comes down to, 'How do we get those great ideas?' "[11] With this kind of "know how" and "whom they know," P&G is likely to be around in another 175 years.

The Doctor Is In—and Innovating

Going where your customers are, is one of the fundamental tenets of social media success. Being involved with the communities in which your customers are active can be a great vehicle for innovation. At times these communities are open—anyone can join for free. Other times they may be password protected or require a paid membership for access.

Sermo, the world's largest online community of physicians, is an example of a gated, or password protected, community. About 112,000 active physicians comprise the community—that's about 20 percent of all U.S. doctors. Physicians are able to join the network for free and, once there, enjoy access to a wide range of experience and expertise. Sixty-eight specialties and all 50 states are represented in the community that spends more than 35,000 hours a month together online.

It's easy to see how the Sermo community can help its members collaborate and make strides toward improving patient care, but how can it augment a company's innovation efforts? Several health care organizations, governmental agencies, and even financial services companies have joined Sermo as clients. These clients pay for access to this physician community. This access allows them to observe ongoing peer-to-peer physician conversations and to be alerted when certain topics—diabetes or antidepressants for example—are being discussed. It also provides them with the opportunity to conduct research within the community, targeting any group of specialists for qualitative and/or quantitative results. Posting questions, conducting surveys, exchanging data, and creating panels are all common practice. Clients can also post specific branded messages to the community, such as new product alerts. Sermo is transparent about these client relationships; physician members are fully aware of this client observation and participation.

Sermo founder and CEO, Dr. Daniel Palestrant, observed that clients are increasingly using the community to conduct what he calls "point shoot point engagement." As he recently explained to *Medical Marketing & Media*:

> A brand team might have an idea, so they decide they want to run a survey, so they might survey 100 cardiologists who are in the top prescribers. They get the result back 48 hours later. Then they want to move to a panel. They start seeing those results in real time, and then they decide they want to scale this up into a 2,000 physician survey. And that whole process might take a week and cost a quarter of what they would have paid to go through a conventional market research or promotion mechanism.[12]

What communities might be useful to your company's innovation efforts?

Brainstorm with Your Competitors

Why would coffee rivals like Starbucks, Dunkin' Donuts, and Tim Hortons collaborate? To find the perfect coffee cup—not the perfect cup of coffee. Jim Hanna, who is director of environmental impact at Starbucks, explained their collaboration to the *Boston Globe*: "We are fiercely competitive but we really want to differentiate ourselves on the quality of our product and level of service in stores. Sustainability [on the other hand] is a problem we all have to solve together."[13]

Turns out that finding the perfect coffee cup is a challenge. Dunkin' Donuts supply chain manager has been looking for an alternative to its Styrofoam cup for four years. Starbucks has been on a similar journey, even holding a "BetaCup" challenge to generate input from its customers. (Of course, the perfect cup is a reusable mug, which to date has not been widely adopted by consumers, even though they are putting pressure on coffee companies to become more sustainable.)

Understanding the irony of consumer behavior and the complexity of the perfect cup challenge, these three rivals are collaborating on cup designs as well as working to address the issue from a different angle—creating an aftermarket for recycled cups. If they can convince paper companies of the value of recycled cup material, so that used cups don't wind up in landfills, they will have made substantial progress by putting their heads and market power together.

Here's another example of formidable competitors partnering together. Procter & Gamble (P&G) and Clorox jointly developed the highly successful Glad Press'n Seal product line. Researchers at P&G discovered the plastic wrap technology behind this product. Although they knew that the product had the potential to be a game-changer in the way food is wrapped and stored, trying to enter such a well-established category did not fit with the company's overall strategy. Instead, P&G approached Clorox, which already had strong presence in the category and the organizational structure to manufacture and distribute the proposed product. Today the plastic wrap is a top-selling product, a billion-dollar brand, of which P&G owns 20 percent.

Rally the Troops

Sometimes organizations are able to find the innovation they are looking for internally, particularly if they have a diverse workforce. If you have ever used an e-book or a car navigation system, or played the video game Guitar Hero, then you know firsthand the creativity that is brewing at MIT's Media Lab.[14] More than 300 new innovations are currently being nurtured in the lab. Cynthia Breazeal, who oversees social robot research, explained that the "secret sauce" to the creativity that is in abundance at their lab is getting people in different fields to share ideas. "It's not just about multiple sciences and multiple engineering," she said. "It's like you've got designers and artists and musicians. I mean, we're all under the same roof."[15]

Nicholas Negroponte, cofounder and chairman of the Media Lab, whole-heartedly believes that innovation comes from differences. "Lateral thinking is key, because 'incrementalism' is the enemy of creativity. By juxtaposing people from very different backgrounds, new ideas are bound to emerge."

Apple has been notorious for developing its products internally. The reason: the conviction that people, in general, tend to think in terms of improvements to what is already out there, not revolutionary new ideas. "It's hard for them [users] to tell you what they want when they've never seen anything remotely like it," explained Steve Jobs, CEO of Apple.[16]

So how is Apple able to develop such game-changing products, over and over again? There are several factors: a provocateur for a CEO, a culture that prizes "thinking differently," and a richly diverse pool of internal talent. To create its best-selling iPhone, for example, Apple brought together a group of employees with expertise in a wide range of areas—camera, music, phone, and touch-screen technology. It also opened up its platform so that outside innovators could develop a seemingly infinite number of applications, making the phone all the more valuable to its end users.

Mixing Baby Shampoo, Medical Devices, and Pharmaceuticals

"It's the ability to work across the boundaries that really brings true innovation," explained William Weldon, CEO of Johnson & Johnson (J&J).[17] He knows that real value is created when collaboration takes place and is actively working to foster cross-pollination across J&J. To give you a sense the scope of this task, consider that more than 200 operating companies comprise the firm, which is divided into three major divisions. Although J&J tends to be known for consumer products like baby powder, band-aids, and shampoo, its has much larger presences in pharmaceuticals and medical device and diagnostics—in fact, its medical device and diagnostics business is the largest in the world. The company enjoys about $61 billion in revenue and a market capitalization of anywhere from $180 billion to $200 billion. There is a lot of knowledge and innovation to be unlocked from within its organizational boundaries alone.

Weldon will be the first to tell you that it is a formidable challenge to realize cross-divisional collaboration when each operating company has their own responsibilities in the markets in which they compete that can more than fill their employees' time. What's remarkable is that a company of this size is able to do exactly that.

In an interview with *Knowledge@Wharton*, Weldon recalled a meeting at which J&J brought together engineers from its medical device and diagnostics business with scientists from its pharmaceutical division. "They came up with putting a drug on a stent . . . for cardiovascular disease, which was a huge breakthrough."[18] Weldon also cites a business that they recently launched that brought together the skills of engineers and scientists to develop a patch that delivers a narcotic for postoperative use. This new technology frees patients of the need to carry around patient-controlled analgesia (PCA) pumps. A battery ensures that the right amount of the narcotic is delivered, within the right timeframe, and with the right frequency. "You look at the convergence of these skills, technologies, and products and then people—and I think that it offers us a distinct competitive advantage," Weldon explained.[19]

How do they do it? The company relies on several formal and informal ways to foster a collaborative environment. Their internal ventures process allows employees within the organization to put forward a recommendation, form a business plan and budget, and present it for further evaluation. If, as they say, the dog can hunt, the group, or "skunkwork" people as they are known colloquially, gets the green light to further develop the idea.

To spur on these initiatives, J&J routinely brings together people from different areas of the company to simply discuss what they are doing. Conversations among these diverse groups often bring product ideas forward. "It's usually better when they [employees] generate them [ideas] rather than when we try and impose upon them," Weldon pointed out.[20] The company has also developed its own Intranet, which has been, in Weldon's eyes, "very successful." This social technology allows scientists to see what others are working on and to discuss their discoveries. By connecting people throughout an organization the size of J&J, and providing platforms for them to cocreate and discuss ideas, social tools can support this dynamic innovation process.

Idea Jams: Getting the Ideas Flowing

IBM regularly brings its entire organization—including clients and external partners—together via social media to brainstorm ideas. The company first conceived of its now famous "idea jams" a decade ago. Its original goal for this online collaboration event was to build a stronger sense of community across its highly disbursed and diverse workforce. Like the jams of jazz musicians, idea jams bring together a diverse group of people to riff on various predefined topics. Moderators help keep the conversation flowing, pointing out threads in the conversation, and conducting polls on certain issues during the process to determine how widespread sentiments are. (Contrary to popular perception, most jazz improvisation is not completely unstructured either; the "background" instruments provide a structured background of rhythm and harmony with which the soloist improvises.)

Forty thousand people participated in IBM's first idea jam that took place around the clock over the course of three days. Employees posted 52,000 comments across interlinked bulletin boards and web pages on the company's intranet. The jam worked so well—several new courses of action were initiated as a direct result of the experiment—that the model has been reactivated to address several other key issues in subsequent years. (It has also been turned into a successful external consulting business for the firm.)

The following year, more than 300,000 IBM employees "jammed" about the company's values, the first such redefinition in more than 100 years. Innovation was the focus of its 2006 jam. More than 150,000 IBM employees, family members, business partners, clients, and university researchers from 104 countries came together over the course of two 3-day sessions to discuss emerging IBM technologies. The first session focused on key technologies and new ways to use them. The second session, which took place two months later, further refined these ideas. Wikis were central to the second session; people were able to begin working on rough drafts for business plans for the most promising ideas immediately.

A plethora of output was generated from these two sessions; it took hundreds of management hours to sort through it all. In the end, it was well worth it. Two months later, the company's CEO,

Sam Palmisano, was able to announce 10 new businesses that are currently being developed including 3-D Internet, smarter transportation systems, intelligent utility systems, and predictive water management, several of which are part of the company's brilliant Smarter Planet initiative.

In 2009, IBM held its first jam for university students, educators, and business professionals: Jamming for a Smarter Planet. Insights from the event are helping the company further refine its Smarter Planet initiative through which it is harnessing some of the world's most creative, inspired, and passionate people to tackle complex, multinational problems. Over the course of 72 hours, the group brainstormed about health care, limited water supplies, smarter electricity grids, attractive and sustainable urban environments, and skill sets that students—our future leaders—will need to better address the challenges that these issues present.

"Students are confident that their future will be a smarter place—a world where they will drive cars that get 100 miles per gallon, learn in virtual classrooms connected with students around the globe, and where they can run their business on a secure, energy-efficient and interconnected grid," said Jai Menon, vice president and chief technology officer of technical strategy for IBM's Systems and Technology Group. "They are boldly challenging the industry to transform that vision into their reality, and IBM is committed to meeting that challenge."[21]

The Smarter Planet movement is an example of collaboration with anyone and everyone that can have an effect on an issue. IBM's experience shows, over and over again, that the creativity that is ready to be tapped within an organization's ecosystem can be quite impressive.

Shopping for Ideas

What opportunities are there for companies that have a specific challenge that they are looking to solve (such as when Colgate-Palmolive wanted to learn how to inject fluoride powder into its toothpaste), but they have exhausted their internal resources? The social web has nurtured the development of a handful of online innovation brokers to help companies in this very situation. These open marketplaces allow companies to access the intellectual property they need from people and organizations around the globe. Perhaps the most well known is InnoCentive, the first global Web community for open innovation, but there are others, including NineSigma, PhilOptima, and Innovation Exchange, each having a slightly different emphasis.

InnoCentive began as a start-up at Eli Lilly and Company in 2001. Looking at the industry's cost structure, the pharmaceutical company realized that the conventional way of funding research was no longer cost-effective; the industry's R&D expenses were going to exceed its overall revenue. In response, they began experimenting with other models to bring new thinking and innovation to the organization.

Eli Lilly was essentially InnoCentive's first "seeker," that is, an organization looking to solve a business or R&D problem through InnoCentive's Open Innovation Marketplace. InnoCentive became a stand-alone company in 2005 as the crowd-sourcing model morphed from an interesting idea to a validated and vital innovation option for and beyond the pharmaceutical industry. Seekers have since posted 1,044 challenges as of the date of this writing, for which 685 awards, amounting to $24.2 million, have been given. Seekers include many household names including P&G, NASA, the Rockefeller Foundation, and the International AIDS Vaccine Initiative. Two hundred thousand people from 200 countries comprise the company's "solvers."

Often the solutions that are provided via e-innovation communities like InnoCentive are derived faster than many in-house R&D departments because multiple minds across a variety of disciplines work simultaneously on challenges, not sequentially as in most in-house R&D departments. Successful solutions are sourced at a lower cost than many internal R&D departments because, after the initial posting fee, companies only pay for their successes.

Show Me the Money

Let's talk about the economics of working with InnoCentive for a moment. Say, for example, that your company is trying to improve a business process or identify a breakthrough technology. To run that challenge, InnoCentive typically charges between $15,000 and $35,000. Much of this upfront fee covers the cost of having a team of PhDs work with you to clearly articulate the problem for which you are looking to their open marketplace to solve. This includes defining what is known and not known about the problem, how a solution might be used across various sectors, and the research paths that have already been taken. This upfront work is vital to the success of any open marketplace challenge.

In addition to the initial fee, there's an award amount that is given to the person or group that solves the challenge. Based on challenges that are active in their marketplace today, these awards can range from $5,000 to $250,000. Finally, there is a pay-for-performance premium, which is calculated as a percentage of the total award amount, which is paid to InnoCentive by the seeker if a solution is provided. For illustrative purposes, let's say that the premium amounts to 40 percent of the established award. The bottom line is this: it is in a company's best interest to hire InnoCentive to solve problems where there is an anticipated market opportunity greater than $500,000. In the worst case, a company is out $15,000 but walks away with a definition of the problem it is trying to solve. In the best case, it pays $85,000 and retains the rights to the solution. It is hard to beat those economics.

The Complete Package

In addition to offering access to its global brain trust, InnoCentive helps companies tap into the creativity and knowledge of their own organizations through its proprietary Innovation@work software. The product, which is integrated into a company's Intranet, provides a platform for companies to establish prize-based open innovation challenges internally, allowing them to harness all of their intellectual assets to tackle business issues and opportunities. The impetus for creation of this product was a CEO who had recently made five acquisitions and wanted to better understand what resources his company had available internally. (If a challenge eventually warrants an externally sourced solution, it can easily be transferred from the internal platform to InnoCentive's external marketplace, allowing a company to take maximum advantage of its innovation capabilities inside and out.) A change management consulting practice, "ONRAMP," rounds out the company's product mix and helps companies to make the cultural changes necessary to embrace a more open innovation model. Syngenta, which is engaged in sustainable agribusiness, launched several challenges through InnoCentive, while also working with ONRAMP on their implementation. The company later launched InnoCentive@Work in its offices in Europe, North America, and India. Syngenta had achieved multiple benefits from working with InnoCentive, resulting in a return on investment (ROI) of 182 percent, with a payback period of less than two months.[22]

The proof is, as they say, in the pudding. "Open form of innovation is vital in this century," said Dwayne Spradlin, InnoCentive's CEO. Spradlin and I both believe that we are in the dawn of a new era, a time when we are seeing a reinvention of business. Spradlin recently said to me, "We live in a wired world where some of the best people available to help solve your challenge may not be located near you or be a part of your organization. You can't be a closed innovation organization any longer. If you don't master the skills to be open and integrate with the rest of the world, you simply can't compete." I couldn't agree more.

Monitizing Your Intellectual Property

What about the university, entrepreneur, engineer, or scientist that has developed early-stage technology that seems to have commercial potential, but doesn't have the capability or resources to single-handedly transform it into a viable product? Or the company that has developed promising intellectual property through its corporate R&D effort, but it did not solve the issue that needed to be solved? Or the discovery that may have addressed a market that is not central to the company's overall strategy, such as when P&G discovered a new calcium formulation or a revolutionary plastic wrap technology?

That's where entities like yet2.com come in. Yet2.com helps companies leverage and extract value from their intellectual property through both consulting and an online licensing marketplace, maximizing the return on companies' initial development expenses. (Obviously, their marketplace also assists companies with the inverse: sourcing IP.) Over the past 10 years, yet2.com has completed more than 100 licensing deals on four continents in fields as diverse as biotech and materials. Sony, Panasonic, DuPont, P&G, and a host of other well-known companies have successfully worked with yet2.com.

Yet2.com president Ben DuPont said in a statement, "Our business keeps expanding as more companies spin out underutilized technology to improve their existing products and solutions."[23] The company estimates that the technology acquisition and licensing market is currently valued at $105 billion and it is growing.[24] Yet2.com's marketplace facilitates the buying and selling of intellectual property, broadening the reach of participants and allowing companies to look beyond their own industries for technology exchange. As the company's web site says, "An engine designer seeking fuel injection technology might not immediately think of obtaining it from a rocket manufacturer—but that's exactly what has happened on the yet2.com marketplace."[25]

Robert Ott, manager of product and technology licensing at The Boeing Company, explained the benefits it has realized from brokering its intellectual property with yet2.com, "Listing portions of our intellectual property portfolio on yet2.com has been providing Boeing with additional exposure to companies of all sizes and industries outside our core sector. Our relationship with yet2.com has enabled us to pursue new revenue opportunities for Boeing in an increasingly more efficient global marketplace."[26]

What does it take to effectively monetize products and technologies through yet2.com's marketplace? It takes well-tested and patented assets, people skills, and a culture that embraces licensing. Independent test data is critical to every investment decision. It makes a potential deal possible. "A licensee will still want to do their own testing with their own customers," explains DuPont, "but strong independent data will convince them to spend the time, money, and reputational risk with their customer to try the technology."[27] Access to the original inventor(s) is also highly valued because it brings an important source of expertise to the transaction.

People skills are also important to getting a deal done because, invariably, additional development work is needed for technology to really meet the need at hand. "If the people don't like working together, a partnership won't develop," DuPont cautioned.[28]

Stay Close to Scientific Communities

Ed Catmull, CEO of Pixar Animation Studios, wrote an article for *Harvard Business Review* in which he described the three pillars that support his company's innovation success: (1) everyone must have the freedom to communicate with everyone, (2) it must be safe for everyone to offer ideas, and (3) we must stay close to innovations happening in the academic community. [29]

Catmull is not alone. During the past few years, companies have been forming partnerships of varying levels of formality with universities and research labs. One of the drivers of these partnerships is a shift in corporate R&D away from long-term and high-risk research toward investing in technologies at later stages of development. According to a report conducted by the Kauffman Foundation, "The vacuum left by this retreat is being filled in large part by creative and productive partnerships between industry and universities."[30]

More often than not corporate/university partnerships are research related. You have already heard about the creativity brewing at MIT's Media Lab; here is a high-level look at the partnerships through which it is sponsored.[31] The idea for the Media Lab came into being in 1980 by Professor Nicholas Negroponte and former MIT President and Science Advisor to President John F. Kennedy, Jerome Wiesner. Today more than 60 sponsors support the Lab, including many well-known corporations. These sponsors—which range in focus from "electronics to entertainment, furniture to finance, and greeting cards to telecommunications"—provide the majority of funding for the lab's $25 million annual budget.

Most sponsors join as members of a consortium, which brings together lab faculty, research staff, and sponsor organizations around a general theme. Rather than funding a project or a group, sponsors fund a consortium. Consortia that are active today include Things That Think, Digital Life, and the Consumer Electronics Lab. The cost of joining a consortium is about $200,000 per year, for a minimum of three years. What do members get for their money?

The most important benefit is access to ideas, in fact, "an abundance of ideas, technologies, and paradigms for the future."[32] Consortium sponsors receive full intellectual property rights—license-fee free and royalty free, in perpetuity—to all work developed at the lab during their sponsorship years. As a reference point, the Media Lab has incubated dozens of new products for sponsors and more than 50 start-up companies, in addition to generating roughly 20 patents a year. Sponsors also have access to lab input on new and existing products and to Media Lab students. (Microsoft, IBM, Motorola, and Samsung have all hired Media Lab graduates.) Many sponsors also use the lab to connect with other companies to form collaborative business partnerships.

Other times industry/university partnerships focus on curriculum development, training, and employee recruitment. Massachusetts's Middlesex Community College (MCC) and the Lahey Clinic, for example, have formed a partnership the goal of which is to address the nationwide nursing shortage. Through the partnership, employees at Lahey can attend MCC's nursing program part time, while continuing to work at the clinic. Similarly, MCC and two other community colleges are working with National Grid, the region's primary provider of electricity, to develop multiskilled technicians to help mitigate the labor shortage facing that industry.

It Sounds Good but . . .

Of course, multiple challenges are involved in successfully implementing these new innovation models. Some of the reasons are cultural: companies are still developing the mind-set for successful open innovation. Tension between "us and them" and sharing and protecting is firmly entrenched and can be limiting. Sometimes the systems and structures for open innovation are not yet in place. Without them it can be next to impossible to get busy employees to think beyond their daily responsibilities to consider cross-organizational innovation initiatives. Tools that can be helpful include linking participation to job performance and carving out time for employees to connect around ideas. Ensuring that the proper social tools are in place to allow for virtual gatherings and ongoing discussions are also critical to capture the insight of people from different functions, locations, business units, and ranks. As we have previously discussed, the ability to speak openly without the fear of repercussion frees employees to more fully participate, expanding the potential effect of the conversation.

Some of the challenges are skill based. The upfront fee charged by InnoCentive funds what is often an extensive process of helping companies articulate the challenges that they are looking to solve in the precise way that "outsiders" find useful. Some of the disappointment is explained by the inherent drawbacks of individual models. Idea jams, for example, can work well for idea generation, but because people don't always follow threads of conversations, especially over an extended period, they are not always as helpful with refining ideas. Sometimes the conflict between the values and motivations of academics and corporate executives can thwart the innovation process. What happens when competitors source the same open innovation market for similar, or even identical, ideas or technology?

I am optimistic that these challenges—and more—will be worked out over time, as social technology and open innovation become a part of companies' new DNA. The rewards are too plentiful to be stymied for long.

Armed with a plethora of open-sourced ideas, the question then becomes how do social tools help companies to better develop and execute strategy? Keep reading for some ideas.

Questions to Consider

- How comfortable are you with the idea of open-sourcing aspects of your innovation process?
- Which of the tools described may be useful to your company?

CHAPTER EIGHT

Strategy Execution

Capitalize on What Your Organization Already Knows

If you have read this far, then you are well aware of the value of being able to effectively leverage networks of stakeholders to your advantage and theirs. You know of the wealth of information that companies' broader ecosystems contain and are generally eager to share. You are also aware that it takes a disciplined process for this information to be converted into knowledge and for that knowledge to be transformed into actionable strategy. You also know how social media tools can help companies make all of this happen. But what about strategy execution? How does social media convert actionable strategy into executed strategy?

This aspect of the social media engagement process is critical. Mark Fuller, chairman of Monitor Group, tells me that in his experience, most chief executive officers (CEOs) are less worried about strategy formation and more concerned about its execution. Fuller is in good company. Thomas Edison, who said, "Genius is 1 percent innovation and 99 percent perspiration," would have agreed. Fuller attributes 80 percent of strategy implementation failure to the friction that exists along the edges of interactions between individuals, departments, business units, regional operations, and the C-suite and the rest of the organization. Social technologies can reduce this friction, providing companies with an unprecedented opportunity to improve the way that they work. How are they able to chip away at this challenge that has baffled managers since organizations began?

Putting Employees on the Same Page

One challenge to strategy implementation is differing perspectives among disparate functions about what is indeed the best strategy. Here's a simplified example of a classic situation. Imagine a company that makes widgets. Its employees are highly charged by the company's vision—something along the lines of changing the world through providing the highest-quality widgets—and the company's commitment to building those widgets in a sustainable way.

Here's the rub. To accomplish this goal, manufacturing wants to make one product, millions of times, and never change the lines. It makes perfect sense: This strategy is the most efficient and cost-effective way to produce widgets. Marketing and sales, on the other hand, want to be able to customize the widgets for every customer. This, too, makes perfect sense. This high level of customization allows the company to meet every customer's widgetary needs and maximize its revenue. Clearly there is some inherent inconsistency in strategy here.

How can social tools resolve this conflict? Conversational data gleaned from social engagement provides each of these functions with access to the same data set. Working with the same information puts management from each of these functions on the same page, leaving less room for functional bias. What's more, social tools allow companies to go back to their customers for further clarification when necessary.

As an example, imagine that our fictional company makes blue widgets and black widgets, but that marketing and sales are convinced that the company needs to also manufacture yellow widgets. Social tools allow companies to speak directly with consumers to ascertain if this desire for yellow widgets is widespread. If yellow widget availability is not a deal-breaker for a large enough number of clients to warrant the costs of changing the line, the conflict between manufacturing and marketing and sales can be resolved quite quickly. Management can get on with focusing on issues and activities that will bring more value to customers and the company. They can also quite easily and inexpensively go back to consumers at a later point in time to determine if demand for yellow widgets has increased. This upfront concurrence goes a long way toward getting multiple functions on the same page, which makes comprehensive strategy design and execution much easier.

Here's another bonus: Social tools allow companies to explain the decisions that they do make directly to their stakeholder communities. They can blog about why they have chosen not to produce yellow widgets at this time—perhaps because the cost of every widget will rise to cover the increased costs of producing yellow widgets since there is not sufficient demand. Or, in an alternative scenario, they can discuss why they chose not to produce yellow widgets, even if plenty of customers are asking for them. It may be the case that the yellow dye that is required for manufacturing yellow widgets is toxic and unable to be disposed of in a way that is safe and sustainable. By explaining the situation to their customers in social environments, companies can engender a better understanding with their customers and the public at large. This decision and the ensuing discussion may even lead to accolades, closer constituent relations, and perhaps some useful ideation about how to more safely and sustainably meet the need that yellow widgets were trying to address. (It can also help reduce the friction between manufacturing and marketing and sales.)

Expanding Employees' Personal Networks

Remember the adage, it's who you know and what they know? It's still true. Relationships still trump impersonal sources of information such as databases, procedure manuals, and even the Internet. Research conducted by Rob Cross, Founder and Research

Director of The Network Roundtable, a consortium of 100+ organizations working with University of Virginia faculty to apply
network techniques to critical business issues, and colleagues found
that 85 percent of managers get information that is critical to project success from their networks of relationships.[1] (Interestingly,
Cross found that the 15 percent that did rely on impersonal sources
were all relatively new to the organization and had not had the
occasion to develop sufficient personal networks.) Similarly, Tom
Allen, a professor of management at MIT, reviewed a decade of
research and found that engineers and scientists are almost five
times as likely to look to people for information than to other impersonal sources.[2] The larger *and more effective* the network, the
better scientists and managers, and anyone else for that matter, are
able to get things done. This is especially true for industries that
are knowledge and innovation driven.

Social tools build the size of employees' networks, extending
their reach beyond an inner circle of relationships to people within
other departments, business units, geographic boundaries, hierarchical
levels, and even across organizations' external boundaries to include
clients, business partners, alumni, and competitors. How do they increase the effectiveness of employees' networks?

Research conducted by Cross and colleagues found that four features distinguish effective from ineffective relationships: (1) knowledge of what another person knows and thus when to turn to that
person; (2) ability to gain timely access to that person; (3) willingness
of the person sought out to engage in problem solving rather than
dump information; and (4) a degree of safety in the relationship that
promotes learning and creativity.[3] Social tools connect faces, interests,
expertise, and conversation with names, thereby smartening and hu-
manizing these networks. By enhancing employees' ability to locate
available resources anywhere in the world, and thereby generate targeted consultations, social tools provide an important initial step in
harnessing the collective capability of an organization. Social technologies also make rapid communication possible by their very nature
and because people are generally more responsive to requests made by
colleagues within their network. (To facilitate this, management can
also set expectations for acceptable response times.)

This connectedness makes for a much more intelligent and efficient organization. It is as if another lane is opened on the freeway: ideas can flow. As a result, employees can better locate expertise, cultivate collective knowledge, and bring together diverse teams to rapidly solve customers' problems, design new products, or put out a fire. In so doing, employees can also expand their spheres of influence, ultimately increasing their value to the company.

A handful of these interactions may have happened through physical rather than social destinations—with friends in a hallway, customers in focus groups, or colleagues at a conference—but they may not have happened as frequently or with as close to zero cost. Social environments that link people who are less connected—an organization's employees worldwide, an elected official with his or her constituency, or a company and its customer base—magnify the opportunity to create value by making these connections possible.

The Buzz on IBM's Beehive

In 2007, IBM launched an internal social network, Beehive, the purpose of which was "to blur the boundaries of work and home, professional and personal, and business and fun."[4] Remember the emerging phenomenon of "weisure"? IBM has embraced it. Their goal in creating Beehive is to encourage sharing of all types, regardless of whether the material is work related or personal, and to study the effect of sharing on employees' relationships.

What has IBM discovered? Usage analysis revealed that employees were actually getting to know each other better through Beehive. The study concluded that, "They have closer bonds to their network, they have a greater willingness to contribute to the company, they have a greater interest in connecting globally, have greater access to new people, and a greater ability to access expertise."[5] What organization wouldn't benefit from having a Beehive?

Connecting Everyone: Cerner and GE

Cerner is using its internal social media platform to link its employees with its clients and business partners. Its platform, uCern, combines collaboration tools with a social networking platform. It allows users to find others through search capabilities for individuals or groups and to share their knowledge within the uCern community by blogging or forming a discussion group. Content is stored in the Learning Center and wikis allow for collaborative documentation.

How does uCern help with strategy implementation? It changes organizational dynamics and improves the company's ability to act. By linking people together who share the same business goals, the company "increases the success that teams are working to achieve. . . . It reduces the time between question, discussion, and decision, and between discovery of new ideas and adoption."[6] That makes strategy formulation and implementation a quicker process.

Similarly, GE's social network, SupportCentral, which came on board in early 2000, has since become the center of the company's global operations. SupportCentral's usage numbers are impressive. Today, all 400,000 GE employees around the world have profiles on the professional network. According to an interview published by ZDNet.com with Dr. Sukh Grewal, Manager of GE's SupportCentral collaboration and workflow environment, people communicate on the platform in 20 languages, it enjoys more hits than Google and Yahoo! combined, and it is home to more than 50,000 communities several of which welcome the participation of external vendors, suppliers, and customers. Employees are encouraged to develop their own business applications and are shifting to a complete online document system. The cost savings to GE are already estimated to be in the "many millions."[7] GE's MarkNet platform that links and develops the skills and experience of its marketing folks around the world will only enhance these results.

Providing Simple Collaborative Tools

A third obstacle to strategy implementation is the challenge of working across different fields and functions to solve complex, multidisciplinary issues. We have already seen how bringing together larger and more diverse minds can be more effective in solving multifaceted problems than less heterogeneous groupings. As business tasks have required employees to become increasingly specialized, the ability to synchronize efforts and blend multidisciplinary expertise has become all the more important. Companies that master this ability to continually refine and reinterpret information will benefit from being more insightful, self-aware, posed for action, and productive. By quickly harnessing the intelligence and know-how that already exists within their organizations and ecosystems, they are more readily able to keep the whole system up-to-date, relevant, and in sync with the marketplace.

Multiple social tools are available to facilitate this collaboration including file sharing, forums, wikis, microblogs like Yammer, instant messaging, and teleconferencing.

Several of these tools offer employees the opportunity to post queries to the broader organization, taking advantage of colleagues' expertise and insight. Others like blogs, videos, and podcasts, provide employees with the opportunity to share their knowledge and expertise and receive feedback in return. Tagging and rating systems augment employees' ability to find the best resources available on a given subject. Teleconferencing shrinks distances bringing people from all around the globe into the same virtual space. Internal communities optimize knowledge creation and capture. Together these tools keep the organization—and often multiple external customer communities—learning and connected.

Using Social Tools to Improve Homeland Security

Most of us can remember exactly where we were and what we were doing on September 11, 2001. I would wager that although many of us may not know where we were and what we were doing when the 9/11 Commission report was released, we probably know the upshot of what they found:

> The FBI's information systems were woefully inadequate. The FBI lacked the ability to know what it knew: there was no effective mechanism for capturing or sharing its institutional knowledge. FBI agents did create records of interviews

and other investigative efforts, but there were no reports for officers to condense the information into meaningful intelligence that could be retrieved and disseminated.[8]

Here's some good news that we may not all be aware of: the United States intelligence community is putting social media tools to use to help experts across intelligence organizations pool their information and be able to make quick assessments, actions that can improve homeland and international security. Sixteen federal agencies, including organizations like the Central Intelligence Agency (CIA) and the Federal Bureau of Investigation (FBI), are using a suite of Web 2.0 technologies that link about 200,000 people at the highest levels across these organizations. Andrew McAfee, a principal research scientist at the Center for Digital Business at the MIT Sloan School of Management and the author of *Enterprise 2.0: New Collaborative Tools for Your Organization's Toughest Challenges*, studied the Intelligence community's use of social media. According to McAfee, these tools include an integrated blogging platform that allows people in one agency to search and comment on blogs created in another; a Facebook-style social network; a microblogging tool similar to Yammer; and Intellipedia, a wiki-based system for collaborative data sharing.

Richard A. Russell, deputy assistant director of National Intelligence for Information Sharing Customer Outreach (ISCO), explained that Intellipedia was created so "analysts in different agencies that work on X or Y can go in and see what other people are doing on subject X or Y and actually add in their two cents worth . . . or documents that they have."[9] Russell is clear that the goal of the system to work together toward "decision superiority," not "information superiority." This is an important distinction. Decision superiority reflects a connection of the dots in a meaningful way that allows for effective and actionable strategy formation. "We have to get inside the decision cycle of the enemy," Russell said. "We have to be able to discover what they're doing and respond effectively."

The system is working. Thomas Fingar, deputy director of National Intelligence Analytics, cited the successful use of Intellipedia to gather observations on Iraqi insurgents. Analysts were able to pull together research in a couple of days on Intellipedia with "no bureaucracy, no mother-may-I, no convening meetings."[10] Sounds like a welcome relief for any organization.

There is another layer to these rewards. McAfee found that social tools allowed analysts to go beyond incremental enhancements to their ability to do their jobs.[11] Social tools have actually made it possible for analysts to accomplish things that were not previously possible. One Defense Intelligence Agency (DIA) analyst told McAfee that the tools allowed him to interact with people that he would never have had a chance to interact with otherwise. A National Security Agency (NSA) analyst said the tools allowed him to know who to go to when he needed to find something out. A CIA analyst said, "The ability to link information and people together, as wikis and blogs do, makes possible an activity that I truly believe will transform our Community."[12] That's real progress.

Beer and Semi-Conductors; Yammer and TelePresence

Knowledge and wisdom, rather than information, can be gathered when collaboration takes place. This is an important distinction. Knowledge reflects a meaningful connecting of the dots rather than just a collection of data, or, as Russell suggests, the difference between decision superiority and information superiority.

Wikis like Intellipedia are one of the tools that allow this collaboration to take place. Yammer, an internal microblog similar to Twitter, is another popular collaborative tool—so popular, in fact, that more than 70 percent of Fortune 500 companies are using it—and that number continues to grow. When Peter Swinburn became CEO of the beverage company, Molson Coors, in June 2008, one of his goals was to better link the company's 15,000 employees that work across three continents. Yammer was part of his solution. Has Yammer helped Swinburn accomplish this goal? Today, 87 percent of Molson Coors employees believe that the company has a "clear vision for the future," up from 73 percent in 2008. Sounds to me like Swinburn has been able to utilize Yammer to clearly communicate and connect with the company's worldwide workforce.

Similarly, a client of Cisco, the IT solutions vendor, has found that use of Cisco's TelePresence system, which provides high-definition and life-size video and document sharing tools, has facilitated money-saving collaboration among one of its client's global operations. The Fortune 100 high-tech semiconductor manufacturer had recently expanded its operations overseas to take advantage of the pools of talent available in Europe, India, and China. This international expansion introduced more complexity into the company's research, development, and engineering processes as it required coordination across cultures, geography, and time zones in addition to function. By making use of the TelePresence system, the company has been able to foster "more frequent and intuitive collaboration."[13] It estimated that the resulting time-to-market improvements increased margins by approximately $18 million and reduced R&D costs by $5 million.

The Company as Wiki

Brad Anderson, vice chair and CEO of Best Buy, uses the metaphor of the company as a wiki to describe Best Buy's relationship with social media. The impetus for their extensive use of social tools was the recognition that the company's business was morphing from distributing products and services to helping customers to better use the products and services that Best Buy sells. To address this market transition, the company took steps to empower its employees to take the lead in sharing their insights and experience to derive customer solutions. Their employee mantra became: I am Best Buy.

Best Buy implemented a whole suite of social media tools internally to help build this insight. Its social network, Blue Shirt Nation, allows employees to get to know each other and better understand where expertise can be found within the company. Online discussions are fostered around the Watercooler—where else?—a discussion forum that the company claims is the most rapid way to distribute information internally. Their wiki is the central knowledge base and contains customer feedback as well as reams of product information from manufacturers, suppliers, and employees. Employees can post their ideas and proposals for how products and processes can be improved in the Loop Marketplace. Their TagTrade prediction market helps the company make more accurate estimates about issues and developments that are critical to its success. (We'll talk more about TagTrade in a few pages.) The foundation for all of this is ramped-up employee engagement and an understanding of the core values of the company, which creates boundaries for the freedom that social media provides. According to Anderson, when these values are firmly entrenched, "you can count on better fundamental behavior from your employee base than you'd have if you weren't engaged in these activities."[14] He also notes that use of these tools has decreased employee turnover, made work much more fun, and enhanced the company's productivity. What are we all waiting for?

Tapping into Employees' Insight

A fourth impediment to strategy execution is what management often refers to as the frozen middle, the at times large population of employees that are not completely aware of or actively involved in a corporation's strategic initiatives. Social tools can help to mitigate this management challenge by getting at the root of the problem: lack of employee engagement. As we have seen, social networks like Beehive, SupportCentral, and uCern help employees to feel more connected to the company and each other, and ignite their willingness to contribute. Social tools can also provide employees with access to the information they need to effectively make more decisions than they have in the past about strategy and its implementation.

"The distribution of decision rights about strategy is no longer in the CEO's office or in the strategic planning department, allegedly being controlled by C-level executives," observed Mark Fuller, who has worked with thousands of companies. "It is going out into the company; anyone in the company can now have an opinion and share that opinion."

Although this may sound alarms for leadership, it is actually good news. Think about it for a moment. Who often has the most up-to-date knowledge about what the market is saying about a company's products and services—employees in the trenches who are interacting with customers, or planners in corporate offices? Don't get me wrong. I am not saying that there is no longer a need for senior management of companies. There absolutely is a need for effective leaders who can listen, inspire, and get things done. But can't the decision making of even the best management teams be improved with the input of those who are in the marketplace daily? Why not take advantage of social media's ability to help keep decision making as close to the market as possible?

Social Tools for Forecasting

One of the ways that companies are keeping decision making closer to the market is to engage employees in predicting profits, sales, and the timing of product launches. In addition to better engaging employees, this process often helps companies to make more accurate forecasts. As Joe Miles, a mathematician for eyeforpharma, a think-tank for the pharma industry, explains, "The opinion of the group as a whole is often better than that of the best member of the group."[15]

As an example of this phenomena, Miles sites the experience of 10 pharma managers from a variety of disciplines within one pharmaceutical company—sales, finance, product, and production—who were asked to estimate sales for a new product launch. The range of their answers was quite broad; however, the collective foresight gathered by the average of those answers was astoundingly accurate.

How do these forecasting tools work? A decision market—also known as a prediction market—is essentially an internal stock exchange where a given "stock" is a proxy for an issue or event of interest to an organization. Such issues or events could be sales forecasts of a given product, the readiness of a product to launch or a new store to open, or the viability of a new product or service.

An organization's employees, and, at times, members from its broader ecosystem, act as traders, buying shares in various forecasts using virtual dollars. Drawing on their understanding of the issue's prospects, they bet on what they believe is the most likely outcome. For example, will a product launch on time or not? Anonymity protects employees so they can trade honestly. An incentive structure linked to the accuracy of estimates motivates employees to garner relevant information to help them maximize the value of their virtual portfolio. When an employee sees that a stock's value differs from his or her expectation, that employee has the opportunity to buy or sell the stock, driving the price up or down. Because the markets operate in real time, they can reflect the most up-to-date information.

Prediction markets are increasingly being used in the corporate world. Several companies, such as Best Buy, Cisco Systems, Google, General Mills, GE Healthcare, HP, and IBM, are using these social tools. A whole host of software and service vendors, such as HP, ConsensusPoint, and NewsFutures, have developed corporate applications.

Best Buy Gets Better Estimates

"There is nothing more important than telling the company what we know," says Jeff Severts, executive vice president of Best Buy. "The Best Buy TagTrade prediction market provides an early warning indicator to help flag potential problems early."[16]

Best Buy created TagTrade, an internal prediction market, in 2006 to capture U.S. employees' insights on a range of topics. The goal of the marketplace was to tap into the insight of employees to provide senior leaders with key indicators for the success of critical initiatives within the company. Since its initial launch, TagTrade has captured quite accurate forecasts about a whole host of issues. For example, trades within the company's prediction market forecasted that a store opening in Shanghai would be delayed. The price of the "on time" share was almost half of the price of the delayed share, reflecting employees' doubt that the store would indeed open on time. TagTrade is used to predict outcomes for short- and long-term initiatives. These predictions are generally more accurate than traditional forecasts—in some cases even as much as 5 percent more accurate. That's money in the bank.

Weighing In on How Strategy Gets Executed

As we have seen, employee ideation and input is vital in and of itself; however, there are several other important byproducts of having employees engaged in the decision-making process. When employees birth, shape, and evaluate ideas, they are generally more invested in their execution. They also become more aware of the strategic vision for the company and can better determine which projects and activities are on-vision.

Engaging employees in the "how it gets done" in addition to the "what should be done" can also bear fruit. Conclusions drawn from multiple studies show that encouraging employees to make decisions about how work gets done enhances their performance. "Instead of having to constantly resort to orders and threats, companies can rely on workers to find new, more efficient ways of getting things done," observes James Surowiecki, the author of *The Wisdom of Crowds, Why the Many Are Smarter than the Few.*[17] Like a muscle, the more this decision-making ability is flexed and utilized, the stronger and more effective it becomes.

Promises, Promises

Thirty years ago, corporate executives were quite taken by the promise of technology and how it might transform their organizations. However, many were disappointed in the results. What sets social media apart from previous generations of information technology that made similar promises about being able to help foster enterprise-wide coordination and collaboration?

Today's tools allow for many-to-many communication. Andrew McAfee, who researches the effect of technology on business, points out that this is distinct from research tools like e-mail and instant messaging (IM) that are used for one-to-many communications and affect personal productivity, but don't enhance group functionality. Popular technologies for consuming information, like Intranets and public web sites, are useful; however, they are created, updated, and maintained by only a few people, not by all of the members of a workgroup. Finally, in the history of corporate computing, the norm has been to impose work structures—to define workflows, interdependencies, decisions rights, and what information is included and how it is presented—in advance. Social tools are much more flexible—McAfee refers to them as "free and easy platforms"—that can be built and edited in a few clicks.[18] Rather than feeling like armor, social tools feel like skin.

McAfee's current research suggests that we can now actually follow through on the promises that previous generations of technologists made. "It's showing up in the data," McAfee told me, "Companies that are doing well at it are pulling away from the laggards. Performance gaps are opening up."

What About Productivity?

With access to all of these internal and external social tools, do employees have any time to get their "real" work done? Absolutely, because, for most employees, social tools facilitate a large component of their work, much like the effect the telephone had when it first came on the scene. Twitter aids companies in resolving customer service issues. LinkedIn helps salespeople and recruiters develop leads. Connections made and maintained through alumni networks build business development opportunities. Internal social networks expand employees' networks and help them to locate expertise more readily.

What about leisure browsing? Can't employees get caught up in tweeting and checking their personal Facebook profiles on company time? Absolutely. To some extent this may be a good thing. Research conducted by Dr. Brent Coker of the Department of Management and Marketing at the University of Melbourne, suggests that this access may actually improve employee productivity. According to Coker, "People who surf the net for fun at work—with a reasonable limit of less than 20 percent of their total time in the office—are more productive by about 9 percent than those who don't."[19] In my personal experience, taking short mental breaks often helps to bring a fresh perspective to my work. That having been said, companies should be clear on what their expectations for their employees are with respect to time spent on external social networks so that there are no surprises. It's not difficult to monitor time spent on these tools.

Leakage and Discoverable Evidence?

What about the leakage of proprietary information and the creation of discoverable evidence that could be used in a court of law against a company? These are real risks that companies face *with* or *without* social media engagement. Any employee can inadvertently leave a carefully disguised prototype of a next generation product—perhaps an iPhone?—at a bar when celebrating his or her birthday with friends. This is despite extraordinary security measures such as products being kept behind doors that can be opened only with security codes that change every few minutes and having members of development teams know only a fraction of the overall plans for the product.

With respect to civil discovery, under U.S. law, each party can request documents and other evidence from companies using subpoenas and depositions. This is nothing new. Companies have been aware of and subject to these procedures since the country's legal framework was put in place. What is different now is that it is much more difficult to destroy evidence, which of course is illegal. The Internet has a long, long memory; its content is permanent. The best defense, in this case, is offense. Employees at all levels of the organization need to clearly understand the company's ethics and the larger ramifications of their violation.

How is social media changing the way companies recruit, train, and retain employees? What is social technology changing in the workscape and the role of human resources? We'll explore these questions in the chapter that follows.

Questions to Consider

- How might your company tap into its own expertise more completely?
- What is your company's current policy regarding social media use for employees?

CHAPTER NINE

Human Capital

Expect Real-Time Resumes
and Create a Twenty-First
Century Workplace

N ot too long ago, my oldest daughter began the college search process. I was the designated parent on the project and did what I
could to "help" her. I dutifully collected all kinds of collateral on
each college visit—campus maps, course catalogs, and listings of arts
and sports events. I even put a new leaf in the dining room table
where I hoped she would organize all of these valuables that I had
carried up and down the East coast upon our return.

Months went by and much to my chagrin she never organized the
material. Actually, if the truth be told, she never even touched it.
Somehow I managed to keep myself from commenting on what I felt
was her lack of engagement in the process. When it came time for her
to refine her search and begin writing the applications, however, I was
shocked. Not only could she articulate the relative strengths and
weaknesses of each school, she knew which schools had the best
food, which professors taught undergraduates and when they were
going on sabbatical, and even which dorms to avoid.

When I asked her how she learned all of this, knowing that she
had never touched the bounty on the dining room table, she said,
"College Prowler, Dad." Turns out that CollegeProwler.com, and a

handful of other digital destinations, draw on current college students' experience to describe and evaluate life on their campuses. Rankings and discussion address academics, housing, food, diversity, nightlife, and even the attractiveness of members of the opposite sex. That's more than most college brochures will tell you.

Social destinations are changing the way that prospective students and employees research and connect with institutions where they might want to study and work. Social enterprises grasp this watershed change and are reaching out, identifying where these decision-making conversations are taking place, and joining in the conversation. Social media's effect goes beyond recruiting, however, to include how organizations grow and retain their employees, and how they stay in touch with them even after they have moved on.

Social Recruiting Is Hot

Social media has become a mainstream recruiting tool for many companies. Of companies who are hiring, 92 percent use or are planning to use social media for recruiting, according to Jobvite's 2010 Social Recruiting Survey.[1] Of this group, 86 percent use LinkedIn, 60 percent use Facebook, and 50 percent use Twitter. Half of these companies plan to invest more in social recruiting going forward, because, for many, adoption has yielded a greater return on investment (ROI) than traditional methods. Not surprisingly, 36 percent plan to spend less on job boards and 38 percent will spend less on third-party recruiters and search firms.

John Campagnino, the head of recruiting for the consulting firm Accenture, plans to make as many as 40 percent of his hires through social media. Campagnino explained to *Fortune,* "If I were going to go out to a major recruiting firm, for example, we could potentially pay upwards of $100,000 to $150,000 for one person. Start multiplying that by a number of senior executives, and you start talking about significant numbers of dollars very quickly. . . . This is the future of recruiting for our company."[2]

What is it about social tools that make them so effective at recruiting? In a word: access. Social media is giving companies unprecedented access to a deeper pool of candidates. Companies can reach potential hires who are actively looking for jobs through job postings, as well as passive candidates, those who are not actively looking to make a change, through their social networks.

Job postings on social sites are quite effective in reaching candidates who are knee-deep in the job search process. Passive candidates, on the other hand, are better found through word of mouth: the right person presenting the right opportunity at just the right time. Lou Adler, president of the Adler Group and author of *Hire with Your Head*, estimates that only 10 percent of passive candidates look at job postings, and most of those do not respond to them.[3] What is more effective in reaching this highly sought-after population? Thirty percent are enticed away from their present jobs through employee referrals, another 30 percent through social networks, and the last 30 percent through LinkedIn's InMail (if you are not familiar with these, hang in there, we will get to them).[4] What is it about these vehicles that can reach passive candidates where job postings may not? Referrals.

As I have said before, we now live in a recommendation economy in which people look to others to find out about everything from products, services, colleges, and jobs to prospective hires. People trust their peers more than any other source, especially when they know them personally. Referrals share that "known quality" as they are generally made between people who are familiar with each other and who feel responsible to each other for the quality of the recommendations that they pass along. Not surprisingly, referrals are 54 times more likely to translate into hires than candidates recruited through a message board and they have a 25 percent higher retention rate.[5] That's essentially money in the bank. Especially when you consider that referred employees don't come with an external recruiter's price tag.

Referrals have long been critical to recruiting. Many companies have a tradition of compensating their employees for making effective referrals. Social media facilitates the employee referral process by making it possible for employees to spread the word about a potential opportunity widely and instantaneously through their personal networks.

This past year we instituted a social media recruiting strategy at my companies to complement our traditional efforts. It has been impressive to see how quickly job opportunities filter through our employee networks and the high quality of the candidates that these social networks uncover. It's almost possible these days, with the help of social media, to find a needle in a haystack.

Social media tools like LinkedIn, Twitter, and Facebook make it possible for companies to go outside of their employees' immediate networks to tap into a gigantic and global pool of talent. (Craigslist can also be quite effective.) A brief summary of basic ways to use each of these tools follows. It is intended only to wet your whistle, not be exhaustive. There are many resources out there that will help you explore the finer details and reap more bang for your social recruiting buck. Of course, there is no substitute for just giving it a try.

You Gotta Be Part of LinkedIn

What has 75 million members, a new professional joining approximately every second, and a membership that includes executives from every Fortune 500 company? LinkedIn. LinkedIn is the world's largest professional network, or as one user said, "an über database of people and the work that they do." It is a global community with over half of its membership coming from outside the United States.[6] Given that more than one quarter of its members are senior executives, it's likely that many of your colleagues, customers, and competitors are part of the network.

LinkedIn is not just a recruiting vehicle; it is designed for professional networking. Approximately 80 percent of LinkedIn members are not actively looking for a job.[7] (For corporate recruiters that represents quite a pool of passive candidates available for the taking, however.)

Reid Hoffman and a group of colleagues started LinkedIn to help people proactively present themselves to the digital world. It is part of what Hoffman describes as a person's "foreground reputation," which includes the images and words that they post, the sites and networks that they join, and the people and causes with which they associate. It is distinct from a background reputation, which is derived from what people learn about a person from other third-party sources. When combined, these foreground and background reputations comprise a personal digital reputation.

"The social web has made it more obvious that everyone is a brand," observes Dan Schawbel, social media expert at EMC and author of the book *Me 2.0*. "Basically, you have to think like a company. It's no longer enough just to have a resume."

Employees at all ranks today must actively manage their personal digital reputations. As they do, they build their social currency and their credibility. One of the ways that social currency is built is through the size and quality of one's personal networks and social engagement. It is quite common these days to be evaluated on the number of followers one has, the volume and value of posts made, and the communities with which one is engaged. David Hayes, the president and founder of HireMinds, a professional and executive search firm, tells me that in the last year, the number of job searches that he has undertaken in which social media fluency and connectedness is required has risen exponentially. Note that these searches have been for generalists, not social media experts. Choosing not to be social media fluent sends a strong, and perhaps unintended, message. It essentially signifies being out of step with where the market has gone.

Profiles and Contacts on LinkedIn

Profiles are at the heart of LinkedIn. A person's profile is essentially his or her digital resume. It captures education, experience, and expertise, along with one simple photo. It also contains space for interests, groups, and honors, as well as links to web sites of organizations with which a person is affiliated and any blogs that the person writes. You won't find photo albums, games, and bumper stickers here. LinkedIn presents its members as professionals. Although it can appear to be a daunting task, it pays to take the time to fully complete one's profile. The more complete the profiles of candidates and hiring managers or recruiters, the more helpful LinkedIn can be.

The "snapshot" portion of a person's profile is, as LinkedIn's web site says, essentially a "next-generation business card."[8] It contains a 30,000-foot overview of a person and includes his or her name, location, current title, past positions, education, recommendations, and related web sites. The snapshot also includes a link to a person's public profile, that is, the profile that will pop up when people look for him or her on Google or other search engines. (It is distinct from the more robust profile that LinkedIn users are able to view.) The "summary" section of the profile provides a more in-depth description of the person's professional experience and skills. Needless to say, this summary is like an elevator speech. It is compact and convinces a person to keep reading through the profile—or not.

A second dimension of a person's LinkedIn profile is his or her network of contacts. The richness of these networks varies depending on the number of direct contacts that a person has and how well he or she has worked LinkedIn's connection process. Let me explain: LinkedIn taps a person's address book to build their initial network. It also helps expand this network by identifying people that may have worked or attended school with a person—it gathers this background information from the profile. Members can augment their list of contacts by searching for other LinkedIn members using keywords, a name, title, company, or industry. The final step in network creation is inviting this list of people to become part of one's personalized network. It's simple: you send them a LinkedIn "invitation" asking if they would like to be a part of your network. If they accept your invitation, you both are automatically a part of each other's networks.

Recruiting Through LinkedIn

LinkedIn is quite effective for recruiting for middle and upper management positions, not necessarily lower-level jobs, simply because that is who comprises the majority of the membership. Whereas it is free to search for a job on LinkedIn, there is a monthly fee for listing a job posting. According to the company, the typical job posting is forwarded 11 times by members and receives more than 30 applications.[9] These job descriptions are search engine optimized and posted on Twitter to tap into the larger social web.

Here's an interesting feature: an internal search engine helps identify potential candidates by linking keywords in a company's job description with those in people's profiles. If it seems like it may be a good match, LinkedIn sets up InMails for recruiters, through which they can reach out, introduce themselves, and present the opportunity. Interested candidates can scan their networks to see if they know anyone who works at the company through which they can gather more information. They can also connect directly with a recruiter or be redirected to a corporate career web site. If these candidates are not interested in the position for themselves, they can forward the job description on to their other connections. And they do.

Companies can also search for candidates without posting a job description. To do so, hiring managers can post an update on their personal profiles, indicating that they are hiring and asking for referrals from their networks. Working through recruiters' networks personalizes the company for potential candidates, providing a sense of familiarity with someone at the hiring institution.

Here's an example of LinkedIn in action.[10] A hiring manager at Yahoo! connected with a LinkedIn member in India about a new lab that Yahoo! was building in his country. He mentioned that Yahoo! was looking for someone to head the initiative and asked for a few names of people that his contact might recommend. The LinkedIn member referred several people to the recruiter; because his interest had been piqued, he also sent along his own resume. In the end, he was hired. The rest, as they say, is history.

Vetting Candidates Through the Social Web

One of the real strengths of LinkedIn is how it assists recruiters in the due diligence process. As you know, a LinkedIn profile lists the positions held and education obtained by an individual. A complete profile also includes selected recommendations from those with whom he or she has worked. With a premium membership, companies can also complete a reference search to see what an applicant's former colleagues have to say about the candidate. This is a good supplement to the recommendations that a candidate has chosen and posted, which we would expect might paint the best picture possible.

It's also helpful to cross-reference a candidate across social platforms comparing his or her Facebook profile, Tweet history, and LinkedIn summary against his or her resume. "You can't imagine how many inconsistencies we find," Hayes tells me.

Of course, due diligence works both ways and potential recruits can use LinkedIn and other sites such as glassdoor.com to investigate companies and their potential bosses. There is nothing like a former employee, especially the one who most recently held the position for which a company is trying to hire, to give up the scoop. This "reverse due diligence" is nothing new, but in the social media age, it is very public. Companies and individuals have to be quite savvy and skilled in managing their digital reputations, pretty much around the clock.

Hayes told me of a time when HireMinds thought that they had found the perfect candidate for a job; the hiring company also thought it was a solid match; the champagne hadn't been chilled, but it was close. While contemplating the offer, the potential hire undertook a bit more research and found an issue that really concerned him about the company that was being discussed on glassdoor .com. Because Hayes had a good relationship with both the candidate and the hiring company, they were all able to sit down and discuss the issue and what the company was doing to remedy the situation. In the end, the candidate's concern was addressed and he accepted the offer.

To avoid situations like these, in addition to combing the Web for negative press, HireMinds directly inquires about potential skeletons in the closet at companies for which they are considering taking on a search assignment. If the circumstances warrant intervention, Hire-Minds works with companies to articulate and remedy the situation at hand, just as Hayes did in the aforementioned situation. What is the takeaway from this story? Monitor what is being said about your company in various forums—don't miss glassdoor.com—and tackle any issues that arise quickly and honestly. Proactively engage in social environments to build your reputation equity. It's the social media age's version of saving for a rainy day.

Tweeting for Hires

Twitter's social network also provides an effective tool for recruiting. The microblogging platform has more than 106 million registered users and is gaining 300,000 users a day. The easiest way to recruit on Twitter is simply to tweet about the hires that you are trying to make. Tweeting about job opportunities is fairly straightforward; the only trick is working within the 140-character limit. Here's an example of a recent tweet from my company, Racepoint Group:

> Do u eat, zzz, luv PR + new media? @racepointgroup, PR agency w/offices in Bos, SF, DC, Lon is hiring! http://bit.ly/bxjDD.

Supplementing the listing with a hashtag or two (#hiring, #recruiting, #job, #jobpost, #NAJ—translation: need a job), which helps to organize information on Twitter, can also help to target potential hires. Using an abbreviated URL (http://bit.ly/bxjDD) requires fewer characters.

Given the limitations on space, job tweets are primarily used for redirecting candidates to companies' career web sites. Other recruiting related uses for Twitter include tweeting about when you may be attending a job fair or college campus, highlighting employee perks and benefits, redirecting candidates to your company's blogs and other social destinations where they can learn more, and retweeting company mentions.

Finding Candidates on Facebook

With more than 500 million active users, 50 percent of whom log on daily, Facebook is *the* social network in terms of reach. Of course, not all Facebook users are professionals who would make for good hires at the moment. (My 13-year-old son and his friends, for example.) But if you are looking to connect with soon-to-be or recent college or post-college grads, this is a great place to build a presence.

Ernst & Young (E&Y) was an early adopter of Facebook for recruiting. Today, Ernest & Young Careers has more than 50,000 people who "like" it (formerly known as *fans*). Its information section contains exactly that, a broad brush-stroke of information that paints a picture of the firm. Under updates, potential candidates can learn about the company's commitment to social responsibility, awards it has received and given, interview tips, and other places to find E&Y on the Web. Specific destinations developed for students and experienced candidates explain career paths, highlight E&Y's thought leadership, and profile some of its people.

Candidates can reach out directly to the company via its wall to inquire about their specific situation and to have their questions answered. E&Y also uses their wall to address rumors and fallacies. For example, one Facebook user questioned the company's pay scale relative to its peers. E&Y was able to refute the misperception directly, but the most powerful message came from the company's own employees who took it upon themselves to explain and praise E&Y's benefits package.

Companies can post a job opportunity for free in the Facebook Marketplace. To do so, all they have to do is scroll over to the jobs section, bypassing the houses, books, cars, and other items that are also for sale in the marketplace. A more targeted option is placing a Facebook Ad.

Citysearch's chief executive officer (CEO), Jay Herrati, recently explained how his firm was using Facebook Ads to *TechCrunch*.[11] Essentially, Citysearch takes out an ad for an opportunity and distributes it, along with a photo of the designated hiring manager, only to the manager's Facebook friends. People within his or her network receive the message, can vote on it, and share it with their friends. If they are actually interested in the job, they can connect directly with the hiring manager. There is familiarity in this process; people feel that they are connected in some way to the hiring manager, even if it is distantly through other friends, which makes the process seem more intimate.

Company Career Portals

A word or two about company career sites is necessary. Many companies are spending big dollars to ramp up these social destinations. The best sites, according to Torgil Lenning, cofounder and CEO of Potentialpark Communications, a Swedish recruitment firm that ranks career sites of large companies, "take them [candidates] from: information via inspiration to a relation."[12]

Potentialpark recently awarded their best career site designation to Bertelsmann, the global media company. A quick glance at their portal, www.createyourowncareer.com, reveals blogs, videos, and podcasts from the company and from its employees; search capabilities for jobs with Bertelsmann around the world; images from company events; outreach to alumni; self-assessments and other resources to help candidates create their own career paths and much more. (It is definitely worth exploring.)

What is it that speaks to candidates? "Job seekers have become used to improved career sites and have increased their expectations and demands," Lenning said in a recent interview. "In order to be competitive, when your dream candidate sits in front of their computer and evaluates you versus your nearest competitor, you have to have a web site that is coming from the candidate's perspective."

What do candidates expect? According to Potentialpark's research, candidates want to hear a company's official story as well as comments from people who have experience with the company. What if there is some negative feedback provided on the site? It's okay. "There are strange people out there that say strange things, and readers understand this . . . if there are employers that tell stories that do not hold true, readers will discover this too," Lenning explained. "Discrepancies and neglect are worse than bad news."

Be Where They Are

Don't overlook other professional communities in which potential hires for your company are active. This includes industry specialist groups—for java developers or medical directors, for example. Another great way to find passive candidates or to just network within your own industry is through LinkedIn groups. It's actually quite easy to do. Just go to the Groups heading and click on Groups Directory. You can search for groups by industry or by key word. When you find a group that you would like to join, click on the "join this group" button. As soon as you are accepted, you can join in the conversation.

Groups are organized so that you can see the range of subjects that have been discussed along with what you have contributed and how others have responded to your comments. Want to know who the most influential people are within the group this week? There's a section on the Group's home page that will tell you. What's more, by hovering over those person's photos, you can learn more about who they are and what they have been saying. You may choose to follow them—or even try to hire them! Want to know who comprises the group? It's quite simple to identify whom they are and what connections you may share. Some groups also have job boards where you can post a job listing. Take a gander at what the types of positions for which other group members are hiring from time to time. It's a good way to stay abreast of where others in the industry are investing resources.

Remember your own alumni as well. "In many cases, alumni themselves are the best candidates for a company's job openings," explains Anne Berkowitch, founder and CEO of SelectMinds, the largest builder of corporate alumni social network communities. "Having an alumni network can help bring them back." In fact, in SelectMinds experience, alumni are twice as likely to rejoin the ranks of a company if they are members of its alumni network. KPMG, which has "a highly engaged and active" alumni network, reports that 16 percent of its overall hires are rehires.[13]

SelectMinds clients find that, on average, 66 percent of their rehires are "star performers."[14] Part of boomerang hires' success is no doubt a result of their familiarity with the company, its culture, and processes—they are able to be productive straight away. They are also highly engaged because they have been on the outside, they have "realized that the grass is not greener," and have returned. SelectMinds has observed that rehiring alumni also has "positive morale implications" for the employee's peers and with customers because it validates their decision to remain engaged with the company.

It goes without saying that the more involved and informed recruiters can be with the social communities from which they may want to tap talent, the more effective they will be. Knowledgeable recruiters will be able to add value to the community, enhancing the company's reputation within the community, and improving their ability to identify and court potential hires. Their voice can supplement that of other company employees—product specialists, developers, corporate finance types—who may already be active in these professional communities.

Successfully Reeling Them In

Increased access has its downsides. It creates a lot of noise and grunt work in the form of many more resumes and inquiries for hiring managers to sort through. "Companies are initially enamored with the volume of resumes that they receive via social media platforms; however, that access often becomes the problem, not the solution, to their recruitment efforts," Hayes explains. "Companies have to be set up to handle a deluge of inquiries and resumes and to be able to separate the wheat from the chaff."

More access does not immediately translate into new hires either. People have to be convinced of an opportunity and decide that it is worth the transaction costs associated with a new position. Social media does provide several more touch points along the way to keep this process moving forward.

The relationship management company, Convergys, finds that mobile text messaging improves the efficiency of this "courting" period. "Not only are these new media the most convenient form of communication as they allow applicants to reach us anytime, day or night, but they also significantly speed up the application process—effectively allowing employees to start a career with Convergys in no time flat," said Sonny Divina, the company's director for recruitment.[15]

Candidates can begin their application process by texting the word "APPLY" and directing it to the company, which, in turn, responds with instructions on how go about the application process. (The company also texts reminders of upcoming interviews and pre-employment requirements to candidates.) Current employees can use text messaging to send referrals to the company. The net result: social media has raised the nationwide yield of applications and referrals for Convergys, according to Divina.

"Social media alone cannot clench most deals," cautions Hayes. "It can pique someone's interest and add color to an opportunity, but in the end, for high level positions, you still have to pick up the phone. Recruiting is still about building relationships and making connections, often long before a potential candidate is even considering a career shift or a new position is contemplated." This is precisely why Hayes is confident that the role of the third-party executive recruiter will not disappear any time soon, just as it didn't when job boards were born. In fact, his company is busier than ever.

One to Watch: Deloitte Services

People are critical to the success of any company, especially a company whose product is its people. To effectively build its human capital, the consulting firm Deloitte is constantly recruiting. As a result, the company receives nearly 147,000 applications for employment per year. After much researching and vetting, 4,000 of these applicants are given the opportunity to interview.[16]

Social media is critical to Deloitte's recruiting efforts. The company uses a variety of social sites to connect with candidates wherever they are, including Deloitte's own career microsite, Facebook, Twitter, LinkedIn, and YouTube. Some of these tools serve as bell ringers, used to grab potential applicants' attention and direct it back to their microsite, where more detailed information is available.

Links to job postings are provided on Twitter as well as on LinkedIn. The company's dedicated Facebook page includes Deloitte Perspectives, the company's global blog; YouTube videos on energy predictions, manufacturing and the global economy, and why Deloitte is the best place to launch a career; Twitter feeds; and a wall, through which the company interacts directly with candidates. One of the partners that is featured under employee profiles on Deloitte's Facebook page receives e-mails regularly from interested applicants, many of whom have added him to their list of Facebook friends.[17]

The company's microsite is full of "official information" as well as employee-generated content. It contains examples of how the company lives out its commitment to corporate responsibility; showcases employees, including some of their favorite TV shows; provides interactive tools to help candidates envision their career progression at Deloitte; and maps when and where Deloitte recruiters will be interviewing. The company even has created campus microsites for targeted universities.

Human Resources Meets Marketing

Social media has brought human resources into the marketing business in a larger and more public way. Human resources now encourages employees to make videos about what it is like to work at a company; creates interactive games for recruiting microsites; and tweets about the company and what makes it a great place to work. Adding human resources' voice to the mix is a good thing; it provides a fuller picture of an organization. However, these additional voices and venues require alignment with the company's overall message, tone, style, personality, and goals. For smaller companies like mine, this is accomplished quite simply. Human resources and marketing are physically located together and they connect all day long. For larger organizations, the social enterprise eforum that we discussed in Chapter 3 can be critical to keeping these multiple voices and efforts coordinated—but not controlled.

Regardless of who is speaking and for what purpose, authenticity remains key. Transparency is part of social media's culture even when it comes to convincing people to come and work for a firm. It's important to have an unscripted presence, to acknowledge imperfections, and to provide opportunities for potential recruits' feedback, questions, and comments. Potential hires can—and will—easily look to multiple sources to test the validity of what recruiters are claiming. Alignment of recruiting messages and day-to-day reality is essential to be perceived as a reliable source of information about a company.

To help potential recruits get to know your company better, ask employees to honestly blog or vlog about working at your company. Post photos of corporate events. Tweet about employee programs and perks: Impact Days, on-campus day care, and internal opportunities—whatever speaks to your potential employee base. Provide in-depth candid profiles about employees. Link to or post articles about your company and its leadership that are written by staff or other third parties. Retweet good mentions about the company and respond to comments and posts about your company on other sites.

With respect to the interview process, list job postings and explain your interview process. Show what is important to your company by providing examples of how what your company is doing makes a difference or about how it effectively and ethically handles challenging situations. List all of your corporate presences—employee blogs, alumni groups, Facebook pages, Flickr photographs, and Twitter handles—so that they are readily accessible to prospective employees. And, of course, tailor your message to the personas of the communities in which you are active.

Accelerating the Onboarding Process

The onboarding process of helping new employees become productive is critical whether employees are brand new to a company or are transitioning from another part of the business. It is vital because it has an effect, both on the employee's initial productivity and on their longer-term retention. Effective onboarding brings an employee into the fold, helping him or her understand and feel a part of an organization's culture and its formal and informal networks. It helps them feel welcome, gives them a sense of how they fit in to the bigger mission of the organization, and reinforces their decision to join. This joining-up process, or lack thereof, can make or break a new hire.

An effective mentoring program is often just what the doctor ordered. Social media training and access is also a significant part of the plan. At my companies, new employees are all taken through a "Social Media 101" training, through which they can become more familiar with the ins and outs and benefits and limitations of multiple social tools. This makes sense for new hires of our companies because we are in the social media business; however, I would argue that this is a great way to start every new professional off in their career at a would-be social enterprise. It says, "these skills are essential to our business" and helps to create a vision for what is possible.

Deloitte uses social media to provide new hires with an innovative orientation experience. Each new hire receives a peer-level onboarding advisor before they report for their first day of work. This relationship continues throughout the hire's first year. The nuts and bolts of orientation are provided via an interactive session—the company's career site makes a point of saying that it is delivered without a single PowerPoint slide—involving gaming, videos, and case studies. There are not any lectures; rather, employees play an interactive board game, "Discovery Map," complete with supporting videos starring "real Deloitte professionals," to learn about the organization. Training also includes personalized coaching from client service and talent leaders; an introduction to an interactive New-Hire Center web site, which offers resources and additional learning opportunities; and assistance in building the all-important network of contacts.

As we saw in Chapter 8, an internal social network can go a long way toward connecting people and getting them active and productive early on in their career transitions. Deloitte has an internal social network called "D Street" where employees can build a social profile and through which they can connect with other employees. This provides them with more readily available access to knowledge (in the form of people), which gets them out of the training mode and into the productive mode faster. The network also keeps employees feeling connected in an industry where employees are often on the road, visiting clients.

Keeping Employees on the Cutting Edge

Social media can also be effective for keeping employees growing over time. Webinars, wikis, training videos, and simulations allow employees to take advantage of training "on demand," when and where it is convenient and at a personalized pace. (Many companies also offer white papers, training videos, and wikis for their customers to better understand how to best use their products and services. As they say at Best Buy, "We need our customers to know all that we know.") These tools generally incur no travel costs and can be used over and over again. They can augment corporate classroom training by offering the capability to conduct polls, in-session quizzes, and pre- and post-course engagement. Those who are most knowledgeable about the subject at hand can also update them continuously, mirroring the constant evolution of corporate policies and procedures.

The Army, for example, is using social tools to capture seasoned employees' knowledge, reducing the costs and improving the knowledge transfer associated with recruitment, training, and development. The organization recently invited about 140,000 soldiers of all ranks to make real-time updates to its wiki to assist in rewriting seven Army training manuals.

"The pace of change driven by ongoing operations has outstripped our ability to keep up with it at the lowest levels of doctrine," says Clinton Ancker, director of the Combined Arms Center's Combined Arms Doctrine Directorate, which shares responsibility for the wiki project in conjunction with the Battle Command Knowledge System. "By opening up these documents to updates by users, we will be able to stay more current with best practices being used in the field."[18]

Keeping the Learning Curve High at GE

GE has long been known for its corporate learning programs. For more than 60 years, GE has been training leaders at its Crotonville, New York, facility. Much has changed over that time: the subject matter of its courses; the duration of its training programs—in the mid-1950s, courses ran for 13 weeks, now the longest is 3 weeks; and the location—in addition to New York, training takes place Munich, Shanghai, and any place that an MP3 player or Webcam can power up. Today, roughly half of the company's 290,000 employees take part in GE's learning programs, which are supported by an annual budget of close to $1 billion.

"We are really trying to leverage and embed technology into learning," explained Susan Peters, GE's Chief Learning Officer, in a recent interview with *Knowledge@Wharton*.[19] The company accomplishes this through making on-demand materials readily available and by creating content that employees can listen to in the car or during lunch. "[We are] making learning a part of everybody's day all the time," Peters explained.[20] Between 50,000 and 60,000 employees a year do some sort of on-demand learning through their computers. Content covers a wide range of topics from management skills to project skills and is generally available in video format.

Not all training at GE takes place via social media, however. "There is an element of our teaching that we recognize will always be face-to-face, and, therefore, probably less technology sensitive," Peters said. "I don't suspect that we will ever go to a place where we have only technology based or e-learning. We really believe that to 'inspire, connect, and develop' happens with real impact when people are physically together."[21]

That having been said, several social tools are used within the context of GE's face-to-face learning events. TelePresence connects leaders around the world with classes in real time; students report using WebEx and Webcams; materials are available on Kindles and global newspapers can be accessed via touch screens throughout the building; electronic whiteboards have replaced flip charts; and an internal social network allows groups to self-organize and connect before, during, and after training.

Engaging with Your Current Employees

It's no surprise that social media is being used internally; effective employee communication is one of the critical success factors in successful employee engagement. Such engagement is widely believed to increase employee productivity, enhance employee retention, and improve employee morale. Research conducted by the HR consulting firm, Towers Watson (TW), consistently shows that the firms that communicate effectively with employees are also the best financial performers. In fact, they have enjoyed 47 percent higher total returns to shareholders over the last five years compared with firms that are the least effective communicators.[22] TW has found that this is especially true during times of rapid change when employees feel unsettled. In such times and situations, the employee value proposition, which essentially outlines expectations for both employees and the firm, needs to be regularly articulated and rearticulated to keep employees engaged in their work and mindful of essential corporate priorities. TW also suggests that companies operating across multiple regions consider how the perception of this proposition may differ across cultures.

"Today's workers are looking for authentic, timely messages that address how business changes affect them personally," explained Kathryn Yates, Global Leader of Communication consulting at Towers Watson in *Employee Benefit News*. "Social media engages employees in real time and on a variety of topics."[23]

TW has observed that highly successful communicators are using social media tools 2 to 3 times more than the low-effectiveness group of companies to reach employees. Not surprisingly, the most effective communicators are more likely to report their social media tools are cost-effective (37 percent versus 14 percent). Highly effective communicators also tend to be strategic. They are 2 to 3 times more likely to have a documented communication strategy than low-performing organizations and are also using metrics to document the success of their communications.[24]

According to the 2010 Employee Engagement Survey conducted by the International Association of Business Communicators Research Foundation and Buck Consultants, the most common forms of communication used to foster engagement across companies are e-mail (83 percent) and an organization's intranet (75 percent). The survey also found that almost half of employers currently communicate through Facebook, instant messaging, and Twitter.[25]

"This year's respondents reported slight increases in the use of social media tools, and more of them say they have established internal and external policies for appropriate workplace use of social media," said Robin McCasland, past chair, IABC Research Foundation and president, Brain Biscuits Strategic Communication. "When managed effectively, social media can be a great addition to an existing employee engagement strategy. Employees and job candidates alike can read employer news and anecdotes that reinforce a strong, positive culture."[26]

Best Buy: Inspiring Young Savers

Here's an example of effective use of communication by human resources. Most employees don't really understand the value of their compensation and benefit programs. It's a shame because research released by Univers Workplace Benefits shows that employees who understand the value of their rewards are 30 percent more likely to be satisfied with them.[27] How are companies using social media to fill this information gap?

Best Buy's human resources department successfully utilized social media to increase enrollment in their 401(k) plan. Working through the company's internal social networking site, BlueShirt Nation, human resources asked employees to submit videos that might help increase employees' knowledge about and interest in its recently revamped savings program. The challenge: Getting its workforce, more than half of which is under the age of 24, to think about retirement. The reward: A three-day trip to the company's corporate offices to present the video to executives and the Board. The challenge was well received; teams submitted twenty-seven videos—a number much larger than was expected. The winning video, "Croft and 401(k), a Fictional True Story," took the form of a movie trailer for a fictional film about a Best Buy employee who refused to join the 401(k). (Check it out on YouTube.) In the end, it was effective: Best Buy increased enrollment in the plan by 30 percent.

Ann Bender, a Best Buy human resource team member told *Workforce Management*, "It was wild to see the creativity and talent among our workers and the buzz throughout the company was amazing. People couldn't believe that something like this came from HR, which is traditionally more conservative."[28] Today there are several user groups at Best Buy actively discussing compensation, benefits, and retirement questions on BlueShirt Nation. "With 22,000 users, the site is a perfect way to get in front of employees to present new benefits or enhancements," Bender says.[29]

McFamily: Connecting Corporate and Crew

McDonald's began using social media internally to engage with its employees several years before it began its external efforts. Its first foray was not very successful, however. After 10 months of effort, only 22 people were taking advantage of its internal blogging platform. What did McDonald's learn? According to Steve Wilson, senior director of global Web communications, it learned that blogging tools were not a great fit for the company's culture. "We think of ourselves as a McFamily," Wilson explained. Tools that are more collaborative are proving to be a better fit at this stage.[30]

The second version of their internal tool, Mindshare, reflected this learning. A social network, wikis, and threaded discussions complement the company's blogs (Wilson said the 22 bloggers are still at it!) and create a vibrant internal community. Mindshare is organized into several neighborhoods including those specifically geared toward restaurant operations, owner operators, and corporate communications. Useful information is shared within these neighborhoods. A franchise owner in Italy, for example, offered his colleagues a definitive method for getting rid of fingerprints on franchise windows and doors. It may not be rocket science, but it is extremely relevant to many McDonald's owner-operators. Mindshare is incorporated into McDonald's corporate portal so that their 700,000 employees don't have to be members of Mindshare to participate; they can reach the neighborhoods with a single sign-on.

What about the other 40,000 McDonald's crew members who are the face of McDonald's at the drive-up windows and counters, but who technically are employed by the franchises? How does McDonald's connect with this vitally important constituency whose names they might not even know?

After surveying many crew members, the company created Station M, a password-protected site designed exclusively for this group. The crew members' most important priority was having a vehicle through which they could get to know each other. A key feature of the site, therefore, is a social network where members can share information about themselves and post photos. The group's second priority was a way for crew members to be heard by their peers, by the owner-operators, and by the McDonald's corporate offices. Topic forums provide the basis for this discussion platform, which are guided by an elected moderator, along with blogs, and other submissions.

Is Station M successful? Seventy percent of employees who use Mindshare say that it makes them feel better about the company and ideas about how to improve operations are continually circulating.[31] The social site's success has been replicated around the world with McLand in Brazil, Our Lounge in the United Kingdom, and, my personal favorite, Ketchup!, in Singapore. It is the only vehicle through which headquarters can reach crew members besides its printed *Manager's News* and, of course, the drive-through window.

The Twenty-First Century Work Environment as a Selling Tool

What will it take to be an employer of choice going forward and how can social media help companies to get there? The Hidden Brain Drain Task Force, a group of 50 multinational companies, recently undertook the task of answering that first part of that very question.[32] Through a variety of methods, the task force recently posed this question to employed college grads and "high-echelon" talent across age groups and sectors. What did they find? Employees of all ages are looking for a "remixed" set of rewards, which includes flexible work arrangements and the opportunity to give back to society—both of which rated higher than the size of the pay package alone.

The twenty-first century workplace looks quite different from yesterday's. A plethora of nontraditional working arrangements satisfy employees' desire for more flexibility and control over their time. Social tools allow some of the basic office functions to take place remotely— employees can have face-to-face interaction on Skype or through teleconferencing, or work collaboratively on documents and projects, or can "attend" company briefings via podcasts and videocasts—making these new work arrangements successful. Surveys conducted by the connectivity experts, Yankee Group, found that in 2009, 43 percent of business employees were mobile (which they define as spending more than 20 percent of their time away from their primary location) and they see no signs of it abating.[33] In fact, their surveys of North American workers show that nearly three-quarters believe that allowing employees to work remotely benefits the company. When asked to identify the single most important thing a company can do to increase its employees' productivity, the most common response was the ability to work from home. When adopted on a large enough scale, remote working arrangements can even reduce real estate costs for companies. IBM saves $110 million per year because more than one third of its employees work from home.[34]

Why Are You Here?

Another important part of the twenty-first century work environment includes creating a work environment in which employees can find meaning. I am not talking about a place where people sit around singing "Kumbaya." What I am talking about is providing a compelling reason for employees to work for you and creating the kind of culture that encourages relationship building, connection, and innovation.

Dr. David Ulrich, a professor at the University of Michigan's Ross School of Business, together with his wife, Wendy, recently authored the book, *The Why of Work: How Great Leaders Build Abundant Organizations That Win*. In it they explore the research surrounding work as a place to find meaning and purpose. What did they find?

"When they [employees] do find meaning [in their workplace], not only do people feel better about themselves, but the organization is more successful," David Ulrich explained. "People are more productive. Customers get better value. Investors get better results. The community gets the results it wants. It's a win–win; one of the magical elixirs we look for."[35]

Companies that are driven by a distinct moral purpose are, of course, ahead of the game. Corporate community service engagements, such as Deloitte's Impact Day or Threadless's "awesome parties," are also important. IBM takes it one step further through programs like its Corporate Services Corps, where they offer high-potential employees from around the world the opportunity to come together to work on month-long projects that address economic development and environmental sustainability.

Weisure: Finding the Balance

Weisure is another aspect of twenty-first century workscapes. New York University Sociologist Dalton Conley coined the phrase to describe the increasing ambiguity between work and leisure, an emerging trend made possible because of social technology. It manifests itself as fielding work-related texts at soccer games and on the beach while on vacation, and by sending corporate job descriptions through personal networks along with photos of weekend fun. "Social networking as an activity is one of those ambiguous activities," Conley says. "It's part fun and part instrumental in our knowledge economy."

It's also part of human resources' agenda to establish guidelines and policies to help organizations, and employees, adapt to essentially always being on. While employees want to mix work with their personal lives, they also want to achieve some level of work/life balance. What's more, they want fun to be an essential part of their working lives, not just something that happens when they leave the office. Don Tapscott, who established the company nGerera to study the impact of Internet on youth, tells the story of Effie, a young Princeton graduate who is thrilled to be working at Google, in his book *Grown Up Digital*. What is it about Google's work environment that is so appealing? Tapscott quotes Effie:

The company is insanely transparent, which feels like a sign of respect and trust. The hours are as flexible as you'd like them to be. . . . The free food and subsidized massages are key. . . . The boundaries between work and play are fuzzy. Unlike in the corporate world, no one thinks twice if you IM with your friends in the middle of the day or go out to play some volleyball at two. The culture is designed to help employees relax into productivity, not stress into it. . . . To me this just seems, well, logical.[36]

Blending Generations and a Global Workforce

Being able to architect cultures that are meaningful and appealing to several different generations of employees is also high on human resources' agenda. Given the sizeable losses incurred in retirement funds during the last economic downturn, it is quite possible that multiple generations, representing a variety of work styles, may be working side by side by 2015.

Bette Price, a human resource consultant, coined the phrase *gen-blending* to describe this confluence of working and learning styles and perspectives within an organization. Early reports suggest that this blending can invigorate companies. Reverse mentoring programs, in which senior managers are "mentored" by younger employees in the ways of social media complement traditional mentoring relationships, leaving almost everyone feeling as if they have something to contribute.

Ann Hambly, president for 1st Service Solutions, which acts as a buyer advocate on real estate restructurings, told the *Financial Times* that gen-blending has improved her company's morale. "There is better buy-in from the staff. The goals are perceived differently within the company because they weren't just top-down mandates."[37] Human resources must consider how best to recruit and develop this diversity of talent at different career stages and ages.

That's not all. As companies continue to hire overseas talent, human resources will also need to help build corporate cultures that can embrace collaboration across geographic and cultural boundaries. It is in their best interest: in addition to benefiting from labor cost arbitrage in certain markets, over the past decade, companies with strong records of inclusion outperformed the NASDAQ stock market by

47 percent, the Standard & Poor's 500 Index by 23.5 percent, and the Dow Jones Industrial Average by 48 percent.[38] What's more, with 60 percent of the world's engineering bachelor degrees coming from China, India, Japan, Russia, South Korea, and Taiwan, I don't expect this trend in hiring overseas to reverse itself any time soon.

Of course, to be an employer of choice, companies will also have to be sophisticated in the way they communicate, employing social tools internally and externally to create innovative and adaptable environments with quick decision-making abilities in order to keep up with the hyper-connected employees. Human resources will need to be actively involved with making sure that appropriate social media tools, policies, and training are in place.

What will a company that is dominated by diverse hyper-connected individuals look like? It will be flatter, faster, virtual, and collaborative—a social enterprise, the evolution of which we consider in the next, and final, chapter.

Questions to Consider

- How is your human resources department currently using social media to promote and present your company?
- Has social media affected your company's recruiting efforts to date?
- How would Potentialpark Communications, the recruiting firm that ranks career sites of large companies, rate your digital recruiting presence?
- Does an alumni community make sense for your company? If you have one, what are you gaining from it?
- How can social tools improve your orientation process? Your training and development efforts? Your employee engagement?
- How is social media changing your company's work environment?
- With what types of communication tools are your new hires comfortable? Will they be frustrated by your organization?
- What is essential to transforming your organization into a twenty-first century employer of choice?

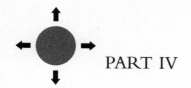

PART IV

The Future of the
Social Enterprise

CHAPTER TEN

Next

What began as a new communication tool used primarily by physicists, techies, and teenagers has gone mainstream, pulling us all—some kicking and screaming—into the throws of the social media era. This era marks a new evolution in the now 40-year-old computing paradigm. First it was mainframes, then personal computers, then the Internet, and now it's the social web. Over time, the emphasis has shifted from the underlying technology itself to the effect that technology is having on the organizations and the people that use these tools. As we have seen, social technology is causing a seismic shift in consumer behavior that is affecting businesses, industries, markets, economies, and cultures everywhere. And it has only just begun. If I had to wager a guess, I'd say that we are in the bottom half of the first inning of this ball game. As such, it is hard to imagine just how far-reaching the effect of the social web will be. What are some of the change trajectories that we are likely to see in the next few years?

Social Enterprises Come of Age

We have seen several examples of companies that are well on their way to becoming social enterprises, those living, breathing entities that are comprised of networks of people, some of whom technically work "for" the company, and many more who do not, that are involved and interested in what a company is and does. Some of these companies were born-on-the-Web like Threadless, Amazon, FaceBook, and Google; others have long, predigital lives and a history of self reengineering like P&G, IBM, Dell, GE, and Johnson & Johnson. Given the rapid rate of innovation that companies are currently experiencing as a result of the explosion of the social web, I expect that in the near term, rather than seeing new leapfrog developments, the focus of management will be on the widespread emergence and refinement of social enterprises. Additional corporate functions will join their company's social engagement efforts and the networks comprising companies' ecosystems will multiply. Many more people within these networks will contribute to companies' success.

As social enterprises become increasingly skilled at developing and collaborating with and within these communities, they will faced with the task of handling volumes of structured and unstructured data. While there is much promise in this data, there is also challenge. Some of the best minds at companies will be charged with finding meaningful ways to aggregate it, determine its value, convert it from data to wisdom, and parse it out to the relevant business areas who can transform it into actionable strategy. From there the job will be to put relevant metrics in place in order to build accountability into this emerging process. But when companies master this process, they will have the capability to readily optimize themselves and their products and processes. Agility will be the norm as will relevant, customer-informed value propositions.

As they make their way up the social enterprise learning curve, companies will improve their cost structures by realizing efficiencies that improve their margins. They'll be able to reduce the uncertainty of operating in highly complex and competitive markets by making better use of new sources of data. The quality of their innovation will have more effect and be more cost-effective. New products and services will be brought to market faster because of shorter development times, assuaging the marketplace's insatiable thirst for innovation.

Efficiencies will be also be gained from integrating aspects of social enterprises' operations with that of their partners. These colleagues may be dispersed physically, even around the globe, but will be closely connected through communication technology. I am no expert on organizational behavior and structure, but research suggests that social enterprises may actually shrink in size because of their active use of communication technology. Thomas Malone, a professor of management at the MIT Sloan School of Management, and his colleagues found that when an industry increases its use of information technology, the average size of companies in that industry tends to decrease after a lag of about two years.[1] Here's the irony: this shrinking of a company's core is likely to take place simultaneously with the expansion of its product and service offerings and a broadening of its global reach resulting from its extended ecosystem of partners.

Leadership of companies will become less paternal. Communication tools will provide employees of social enterprises with access to information that will allow them to make more and better informed decisions. Although it is inherently an empowering movement, building and shaping social enterprises will still require bold and insightful leaders who can ask the right questions, listen to myriad responses, prioritize initiatives, and allocate resources. What will be different is their dominant leadership style. "Inspire and enable" will be more prevalent than "command and control."

Here's an interesting leadership example to consider. Each year, Arkadi Kuhlmann, chairman and president of the bank ING Direct USA, asks his employees, "Would you vote for me to serve you another year?" Although his colleagues and board think that he's "nuts" to do so, Kuhlmann explained his rationale to the New York Times: "I don't want to serve here unless I've got the commitment of people genuinely wanting me to serve."[2] By putting himself up for a vote, Kuhlmann hopes he is communicating that he doesn't take his job for granted and that, in addition to being accountable to the company's shareholders, board, regulators, and customers, he is willing to be held accountable to those who work for him. As Kuhlmann said, "So if I keep walking around saying all the time that our associates are so important, then why don't they have a say in terms of whether or not I'm leading?" Interesting food for thought, isn't it?

In addition to leadership styles morphing, new approaches to organizing work will continue to emerge. Here's another interesting example to consider. W.L. Gore & Associates (Gore), the maker of GORE-TEX fabric and ELIXIR guitar strings, has been letting many of its leaders emerge naturally for some time. In this "team-based, flat lattice" company, there are no traditional organizational charts. Instead, teams organize around opportunities and from there leaders emerge. While some leaders are appointed, more often than not, leaders are defined by their "followership." According to the company, "Leaders emerge naturally by demonstrating special knowledge, skill, or experience that advances a business objective."[3]

Gore is clear that it hires Associates, not employees. Associates are hired for general work areas and work with sponsors (not bosses) to develop an understanding of business opportunities and objectives and to chart a course for their professional development. "Everyone can earn the credibility to define and drive projects" at Gore.[4] While this is the type of work environment that you may expect for a small, entrepreneurial start-up company, consider that Gore is no small start-up: the company was founded in 1958; enjoys worldwide sales of more than $2.5 billion; and employs over 9,000 Associates in 30 countries. It's no wonder that the company regularly earns a position on *Fortune's* annual list of the "100 Best Companies to Work For" in addition to being recognized by several other workplace evaluators across multiple countries.

Successful social enterprises will develop a comprehensive digital strategy as they become engaged on more fronts and with more frequency. This strategy will not be designed in a corner office and imposed on employees from above; rather, it will flow from the bottom upward and horizontally across an entire enterprise. Ultimately, social media will become as familiar to companies as telephones and fax machines; a nonevent that is absolutely fundamental; just another ripple, albeit profound, in the way companies work.

As social media becomes a part of their DNA, companies will naturally better understand themselves, their abilities, and their stakeholder communities, and the marketplace will better understand them. This knowledge will lead to improved stakeholder relationships and more accurate and comprehensive valuations.

The result of becoming a social enterprise is this: organizations will realize significant competitive advantage. Companies that get on the social media train today will be a part of what I truly believe is nothing short of a revolution in the way businesses operate. I have no doubt that social enterprises will be the leading companies of the next generation—they are already pulling away from the pack.

Consumers Are at the Center

We will continue to see customers at the center of successful companies. Understandably, customers are quite comfortable with their newfound centrality. They enjoy the plethora of information that is readily available to them, their ability to consult directly with their peers about products and services, and their increasing ability to negotiate their own terms. Who wouldn't? Companies that embrace this market shift will enjoy a decisive competitive advantage going forward. This customer-orientation will keep companies in closer sync with the marketplace, while building stronger and increasingly trustworthy relationships with multiple communities of interest that can act as their advocates.

The ability to provide remarkable customer experiences is fundamental to making the shift. It is through these online and offline encounters that the dialogue will take place that will both inform companies of market trends and preferences and build ongoing customer interaction and loyalty. Compelling content is at the root of these experiences rather than flashy advertising. Authentic, transparent, and informative, this content will provide customers with value that they will not want to be without. As a result, every company, regardless of its industry, will be in the content-creating business. This content-creating skill set will need to include capabilities in video, physical events, and their integration across multiple platforms.

To augment this core content, we will also see a proliferation of digital couponing and other reward programs for loyal customers. This is not a new development really, just an enhanced technique that will be able to be delivered directly to customers via multiple devices. The most effective of these will be smart; they will recognize past purchases and offer prompts at reasonable times when purchases are likely to be made again (e.g., when a lease is up on a car, or a child goes to kindergarten). Location-based social networks are likely to figure prominently in their delivery.

Name Your Price

Customers will increasingly be offered the opportunity to customize the terms and conditions of their sale and to purchase group discounts. While this may evoke images of companies being forced to sell products and services below their cost, if structured correctly, it is anything but that. Customized product offerings not only meet consumers' needs best, but offer companies opportunities to optimize prices proactively. Similarly, group purchasing sites provide companies with access to thousands of potential customers, with money to burn, and their friends, all via the social web. What's more, these sites are designed to take advantage of peer sharing and recommendations, which we know, are the cat's meow. If structured correctly, these sites can help offset price discounts with increased volume.

Take Groupon, for example. Groupon features one deal with one local company a day in its social environments, which include Facebook, Twitter, and Groupon.com. Members of the Groupon community, of which there are thousands, look forward to receiving daily offers from Groupon to learn more about local businesses and to perhaps "get a deal" at a spa, restaurant, museum, or other attraction. If enough consumers bid on the offer that has been set by the company so that it reaches its predetermined tipping point, the deal goes through. As you can see, customers have the incentive to share the deal with their friends and acquaintances to make the deal happen. It works when the deals are well structured; 97 percent of all businesses selling their services through Groupon come back for more.

From Customer Relationship Management to Vendor Relationship Management

Much of what we have been talking about in this book is really a form of advanced customer relationship management (CRM). Indeed, many CRM vendors are incorporating social features into their product offerings to capture these new sources of customer information and lead generation. Doc Searls, one of the four authors of *The Cluetrain Manifesto,* envisions another complete shift resulting from the social web: the movement from CRM to vendor relationship management (VRM). Let me explain the difference.

The authors of *The Cluetrain Manifesto* were energized by the words of Jakob Nielsen, the king of Web usability, who said, "We are not seats or eyeballs or end users or consumers. We are human beings—and our reach exceeds your grasp. Deal with it." (Nielsen's words formed the preamble of the Cluetrain discourse.) What Searls envisions, and what Nielsen's words hint at, is the emergence of an intentional economy; that is, an economy that "grows around buyers, not sellers." In an intentional economy, the buyer notifies the market of his or her intention to buy and the sellers compete for the buyers' purchase. This is distinct from an attention-driven economy, in which companies find or "capture" buyers, using advertising to be noticed. (You know, the you-need-this, buy, buy, buy message.)

Searls coined the phrase, *vendor relationship management* to describe this next shift of the social web. Essentially the inverse of CRM, in VRM buyers manage their digital profiles asking for what they want directly from the market. Remember the orthodontist example in Chapter 2? Here's another that comes directly from Searls, "A car rental customer should be able to say to the car rental market, 'I'll be skiing in Park City from March 20 to 25. I want to rent a 4-wheel drive SUV. I belong to Avis Wizard, Budget FastBreak, and Hertz 1 Club. I don't want to pay up front for gas or get any insurance. What can any of you companies do for me?'" With this information in hand, sellers can then compete for the buyer's business.

As the car rental example illustrates, VRM takes the guesswork out of company and consumer interactions. "Every single customer is going to come equipped with far more information than any survey could possibly reduce," Searls said. "It's going to be an easier process to follow the actual demand of customers than to try and force that demand into existence [through advertising]."

For VRM to move beyond theory and into practice, new tools will need to be developed that are independent of sellers. A new category of player is likely to come onto the scene, which Searls describes as *fourth parties*. Whereas third parties essentially work on behalf of sellers, fourth parties will work on behalf of buyers. A current example of this is Lending Tree. This financial services company works on behalf of people looking for a loan, connecting them with multiple lenders who then compete for their business. Over time we'll see many more buyer-centric digital destinations like Lending Tree. Not many are out there at the moment, but they are within view.

What happens to social media conversation in a more intentional economy? It thrives. As Searls explained,

> The Intention Economy is built around more than transactions. Conversations matter. So do relationships. So do reputation, authority, and respect. Those virtues, however, are *earned* by sellers (as well as buyers) and not just "branded" by sellers on the minds of buyers like the symbols of ranchers burned on the hides of cattle.

What role does social analytics play in a more intentional economy? Is there any need for companies to analyze demand if it is expressed directly by the buyer? Yes, but it takes on a different focus. It concentrates on whether buyers actually purchase what they have indicated that they desire.

There Is No Place Like Home

As the social web matures, it will continue to fragment into many microsites in order to best meet consumers' needs. Why is this the case? It's where people feel most at home. Consumers' interests are often quite specific. For example, while most gardeners have green thumbs, their gardening interests are often more specific, such as shade, butterfly, or English gardens. Similarly, while social communities have become lifelines for many living with chronic disease, the communities that are often the most helpful are generally illness-specific, such as a community for people with cystic fibrosis or for families impacted by muscular dystrophy. To connect with one or multiple customer groups, companies will increasingly have to expand their presence on the social web, earning their way into multiple communities. Some of these destinations may be open, others may be gated or password protected.

I expect that before too long, corporate web sites will become traffic directors, links rather than encyclopedias. Interested parties will visit corporate sites to be redirected to the microsites, social network pages, and other venues where they can find the highly segmented content and communities for which they are searching. I also expect continued growth in social search, that is, searching for information within one's network, rather than on a broader and impersonal search engine like Google. What's better than the suggestions and advice of one's own friends?

Another development of which companies need to be cognizant is what I call *home basing*. This happens when people choose to "hang out" in a preferred digital destination such as Facebook or LinkedIn. Again, this behavior is nothing new. People have always had places where they feel comfortable, both online and offline, as well as personal communications preferences. What is new is having people use these social networks as their primary communication platform. Rather than regularly checking their e-mail and using it for daily communications, home basers are continuously connected to and communicating via their social network. It's always on, just like our television was when I was growing up. It's how they stay plugged in to their communities.

There are multiple reasons for home basing. Communication can be easy and widespread within social environments like Facebook or LinkedIn. Given their size, it's quite likely that most of one's contacts are already friends or connections and it takes only a few clicks to add another to the pack. All of one's contacts can be reached via a simple update to one's status or a new posting on one's wall, everything ranging from "lost my phone" to "we've been acquired." Communication may also take the form of a traditional, private e-mail sent within the boundaries of the social network. (Now that Facebook is providing users with an "@facebook.com" e-mail address, users can manage all of their communications through a single inbox, if they elect to participate.) Responses can be made quickly—almost reflexively. Third-party links can be shared effortlessly—no attachments! And of course, it works both ways. Home basing allows one to be constantly connected to everyone within one's circle. I would wager that most home basers don't think of themselves as being logged in to LinkedIn or Facebook; rather, they think of themselves as simply being at work or in the company of friends.

What does this new behavior mean for companies? Once again, they have to be where their customers are to effectively hear and reach them. Companies will have to direct content to customers in their home bases, rather than expecting them to come searching for it on companies' domains. Dell, for example, has made it possible for Facebookers to participate on IdeaStorm without ever having to leave the comfort and convenience of the social network. Similarly, Oreo, the cookie brand, feeds its fans comedy videos and recipes and celebrates its "Fan of the Week" with its customer community via Facebook.

This need to go where the people are applies to individuals as well. I have found that if I send certain friends an e-mail through my Internet service provider, it can take them much longer to get back to me than if I send them an e-mail through LinkedIn. Why? They are home basing in LinkedIn. The same is true for connecting with my kids. They don't usually respond to an e-mail from me in the summertime because they view e-mail as a school-related form of communication. In nonacademic periods, they prefer communication through Facebook, SMS, BBM, or silence, which, believe me, can at times be golden.

Expanded Challenges for Corporations to Tackle

Going forward we will continue to see companies involved in new types of partnerships, the purpose of which will be to tackle societal challenges like the environment, health care, and poverty. These problems are too complex, interconnected, and critical for companies to ignore and for any one entity or sector to tackle single-handedly. They can also provide significant financial opportunities for companies.

Sam Palmisano, CEO of IBM, describes this new focus for companies:

> I believe public sector leaders will find in business a willing partner to reform health care and education, secure trade lanes and electronic commerce, advance innovation, train and enable the displaced and dispossessed, grapple with environmental problems and infectious diseases, and tackle the myriad other challenges that globalization raises.[5]

IBM's Smarter Planet initiative, which you have already heard about, and GE's Healthymagination are examples of companies that are doing just that.

GE recently made a 6-year, $6 billion commitment to health care innovation. Their goal is to "substantially lower costs, increase access, and improve the quality of health care."[6] At the end of their first year, the company had validated 24 healthymagination products, established a $250 million equity fund, invested $700 million in R&D, and launched a consumer health campaign, actions which the company estimates have already touched 15 million lives in new ways.[7]

Two of the exciting products to come through their pipeline are a $1,000 handheld electrocardiogram device and a portable, PC-based ultrasound machine that sells for less than $15,000. These products fall into the category of reverse innovation because they are developed for markets in emerging economies. This is the opposite of *glocalization*, in which companies develop products primarily for their home market and then modify them to local conditions, an approach which GE has long employed. Developing products specifically for the needs and budgets of heavily populated places like China and India, represents tremendous growth opportunities for GE while addressing some of the world's most challenging issues.

Here is another one my favorites, TOMS Shoes. Its founder, Blake Mycoskie, refers to himself as the company's chief shoe giver because that is what his company does. Mycoskie created the company to meet a need: to supply children who don't have adequate footwear—or any for that matter—with shoes. Through the company's "One-for-One" movement, TOMS gives away a pair of shoes for every pair that is sold. To date, working through local partners, TOMS has given more than 1 million pairs away to children in 25 countries. As if that is not enough of a reward, the company has also received design awards for their shoes and the Secretary of State's Award for Corporate Excellence, which recognizes U.S. businesses for advancing good corporate citizenship, innovation, and democratic principles.

InnoCentive's open marketplace includes challenges that address global health, emergency response, nature, education, and more. The company's president and CEO, Dwayne Spradlin summarized the promise of this open collaboration in a recent conversation that we had,

> I don't know of a world problem that is hurt by more collaboration, more communication, and more ideas. I think it's quite the contrary. . . . You can take big challenges and break them into smaller problems and different people can work on them and localize them for certain locations. I am impressed with what's already happening. This may very well be a path to a better world.

Other sectors are part of these "issue-addressing ecosystems." One of Clay Shirky's design classes at NYU is working with UNICEF to rethink the way information is gathered and distributed about children who are separated from their families during times of crisis. The project is called RapidFTR, for Rapid Family Tracing and Reunification; it looks at inexpensive ways to take what we've learned from the Web, which generally involves high-cost devices, and re-imagines how those services could be delivered via a low-cost device like a mobile phone. "Since the mobile phone population is nearly double that of the Internet-connected population, there is an enormous population to be reached in various ways whether it's with non-profit services or for a profit enterprise," Shirky observes. (Consider that, in addition to location, most handsets are also able to record light, proximity, acceleration, and soon temperature. The possibilities for how these tools will be able to be put to work are mind-boggling.)

Here's another interesting issue-tackling ecosystem. The Kauffman Foundation, the world's largest foundation devoted to entrepreneurship, recently announced that it was joining forces with the likes of Google, Autodesk, and ePlanet Ventures to support the development of Singularity University. This young university's primary goal is to prepare the next generation of leaders to address "humanity's greatest challenges" including sustainable water, renewable energy, and world poverty. A hallmark of the program is the University's "Ten to the Ninth Power" projects ("10^9+") that ask students to develop an idea that will positively impact at least one billion people within the next 10 years. Salim Ismail, Executive Director and CEO recently described the Kauffman addition to the partnership, "The Kauffman Foundation deeply understands how the convergence of entrepreneurship and exponential technologies will drive growth in the global economy. The opportunities are seemingly endless for keen entrepreneurs to disrupt entrenched industries and cause positive change to the world's grand challenges."[8]

These are hopeful, passion-tapping, and inspiring developments for which every organization in every sector can play a part. This boundary crossing may just be a new stage in the evolution of capitalism.

Keeping the Internet Open and Accessible

We'll continue to see an expansion in connectivity—connection to the global digital network—and hopefully a continued openness of the Web. Part of the social web's success has been because of its accessibility. Connectivity has become ubiquitous and its capabilities are seamlessly intertwined in most people's lives in the developed world. It's hard for us to even imagine life without being able to easily and readily connect with this invisible digital network. It has become a necessity, almost like air.

According to the connectivity experts at Yankee Group, which publishes an "Anywhere Index" that measures countries' wiredness,

North America enjoys a relatively high level of connectedness: 87 percent.[9] (This percentage comes from comparing the number of broadband fixed and wireless digital lines in a region to that region's population.) The most connected countries in the world are Australia, Hong Kong, Japan, South Korea, and Sweden. By contrast, the world's Anywhere Index is 22 percent, reflecting the massive disparity in digital connectedness across regions.

It is in every company's best interest to be on the side of expanded and inexpensive connectivity; it facilitates commerce, opening up markets for labor, supplies, and customers. It pulls countries into the global economic community. (A study conducted at the London School of Economics found that a country's gross domestic product rises by 0.6 percent for every 10 mobile phones per 100 people.[10]) There is also a lot of money to be made from connectivity expansion. Yankee Group estimates that the financial contributions to the global economy—in terms of revenue, jobs, and profit—from growing connectedness will be in the tens of trillions of dollars.[11] Value creation will come in from both development of the network itself and from the devices and services that will make use of the network.

At the moment, the economics are in place for mass penetration of voice and SMS via smart phones in many areas of the world. There is, however, a hefty premium charged for data services. The question remains: how long will it take for the price/volume relationship to turn in favor of selling more access at a lower price? In Asia and some places in Europe that time is now. In other places it may take as long as a decade.

Open for Business

How open does the Web need to be? This is a question that will be debated over the next few years as the Web continues to evolve. We talk of the Web as if it were a single network. In reality it is a network of networks that are connected by open standards. As you may know, Sir Tim Berners-Lee, a young British scientist at the European Organization for Nuclear Research (CERN) in Switzerland, developed the World Wide Web and HyperText Markup Language (HTML), to facilitate information sharing among physicists at CERN and other universities around the world. In 1991, he posted the following summary of what was then the Web project:

> The World Wide Web (WWW) project aims to allow all links to be made to any information anywhere. The WWW project was started to allow high energy physicists to share data, news, and documentation. We are very interested in spreading the Web to other areas and having gateway servers for other data. Collaborators welcome![12]

Berners-Lee made another pivotal contribution a few years later when he founded the World Wide Web Consortium at MIT to develop standards to improve the quality of the Web. He made the critical decision then to make the Web freely available to any and all users, which is why it can enable massive global connectivity today.

Several forces are challenging the openness of the Web today: governments that want it censored and policed; companies that want to gain control; and antiquated laws that were designed for a time of relative scarcity. David Weinberger, one of the authors of *The Cluetrain Manifest,* recently expressed his opinion to me of the danger that a more restricted Web presents, "We could be having a renaissance right now that would make the previous renaissance look like a ball game. This could be way bigger than it is, even."

Nevertheless, I do think that we are heading for what Josh Bernoff, senior vice president of idea development at Forrester Research, described as the *Splinternet,* a splintering of the Web as a unified system.[13] Think of the thousands of applications that are only available to Apple device users and the increase in the number of password-protected sites on the Web. I understand and appreciate the growth of the latter, what I call *gated communities.* People often feel more comfortable in protected social environments. In many cases, it can better meet their needs. But splintering does chip away at the foundation of the Web. This tension among varying levels of openness will continue as the Web matures into a more organized environment.

It Is Not Necessary to Change

It is a time of disruptive change that will strengthen some companies and weaken others. Several years ago at another climactic point in business management, quality guru W. Edwards Deming told leaders that despite an unavoidable change in the external operating environment, it was not necessary to change. But, he was quick to add: survival is not mandatory.

Our employees, customers, shareholders, and other stakeholder communities trust that you and I will recognize these unanticipated and unavoidable structural adjustments and embrace them, even as they cause us discomfort—sometimes profound discomfort. Although these changes pose challenges for companies and their leadership, that's only part of the story. The opportunity they present is also profound.

Companies that are doing the work of building a comprehensive digital strategy will reap the rewards of a budding business renaissance. This strategy will bring them into better alignment with the stakeholder communities with which they are engaged, creating invigorating and meaningful work places, promoting robust innovation and growth, and potentially solving some of society's most urgent challenges. In time, these companies will be transformed into social enterprises and their comprehensive digital strategies will no longer be strategies at all, just the way they do business.

Questions to Consider

- What are your personal next steps?
- What questions still remain?
- How will your company's social media engagement strategy impact its performance in the next six months? Two years?

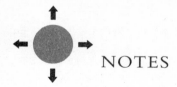

NOTES

Introduction

1. Brian Morrissey, "Q & A: Erin Nelson," *Adweek,* April 27, 2010, www.adweek
.com/aw/content_display/news/digital/e3iacb41595e9be670218a93e1692252a64.
2. David Gardner, "Dell Customer Advisory Panel Executive Summary,"
FastCompany, June 17, 2010, www.fastcompany.com/1661180/dell-customer-
advisory-panel-executive-summary.
3. Booz Allen Hamilton, "Employees Connect, Contribute on Enterprise 2.0
Portal," May 1, 2009, www.boozallen.com/about/article_news-ideas/42033790.
4. For more information on ARM, see www.arm.com.
5. Mike Harvey, "Warren East: ARM Believes Its Strength Lies in Sharing,"
The Times, February 16, 2009, http://business.timesonline.co.uk/tol/business/
movers_and_shakers/article5740769.ece.
6. David Meerman Scott. *Real-Time Marketing and PR* (Hoboken, NJ: John Wiley
& Sons, Inc., 2010).
7. The report, which was published in July 2009, can be found at: www
.engagementdb.com/downloads/ENGAGEMENTdb_Report_2009.pdf.
8. McKinsey & Company, "How Companies Are Benefiting from Web 2.0:
McKinsey Global Survey Results," *McKinsey Quarterly*, September 2009,
www.mckinseyquarterly.com/How_companies_are_benefiting_from_ Web_20_
McKinsey_Global_Survey_Results_2432.
9. Leah Bourne, "Social Media Is Fashion's Newest Muse," *Forbes,* September 7,
2010, www.forbes.com/2010/09/07/fashion-social-networking-customer-
feedback-forbes-woman-style-designers.html.
10. Marka Hansen, "The Gap's New Logo," *Huffington Post*, October 7, 2010,
www.huffingtonpost.com/marka-hansen/the-gaps-new-logo_b_754981.html.
11. Comments taken from conference notes, "Enabling a Customer-Focused Organization," Executive Roundtable Series, Thought Leadership Summit on Digital Strategies, Tuck School of Business at Dartmouth, Hanover, NH, September
9, 2003.

12. Jeff Howe, "The Rise of Crowdsourcing," *Wired*, June 2006, www.wired.com/wired/archieve/14.06/crowds_pr.html.

13. "Innovation: Sometimes It Takes a Village," *Knowledge@Wharton*, June 24, 2009, http://knowledge.wharton.upenn.edu/printer_friendly.cfm?articleid=2272.

14. Nielsenwire, "Global Advertising: Consumers Trust Real Friends and Virtual Strangers the Most," July 7, 2009, http://blog.nielsen.com/nielsenwire/consumer/global-advertising-consumers-trust-real-friends-and-virtual-strangers-the-most.

15. Social commerce statistics provided by *Internet Retailer*, September 2009, www.bazaarvoice.com/resources/stats.

16. Social commerce statistics provided by Rubbermaid case study, April 2010, www.bazaarvoice.com/resources/stats.

17. Mark Addicks, "General Mills Going Social," paper presented at BlogWell's How Big Brands Use Social Media Conference, Minneapolis, MN, August 13, 2009, www.socialmedia.org/blog/social-media-case-study-from-mark-addicks-of-general-mills.

18. Brant Cruz and Josh Mendelsohn, "Why Consumers Care and What Works," August 11, 2010, http://blog.cmbinfo.com/in-the-news-content/bid/47290/Quirks-Creating-Consumer-Brand-Connections-via-Social-Media.

19. Sean Corcoran and others, "The Broad Reach of Social Technologies," April 25, 2009, www.forrester.com/rb/Research/broad_reach_of_social_technologies/q/id/55132/t/2.

20. Maggie Shiels, "YouTube at 5—2bn Views a Day," May 17, 2010, http://news.bbc.co.uk/2/hi/8676380.stm.

21. Nielsen blog, "Social Networks/Blogs Now Account for One in Every Four and a Half Minutes Online," June 15, 2010, http://blog.nielsen.com/nielsenwire/online_mobile/social-media-accounts-for-22-percent-of-time-online.

22. Ross School of Business at the University of Michigan, "Twitter Helps Smaller Firms Level the Information Playing Field," September 16, 2010, www.bus.umich.edu/NewsRoom/ArticleDisplay.asp?news_id=2040.

23. Booz Allen Hamilton, "Employees Connect, Contribute to Enterprise 2.0 Portal," May 1, 2009,www.boozallen.com/about/article_news-ideas/42033790.

24. For more information see Greg Piche's paper presentation, "How Clorox Uses Gaming Mechanics in Social Networks," at BlogWell, San Diego, CA, March 30, 2010, www.socialmedia.org/blog/how-clorox-uses-gaming-mechanics-in-social-media-live-from-blogwell.

25. The 2009 survey can be accessed at: www.edelman.com/trust/2009.

26. The 2010 Edelman Trust Barometer Executive Summary can be accessed at www.scribd.com/full/26268655?access_key=key-1ovbgbpawooot3hnsz3u.

27. Jeremy Liew, "Why the Economics of Social Gaming Are So Attractive to Investors," *PaidContent,* December 1, 2009, http://paidcontent.org/article/419-why-the-economics-of-social-gaming-are-so-attractive-to-investors.

28. United States Department of Labor, Bureau of Labor Statistics, "Occupational Outlook Handbook," 2010–2011 Edition, www.bls.gov/oco/oco2003.htm.

29. For more information, see www.nationalguard.com/?kw=united+states+army +recruiters.

30. Ellen Messmer, "Lockheed Martin Tries Homegrown Social Networking Platform," *IT News*, March 11, 2009, www.itnews.com/security/1025/lockheed-martin-tries-homegrown-social-networking-platform.

31. Don Tapscott, "Netting Young Employees," *What Matters*, February 26, 2009, http://whatmatters.mckinseydigital.com/organization/netting-young-employees.

32. Mark Addicks, "General Mills Going Social," paper presented at BlogWell's How Big Brands Use Social Media Conference, Minneapolis, MN, August 13, 2009, www.socialmedia.org/blog/social-media-case-study-from-mark-addicks-of-general-mills.

Chapter 2: Toward a Comprehensive Digital Business Strategy

1. Gavin O'Malley, "Look Ma, No Hands: More Than Half of Companies Say They Are Using Social Media with No Strategy," *Online Media Daily,* June 22, 2010, www.mediapost.com/publications/?fa=Articles.showArticle&art_aid=130723.

2. For more information on R2integrated's Social Media Survey, see www.r2integrated.com/LinkClick.aspx?fileticket=54H54fg3NsE%3D&tabid=215.

3. "Enabling a Customer-Focused Organization," Executive Roundtable Series, Thought Leadership Summit on Digital Strategies at the Tuck School of Business at Dartmouth College, Hanover, NH, September 9, 2003.

4. For more information see Peter Whoriskey and Kimberly Kindy, "Toyota Faces $16.4 Million U.S. Fine for Waiting to Warn of Defect," *The Washington Post*, April 6, 2010, www.washingtonpost.com/wpdyn/content/article/2010/04/05/AR2010040503200.html.

5. Eliot Spitzer, "We Own You," *Slate,* January 12, 2010, www.slate.com/id/2241191.

6. For more information, see Jeff Jarvis's blog at www.buzzmachine.com/2007/10/18/dell-hell-the-end.

7. Brian Morrissey, "Q & A: Erin Nelson," *Adweek*, April 27, 2010, www.adweek.com/aw/content_display/news/digital/e3iacb41595e9be670218a93e1692252a64.

8. http://gaspedal.com/blogwell.

9. For more information, see www.drivingsales.com.

10. Sean Corcoran, "Using Paid and Earned Media Together," Forrester Research report, August 24, 2010, http://www.forrester.com/rb/Research/using-paid-and-earned-media-together/q/id/57408/t/2.

11. To follow Starbucks on Twitter, see www.twitter.com/starbucks.

12. Alexandra Wheeler and Matthew Guiste, "Starbucks: Building Meaningful Customer Engagement," paper given at the BlogWell conference, "How Big Brands Use Social Media," Minneapolis, MN, 2/16/2010, www.vimeo.com/9718741.

13. To follow Robert Gibbs on Twitter, see http://twitter.com/presssec.
14. Politico, "Gibbs on Twitter: Not as Easy as It Looks," April 18, 2010, www
    .politico.com/blogs/politicolive/0410/Gibbs_on_Twitter_Not_as_easy_as_it_
    looks.html?showall.
15. Jessica Hogue, "Building a Better Burger? Try Social Listening for Product
    Development," *Nielsen Wire*, April 9, 2010, http://blog.nielsen.com/nielsen
    wire/online_mobile/building-a-better-burger-try-social-listening-for-product-
    development.
16. For more information, see Jeremiah Owyang, "Evolution: The Eight Stages of
    Listening," *Web Strategist*, November 10, 2009, www.web-strategist.com/blog/
    2009/11/10/evolution-the-eight-stages-of-listening.
17. For more information, see http://networkedinsights.com/pov/whitepapers.
18. Natalie Zmuda, "Inside Gatorade's Social Media 'Mission Control,'" *Advertising
    Age*, September 28, 2010, http://adage.com/article?article_id=146149.

Chapter 3: Building Enterprise-Wide Engagement Capability

1. "Live from IABSM, Coke's Ingredients for Social Media," *Smartblogs,* April 5,
   2010, http://smartblogs.com/socialmedia/2010/04/05/live-from-iabsm-
   cokes-ingredients-for-social-media.
2. To follow Humana's Social Media Chamber of Commerce on Twitter, use their
   hashtag (#hcoc).
3. Chris Hall, "Meeting of the Minds," *Crumpleitup,* February 16, 2009, http://
   crumpleitup.com/b/2009/02/meeting-minds.
4. Casey Hibbard, "How IBM Uses Social Media to Spur Employee Innovation,"
   Social Media Examiner, February 2, 2010, www.socialmediaexaminer.com/how-
   ibm-uses-social-media-to-spur-employee-innovation/#more-1661.
5. Adam Christensen blog, "Introducing the IBM Expert Network on SlideShare,"
   November 17, 2010, http://adamchristensen.com.
6. Casey Hibbard, "How IBM Uses Social Media to Spur Employee Innovation,"
   Social Media Examiner, February 2, 2010, www.socialmediaexaminer.com/how-
   ibm-uses-social-media-to-spur-employee-innovation/#more-1661.
7. "Web 2.0 and the Corporation," comments taken from conference notes, an Executive Roundtable Series, Thought Leadership Summit on Digital Strategies at the
   Tuck School of Business at Dartmouth College, Hanover, NH, June 19, 2007.
8. bookingmama.blogspot.com.
9. Ibid.
10. Much of the information from this section is based on a white paper pub-
    lished by my company, Digital Influence Group. Jackie Lustig, Scott Rozic,
    and Liz McCormick, "Measuring Social Media ROI," March 2010, http://
    digitalinfluencegroup.com/white-paper-social-media-roi.
11. Babson Executive Education and Mzinga, "Survey: Social Software in Business,"
    September 2009.

12. Much of this section has its roots in a white paper published by my company, Digital Influence Group. Jackie Lustig and Liz McCormick, "Organizing for Social Media," June 2010, http://digitalinfluencegroup.com/register-now-organizing-for-social-media-june-4-webinar.

Chapter 4: Developing a Digitally Driven Company

1. Andy Piper, "Social Media at IBM," www.slideshare.net/andypiper/social-media-at-ibm.
2. Tony Hsieh, "Zappos.com Update," posting to CEO and COO Blog, March 10, 2010, http://blogs.zappos.com/blogs/ceo-and-coo-blog.
3. "Zappos a Social Media Success Story: An Interview with Tony Hsieh," www.davemadethat.com/2008/07/09/communication-20-zappos-a-social-media-success-story-interview-with-tony-hsieh.
4. Yochai Benkler, "The Collaborative Company," *What Matters,* February 26, 2009, http://whatmatters.mckinseydigital.com/internet/the-collaborative-company.
5. Umair Haque, "Twitter, SXSW, and Building a 21st Century Business," March 17, 2010, http://blogs.hbr.org/haque/2010/03/twitter_sxsw_and_building_a_21.html.
6. Mark Kramer and Michael Porter, "Corporate Advantage and Corporate Responsibility," *Harvard Business Review,* December 2006, p. 13.
7. Ibid.
8. McKinsey & Company, "McKinsey Conversations with Global Leaders: John Chambers," *McKinsey Quarterly,* July 2009, www.mckinseyquarterly.com/Strategy/Strategic_Thinking/McKinsey_conversations_with_global_leaders_John_Chambers_of_Cisco_2400.
9. Ibid.
10. Peter Hirshberg, "Best Buy CEO Brad Anderson in Conversation with Peter Hirshberg at Google Zeitgeist," September 17, 2008, http://vimeo.com/2085435.
11. Consensus Point Blog, "Best Buy Prediction Market Videos," October 19, 2008, www.consensuspoint.com/prediction-markets-blog/best-buy-prediction-market-video.
12. Peter Hirshberg, "Best Buy CEO Brad Anderson in Conversation with Peter Hirshberg at Google Zeitgeist," September 17, 2008, http://vimeo.com/2085435.
13. Tessa Finlev, "10 Workplace Skills of the Future; the Skills Workers Should Strive to Have and the Skills Employers Should Seek Out and Promote," *The Future Is Now Blog,* May 8, 2009, www.iftf.org/node/2774.
14. Charlene Li, "The Failure Imperative," *The Strategist,* Spring, 2010, p. 34.
15. Danah Boyd, "Social Media Is Here to Stay . . . Now What?," paper presented at the Microsoft Research Tech Fest, Redmond, WA, February 26, 2009, www.danah.org/papers/talks/MSRTechFest2009.html.

16. To explore the site, go to www.googlelabs.com.

17. Kimberly Maul, "CEO Q&A: Alan Mulally, CEO, Ford," *PRWeek*, August 1, 2010, www.prweekus.com/pages/login.aspx?returl=/ceo-qa-alan-mulally-ceo-ford/article/175035/&pagetypeid=28&articleid=175035&accesslevel=2&expireddays=0&accessAndPrice=0.

18. To see the video, go to www.youtube.com/watch?v=-r_PIg7EAUw.

19. Richard Smith, "Know What You Don't Know," *Newsweek*, June 4, 2010, www.newsweek.com/2010/06/04/know-what-you-don-t-know.html.

20. McKinsey & Company, "McKinsey Conversations with Global Leaders: John Chambers," *McKinsey Quarterly*, July 2009, www.mckinseyquarterly.com/Strategy/Strategic_Thinking/McKinsey_conversations_with_global_leaders_John_Chambers_of_Cisco_2400.

21. Forbes, "The Rise of the Digital C-Suite: How Executives Locate and Filter Business Information," June 2009, http://images.forbes.com/forbesinsights/StudyPDFs/DigitalCsuite.pdf.

22. Fawn Fitter, "The Sizzling Success of Naked Pizza," *Entrepreneur*, September, 2010, www.entrepreneur.com/article/217362.

23. Ted Leonsis, *The Business of Happiness* (Washington, DC: Reegnery Publishing, Inc, 2010), p. 210.

24. Richard Smith, "Know What You Don't Know," *Newsweek*, June 4, 2010, www.newsweek.com/2010/06/04/know-what-you-don-t-know.html.

25. McKinsey & Company, "McKinsey Conversations with Global Leaders: John Chambers," *McKinsey Quarterly*, July 2009, www.mckinseyquarterly.com/Strategy/Strategic_Thinking/McKinsey_conversations_with_global_leaders_John_Chambers_of_Cisco_2400.

Chapter 5: Marketing, Sales, and Service, Step 1

1. David Court, Dave Elzinga, Susan Mulder, and Ole Jørgen Vetvik, "The Customer Decision Journey," *McKinsey Quarterly*, June 2009, www.mckinseyquarterly.com/The_consumer_decision_journey_2373.

2. Chadwick Martin Bailey, "Consumers Engaged via Social Media Are More Likely to Buy, Recommend," March 10, 2010, www.cmbinfo.com/news/press-center/social-media-release-3-10-10.

3. Social commerce statistics provided by *Internet Retailer,* September 2009, www.bazaarvoice.com/resources/stats.

4. Social commerce statistics provided by Rubbermaid case study, April 2010, www.bazaarvoice.com/resources/stats.

5. Jennifer Van Grove, "How 5 Brands Are Mastering the Game of Foursquare," April 2, 2010, http://mashable.com/2010/04/02/foursquare-brands.

6. Melissa Parrish, "Location-Based Social Networks: A Hint of Mobile Engagement Emerges," Forrester Reports, July 27, 2010, www.forrester.com/rb/Research/location-based_social_networks_hint_of_mobile_engagement/q/id/57334/t/2.

7. "Doctors Embrace Social Networking," *Miami Herald*, November 9, 2009, http://pd.miami.com/sp?aff=1100&keywords=doctors-embrace-social-networking&submit.x=0&submit.y=0.

8. "Miami Children's Hospital Posts Surgical Triumphs on YouTube," *Miami Herald*, November 9, 2009, http://miamiherald.com/2009/11/09/1322851/miami-childrens-hospital-posts.html.

9. Ibid.

10. Andy Sernovitz, "Andy's Answers: How to Use Social Media During a Product Recall," SmartBlog on Social Media, August 18, 2010, http://smartblogs.com/socialmedia/2010/08/18/andys-answers-how-to-use-social-media-during-a-product-recall.

11. Example provided by Twitter, http://business.twitter.com/twitter101/case_nakedpizza.

12. James A. Martin, "Get Real Business Results from Social Media," *PC World*, November 26, 2009, www.pcworld.com/businesscenter/article/182927/get_real_business_results_from_social_media.html.

13. Jon Gibs and Sean Bruick, "Nielsen/Facebook Report: The Value of Social Media Ad Impressions," *Nielsen Wire*, April 20, 2010, http://blog.nielsen.com/nielsenwire/online_mobile/nielsenfacebook-ad-report.

14. Larry Weber, Greg Matthews, and Steve Goldbach, "Organizing for Social Media: Webinar and White Paper," June 4, 2010, http://digitalinfluencegroup.com/register-now-organizing-for-social-media-june-4-webinar.

15. Accenture, "Onward and Up: How Marketers are Refocusing the Front Office for Growth," www.accenture.com/NR/rdonlyres/3464EBF6-AA1A-4830-BD46-6A19ED4EAD44/0/Accenture_Marketing_Onward_and_Up.pdf.

16. Lionel Menchaca, "Blending Community and E-Commerce," presented at the BlogWell conference, "How Big Brands Use Social Media," San Francisco, CA, June 23, 2009, http://vimeo.com/5484057.

17. For more information, see Dell's own blog post at http://en.community.dell.com/blogs/direct2dell/archive/2009/06/11/delloutlet-surpasses-2-million-on-twitter.aspx.

18. For more information, see http://developers.facebook.com/plugins.

19. Mary Jane Credeur, "Delta Monitors Twitter to Remedy Customer Complaints," *Bloomberg BusinessWeek*, August 16, 2010, www.businessweek.com/technology/content/aug2010/tc20100813_527916.htm.

20. Ibid.

21. Forrester, "Case Study: Lenovo Takes Ownership of Social Media to Reduce Customer Service Costs," August 14, 2009, www.forrester.com/rb/Research/case_study_lenovo_takes_ownership_of_social/q/id/54318/t/2.

22. Ibid.

23. Natalie Petouhoff, "Adding Social Media to Customer Service Initiatives Can Break Down Barriers to Change," *Forrester*, February 11, 2010, www.forrester.com/rb/Research/customer_experience_pays_off_as_social_media/q/id/56083/t/2.

Chapter 6: Marketing, Sales, and Service, Step 2

1. Clay Shirky, *Here Comes Everybody: The Power of Organizing Without Organizations* (New York: Penguin Books, 2008), p. 17.
2. For more information, see bestbuyin3d.com.
3. Clay Shirky, *Here Comes Everybody: The Power of Organizing Without Organizations* (New York: Penguin Books, 2008), p. 20.
4. Statistics updated as of July 31, 2010, http://stats.wikimedia.org/EN/Sitemap.htm.
5. Andrew McMains, "Facebook Brand Pages Pay Off," *Adweek*, October 11, 2010, www.adweek.com/aw/content_display/news/agency/e3id9de17c1ffdb 95511a66ac1f6619e1ff?imw=Y.
6. Mark Twain, "Letter to Emeline Beach," February 10, 1868.
7. Saritha Rai, "India: More Mobile Phones than Toilets," *Global Post*, May 9, 2010, www.globalpost.com/dispatch/india/100507/mobile-phones-toilets-sanitation-health.
8. Emily Nagle Green, *Anywhere: How Global Connectivity Is Revolutionizing the Way We Do Business* (New York: McGraw Hill, 2009).
9. Morgan Stanley, *The Mobile Internet Report*, December, 2009, www.morganstanley .com/institutional/techresearch/mobile_internet_report122009.html.
10. Matt Rhodes, "Japanese Social Networking—It's All Mobile," *Social Media Today*, January 7, 2010, www.socialmediatoday.com/SMC/163718.
11. Ruder Finn, "Mobile Intent Index," February 12, 2010, http://intentindex .com/mobile.
12. American writer Marc Prensky first coined the phrase "digital native" to refer to those people who grew up surrounded by digital technology such as computers, the Internet, mobile phones, and MP3 players. Prensky argues that the profile of digital natives is distinctly different from their predecessors, "digital immigrants." His use of the term *native* suggests that digital language, mores, and behaviors are natural to those who were raised in the twenty-first century, whereas they have had to be adopted and assimilated by digital immigrants. In keeping with the analogy, Prensky proposes that digital immigrants retain a "thick accent" despite our years of hanging out in digital environments. Digital natives, on the other hand, look and sound completely at home and operate with astounding ease merging the physical and digital worlds.
13. For more information, see www.houseparty.com/hersheysbliss.
14. Sean Corcoran and others, "The Broad Reach of Social Technologies," August 25, 2009, www.forrester.com/rb/Research/broad_reach_of_social_technologies/q/id/ 55132/t/2.
15. Stan Joosten, "Marketing in the Age of Social Media—Examples from Procter & Gamble," presented at the BlogWell conference "How Big Companies Use Social Media," Chicago, IL, Jan 22, 2009, http://vimeo.com/7056109.
16. Ed Nicholson, "How Tyson Food Uses Social Media to Build Community Around the Issue of Hunger," presented at the BlogWell conference, "How Big

Companies Use Social Media," New York, NY, April 29, 2009, http://vimeo .com/4761277.

17. To follow Tyson on Twitter, see http://twitter.com/TysonFoods.

18. Ed Nicholson, "How Tyson Food Uses Social Media to Build Community Around the Issue of Hunger," presented at the BlogWell conference, "How Big Companies Use Social Media," New York, NY, April 29, 2009, www.slideshare .net/GasPedal/blogwell-new-york-social-media-case-study-tyson-foods-presented-by-ed-nicholson.

19. Ibid.

20. Ed Nicholson, "How Tyson Food Uses Social Media to Build Community Around the Issue of Hunger," presented at the BlogWell conference, "How Big Companies Use Social Media," New York, NY, April 29, 2009, http://vimeo .com/4761277.

21. For more information, see FishPhone at www.BlueOcean.org.

22. For more information, see http://blogs.starbucks.com/blogs/customer/archive/ 2010/01/18/donate-to-the-haiti-relief-effort-at-starbucks.aspx.

Chapter 7: Innovation

1. Marisa Taylor, "Winning Netflix Team Draws from AT&T, Yahoo!," *The Wall Street Journal*, September 21, 2009, http://blogs.wsj.com/digits/2009/09/21/ winning-netflix-team-draws-from-att-yahoo.

2. Ibid.

3. For more information, see www.app-my-ride.com.

4. For more information, see https://huggiesmominspired.com.

5. For more information, see https://huggiesmominspired.com/Invent/Inventor-Akemann.aspx.

6. For more information, see http://mystarbucksidea.force.com.

7. http://blogs.starbucks.com/blogs/customer/archive/2008/08/19/coffee-ice-cubes.aspx.

8. https://secure3.verticali.net/pg-connection-portal/ctx/noauth/PortalHome.do.

9. "Innovation: Sometimes It Takes a Village," *Knowledge @ Wharton*, June 24, 2009, http://knowledge.wharton.upenn.edu/article.cfm?articleid=2272.

10. https://secure3.verticali.net/pg-connection-portal/ctx/noauth/0_0_1_4_83_ 4_10.do.

11. Sandy Staggs, "Connect + Develop with Procter & Gamble," *IdeaConnection*, November 20, 2008, www.ideaconnection.com/interviews/00070-Connect-Develop-with-Procter-Gamble.html.

12. Matthew Arnold, "Sermo Revamp Aims for Faster Searches, Better Filters, Alerts," *Medical Marketing & Media*, July 14, 2010, www.mmm-online.com/ sermo-revamp-aims-for-faster-searches-better-filters-alerts/article/174608.

13. Jenn Abelson, "A Cup Good to the Last Drop-Off," *Boston Globe*, September 5, 2010, p, A1.

14. For more information, see www.media.mit.edu.
15. Susan Spencer, Well Spring of American Creativity, January 10, 2010, www
    .cbsnews.com/stories/2010/01/10/sunday/main6078280.shtml.
16. Fred Callopy, "Innovation Tip: Step Back to Step Forward," *BusinessWeek*,
    January 6, 2010, www.businessweek.com/innovate/content/jan2010/id2010015_
    791654.htm.
17. "Johnson & Johnson CEO William Weldon: Leadership in a Decentralized
    Company," June 25, 2008, http://knowledge.wharton.upen.edu/article.cfm?
    articleid=2003.
18. Ibid.
19. Ibid.
20. Ibid.
21. www-03.ibm.com/press/us/en/pressrelease/28096.wss.
22. Michelle Bishop, "The Total Economic Impact of InnoCentive's Enterprise
    Solution: Challenges, InnoCentive@Work, and ONRAMP: A Single-
    Company Case Study," February 2010, www2.innocentive.com/files/node/
    casestudy/total-economic-impacttm-innocentives-enterprise-solution-challenges-
    innocentivework-and-onramp.pdf.
23. Chris Ridey, "Yet2.com's Tech Licenses on the Upswing" Feb 7, 2008, www
    .boston.com/business/ticker/2008/02/yet2coms_tech_l.html.
24. http://www.yet2.com/app/about/about/com.
25. Ibid.
26. For more client testimonies, see www.yet2.com/app/about/about/quotes.
27. http://bendupont.yet2.com/2010/05/26/yet2-com-5-learnings-on-selling-
    early-stage-technology/#more-908.
28. Ibid.
29. Ed Catmull, "How Pixar Fosters Collective Creativity," *Harvard Business Review*, Sep-
    tember 2008, http://hbr.org/2008/09/how-pixar-fosters-collective-creativity/ar/1.
30. "Encouraging Industry-University Partnerships, Report from The Engineering
    Advisory Committee, Subcommittee on Industry, University Partnerships,"
    April 10, 2008, www.kauffman.org/uploadedFiles/EAC_UIP_report_v4.pdf.
31. For more information, see www.media.mit.edu/about/about-the-lab.
32. www.media.mit.edu/sponsorship/getting-value.

Chapter 8: Strategy Execution

1. Rob Cross and others, "Knowing What We Know: Supporting Knowledge Creation and Sharing in Social Networks," *Organizational Dynamics*, Vol. 30, No. 2,
   p. 102, www.analytictech.com/borgatti/papers/borgatti%20-%20knowing%20
   what%20we%20know.pdf.
2. Ibid.
3. Ibid.

4. Joan M. DiMicco and others, "Research on the Use of Social Software in the Workplace," January 14, 2009, www.headshift.com/blog/2009/01/14/IBM%20Social%20Networking%20Research.pdf.

5. Ibid.

6. Cerner, "uCern Overview Video," www.youtube.com/watch?v=nyHNail9xuM.

7. Oliver Marks, "GE's Enterprise Collaboration Backbone," *Collaboration 2.0*, July 17, 2008, www.zdnet.com/blog/collaboration/ges-enterprise-collaboration-backbone/126.

8. 9/11 Commission Report, p. 77.

9. Stew Magnuson, "Feds Lagging in Most Disaster Scenarios, McHale Says," *National Defense*, November 2006, www.nationaldefensemagazine.org/archive/2006/November/Pages/SecurityBeat2819.aspx.

10. www.dni.gov/speeches/20070905_speech.pdf.

11. Andrew McAfee, *Enterprise 2.0* (Cambridge, Massachusetts: Harvard University Press, 2009), p. 116.

12. Ibid, p. 117.

13. Cisco, whitepaper, "The Necessity of Pervasive Collaboration," www.cisco.com/en/US/services/ps2961/ps2664/Necessity_of_Pervasive_Collaboration.pdf.

14. Peter Hirshberg, "Best Buy CEO Brad Anderson in Conversation with Peter Hirshberg at Google Zeitgeist," September 17, 2008, http://vimeo.com/2085435.

15. Shannon Perry, "Prediction Markets—Reinventing Pharma Forecasting?" September 15, 2007, http://social.eyeforpharma.com/story/prediction-markets-%E2%80%93-reinventing-pharma-forecasting.

16. ConsensusPoint Case Study, http://consensuspoint.net/images/BestBuy-Case-Study-Approved.pdf.

17. James Surowiecki, *The Wisdom of Crowds: Why the Many Are Smarter Than the Few and How Collective Wisdom Shapes Business, Economies, Societies, and Nations* (New York: Random House, 2004).

18. For more information, see Andrew McAfee, *Enterprise 2.0* (Cambridge, Massachusetts: Harvard University Press, 2009).

19. The University of Melbourne, "Freedom to Surf: Workers More Productive if Allowed to Use the Internet for Leisure," April 2, 2009, http://uninews.unimelb.edu.au/news/5750.

Chapter 9: Human Capital

1. Jobvite 2010 Social Recruiting Survey, www.recruiting.jobvite.com/resources/social-recruiting-survey.php.

2. Jessi Hempel, "How LinkedIn Will Fire up Your Career," *Fortune*, March 25, 2010, http://money.cnn.com/2010/03/24/technology/linkedin_social_networking.fortune.

3. https://linkedinwebinar.webex.com/linkedinwebinar/lsr.php?AT=pb&SP=EC&rID=1998887&rKey=b5baa0d9e7bfcc64.

4. Ibid.

5. SelectMinds whitepaper: "Referral Programs 2.0: How Social Networking Maximizes Referrals," http://selectminds.com/download-referral-programs-2_0-white-paper.htm.

6. Leena Rao, "LinkedIn Now 60 Million Strong," *TechCrunch*, February 11, 2010, http://techcrunch.com/2010/02/11/linkedin-now-60-million-strong.

7. https://linkedinwebinar.webex.com/linkedinwebinar/lsr.php?AT=pb&SP=EC&rID=1998887&rKey=b5baa0d9e7bfcc64.

8. http://learn.linkedin.com/profiles.

9. www.linkedin.com/hiring%3Ftrk%3Dtab_hire.

10. This example came directly from LinkedIn. To see the original posting, go to http://press.linkedin.com/IndiaYahooJob.

11. Erick Schonfeld, "How to Use Facebook Ads for Social Recruiting," *TechCrunch*, May 12, 2010, http://techcrunch.com/2010/05/12/facebook-ads-social-recruiting-tool.

12. Saatkorn, "Exclusive: Torgil Lenning, CEO, Potentialpark, About Employer Branding and Social Media," March 28, 2010, http://saatkorn.wordpress.com/2010/03/28/exclusive-torgil-lenning-ceo-potentialpark-about-employer-branding-and-social-media.

13. SelectMinds white paper, "Corporate Alumni Social Networking," www.selectminds.com/download-corporate-alumni-social-networking-white-paper.htm.

14. SelectMinds white paper, "Referral Programs 2.0: How Social Networking Maximizes Referrals," www.selectminds.com/download-referral-programs-2_0-white-paper.htm.

15. Convergys, "Convergys' Innovative Recruitment Techniques Keep Applications Coming in Beyond Expectations," December 2, 2009, www.convergys.com/company/news-events/newsroom/news-release.php?newsid=4725.

16. Jeffrey Cohen, "Deloitte Using Social Media for Recruiting and Retention," *Social Media B2B*, October 16, 2009, http://socialmediab2b.com/2009/10/deloitte-uses-social-media-for-recruiting-and-retention.

17. Shareen Pathak, "Finance Firms Spruce up Online Recruitment Efforts," *FINS*, June 23, 2010, www.fins.com/Finance/Articles/SB127721873830209381/Finance-Firms-Spruce-Up-Online-Recruitment-Efforts.

18. Marlene Prost, "Using Social Networks for Training," *Human Resource Executive* August 27, 2009, http://hronline.com/HRE/printstory.jsp?storyid=246750617.

19. Wharton, "How GE Builds Global Leaders: A Conversation with Chief Learning Officer Susan Peters," May 12, 2010, http://knowledge.wharton.upenn/printer_friendly.cfm?articleid=2488.

20. SelectMinds white paper, "Referral Programs 2.0: How Social Networking Maximizes Referrals," www.selectminds.com/download-referral-programs-2_0-white-paper.htm.

21. Ibid.

22. Towers Watson, "Capitalizing on Effective Communication," Communication Study Report 2009/2010, www.towerswatson.com/assets/pdf/670/NA-2009-14890.pdf.

23. Kathleen Kostner, "Social Media Benefit Communication Picks Up Speed," *Employee Benefit News*, March 1, 2010, http://ebn.benefitnews.com/news/social-media-benefit-communication-picks-up-speed-2683010-1.html.

24. Towers Watson, "Capitalizing on Effective Communication," *Communication Study Report 2009/2010*, www.towerswatson.com/assets/pdf/670/NA-2009-14890.pdf.

25. International Association of Business Communicators, "E-mails and Intranet Are Top Communication Methods Used to Engage Employees," August 3, 2010, http://news.iabc.com/index.php?s=43&item=239.

26. Ibid.

27. Leah Carlson Shepherd, "Benefits Knowledge Leads to Retention and Benefits Satisfaction," *Employee Benefit News*, January 1, 2009. http://ebn.benefitnews.com/news/benefits-knowledge-leads-retention-and-benefits-2651411-1.html.

28. Jessica Marquez, "Best Buy Finds Social Networking and 401(k)s Can Be a Good Fit," *Workforce Management*, October 2008," www.workforce.com/section/benefits-compensation/feature/best-buy-finds-social-networking-401(k)s-can-be-good/index.html.

29. Ibid.

30. Heather Oldani and Steve Wilson, "Collaboration 2.0," paper presented at Blog-Well, August 13, 2009, Minneapolis, MN, http://vimeo.com/6677308.

31. The Employee Factor, "McDonald's Leverages Social Media to Engage Employees," May 14, 2010, www.employeefactor.com/?p=2658.

32. Sylvia Ann Hewlett, Laura Sherbin, and Karen Sumberg, "How Gen Y & Boomers Will Reshape Your Agenda," *Harvard Business Review*, July 2009, http://hbr.harvardbusiness.org/2009/07/how-gen-y--boomers-will-reshape-your-agenda/ar/pr.

33. Emily Nagle Green, *Anywhere: How Global Connectivity Is Revolutionizing the Way We Do Business* (New York: McGraw-Hill, 2010), p. 151.

34. Ibid, p. 153.

35. Mary Ellen Slayter, "Dave Ulrich on Getting More Than a Paycheck out of Work," July 14, 2010, http://smartblogs.com/workforce/2010/07/14/dave-ulrich-on-getting-more-than-a-paycheck-out-of-work.

36. Don Tapscott, *Grown Up Digital: How the Net Generation Is Changing Your World* (New York: McGraw-Hill, 2009), p. 165.

37. Rebecca Knight, "Rewards of 'Gen-blending,'" *Financial Times*, September 14, 2009, www.ft.com/cms/s/0/e82acd60-a156-11de-a88d-00144feabdc0.html?nclick_check=1.
38. Cisco white paper, "The Necessity of Pervasive Collaboration," 2010, www.cisco.com/en/US/services/ps2961/ps2664/Necessity_of_Pervasive_Collaboration.pdf.

Chapter 10: Next

1. Thomas Malone, *The Future of Work: How the New Order of Business Will Shape Your Organization, Your Management Style and Your Life* (Cambridge, Massachusetts: Harvard Business School Press, 2004), p. 34.
2. Adam Bryant, "Putting Himself Up for Re-Election (by His Staff)," *New York Times*, October 31, 2010, www.nytimes.com/2010/10/31/business/31corner.html.
3. For more information, see www.gore.com/en_xx/aboutus/culture/index.html.
4. Ibid.
5. www.ibm.com/ibm/ideasfromibm/us/library/pdfs/IFI_GIE_06052006.pdf.
6. GE, Healthmagination 2009 Annual Report, http://files.gecompany.com/healthymagination/ar/healthymagination_annual_report.pdf.
7. Ibid.
8. Kauffman Foundation, "Kauffman Foundation Partners with Singularity University as Corporate Founder," August 26, 2010, www.kauffman.org/newsroom/kauffman-foundation-partners-with-singularity-university-as-corporate-founder.aspx.
9. Emily Nagle Green, *Anywhere: How Global Connectivity Is Revolutionizing the Way We Do Business* (New York: McGraw Hill, 2010), p. 50.
10. Ibid, p. 55.
11. Ibid, p. 16.
12. http://websearch.about.com/od/searchingtheweb/qt/web-history.htm.
13. Josh Bernoff, "The Splinternet Means the End of the Web's Golden Age," January 26, 2010, http://forrester.typepad.com/groundswell/2010/01/the-splinternet-means-the-end-of-the-webs-golden-age.html.

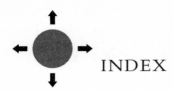

INDEX